HOW TO RAISE
A CHILD OF GOD

HOW TO RAISE
A CHILD OF GOD

Tara Singh

LIFE ACTION PRESS
Los Angeles

The First Edition of *How To Raise A Child Of God* was published in June, 1983
by the Foundation for Life Action.

Library of Congress Cataloging in Publication Data
Singh, Tara, 1919-
How to raise a child of God.
1. Parenting — Religious aspects — New Age movement.
2. New Age movement. I. Title.
BP605.N48S56   1987   649'.7   86-82911
ISBN 1-55531-008-7 Limited Edition, Hardbound
ISBN 1-55531-009-5 Softcover

The material from *A Course In Miracles* and *The Gifts Of God* is used by
permission of the copyright owner, the Foundation for Inner Peace,
P.O.Box 635, Tiburon, California 94920. Quotations from *Think On These
Things* by J. Krishnamurti, © Krishnamurti Foundation of America, are
reprinted by permission of Harper and Row, Publishers, Inc.

We would like to express our appreciation to St. Matthews Church,
Northampton, England, for allowing us to use the photograph of ''Mother
and Child'' by Henry Moore on the cover. Back cover photograph by
Richleigh Heagh.

ACKNOWLEDGMENTS

I would like to express my appreciation to Aliana Scurlock for her long hours of devoted work in the preparation of this book.

In addition, I am grateful to the following friends for their help with tape production, transcribing, editing, proofing, graphic design, and layout: Jim Cheatham, Frank Nader, Clio Dixon, Charles Johnson, Melanie Coulter, Rachel Logel, Norah Ryan, Lucille Frappier, Johanna Macdonald, Susan Berry, Kris and Richleigh Heagh, Sandra Lewis, Connie Willcuts, John and Acacia Williams, Joann Nieto, Nancy Marsh, and Selina Scheer.

For their cooperation and interest in our work, I would like to thank Johanna Macdonald, Fred and Nancy Marsh, Victoria Berry-Wai, and William McClintock.

CONTENTS

THE LAST JUDGMENT

Peace be to you. There is no instant when
You stand alone; no time when God will fail
To take your hand; no moment when His Love
Does not surround you, comfort you and care,
Along with you, for every wish you have,
Each little joy or tiny stab of pain.
At one with you forever, He remains
Your one relationship; your only Friend.
You are the holy Son of God Himself.
Peace be to you, for what is His is yours.*

*This poem is from *The Gifts Of God* by Helen Schucman, the Scribe of *A Course In Miracles* (Foundation for Inner Peace, 1982), page 4. It is an incomparable book of poetry containing some of the most important words ever spoken.

INTRODUCTION

This is not merely an introduction but the very premise and background out of which this book has emerged. It is a statement of the possibility of learning from every encounter.

Learning, in reality, means to undo. It is not accumulation of information, but inner awakening. And in each encounter is the learning/teaching relationship.

Your child would never be without a Teacher of Life if this is your intent. Intent is of purer energy than thought. A sense of helplessness is subject to the externals, but intent is not. To the wise, justifications are never valid. He is aware of the glory of creation and does not limit himself to a sense of lack.

*A Course In Miracles** points out:

I am not the victim of the world I see.

Today's idea is the introduction to your declaration of release. ...the idea should be applied to both the world

---

*A Course In Miracles is a contemporary scripture which deals with the psychological/spiritual issues facing man today. It consists of three volumes: Text, Workbook For Students, and Manual For Teachers. The Text, 622 pages, sets forth the concepts on which the thought system of the Course is based. The Workbook For Students, 478 pages, is designed to make possible the application of the concepts presented in the Text and consists of three hundred and sixty-five lessons, one for each day of the year. The Manual For Teachers, 88 pages, provides answers to some of the basic questions a student of the Course might ask and defines many of the terms used in the Text. (Editor)

you see without and the world you see within . . . . You
will escape from both together, for the inner is the cause of
the outer . . . . Remind yourself that you are making a
declaration of independence in the name of your own
freedom. And in your freedom lies the freedom of the
world. [1]

Now that *A Course In Miracles* is here, parents have True
Knowledge to help them raise a child of God. Miracles are
flashes of insight. They are of Divine Intelligence — ever
meeting the need of those eager to come to wholeness. Man's
own driving force towards the truth that he is, is at work in
the Universe. His own purity of intent draws Universal Forces
to itself.

Wise parents impart True Knowledge to the child
and all power in heaven is there for the asking.
But if they would compromise
their asking is not valid.

Do not undermine virtue.
Without conviction, nothing is possible.

*   *   *

I DID NOT GO TO SCHOOL
BUT ALL THROUGH MY LIFE I LEARNED
THROUGH ENCOUNTERS WITH GREAT BEINGS

Only a small number of children went to school in rural
India where I grew up. A child still had options. I felt false
and unhappy going to school, forced to violate my own self
and comply from fear. So, I would run away. I learned that
when you wanted to urinate you stood before the teacher
with one finger up. That gave you permission to go out into
the cornfields surrounding the school. I would go and not
come back.

For a good while I would get all ready to go to school and leave with the other children, but would never wind up there. I would go to the water pond or the fields instead. At the end of the day, when I heard the school bell ringing, I joined the other children and went home with them.

When the adults caught up with me, I told my mother that I did not want to go to school. My mother heard what I said and valued how I felt — that learning numbers and the alphabet had no meaning for me — and she protected me from going to school. My grandmother, who stood by me as well, said that I had enough land to live like a prince. Why did I need an education to be like a pale-faced clerk? My father, who was insistent on education, was abroad, and my compassionate uncle, who was then the head of the family, was indifferent. Not having gone to school himself he didn't see the importance of it and he loved me too much to hear me cry. God was on my side.

Even though India was ruled by England, they did not own the people. The villagers had their own resources and the children their freedom.

Absolutely vulnerable, simple and direct, completely without guile, my mother had never attended school; she could not even sign her name. But she had stillness to impart and introduced me to the love of God. The Indian wife who married a husband she'd never seen was reared to give. That was all she knew. And she knew everything. Then as a mother she knew wholly to give to the child.

In 1955, when my mother died, I was not in India. My daughter told me that she had walked with her to the city of Phagawara, three miles away from our village of Birak. My mother bought cloth to have a suit made for my daughter and some cloth for herself. On the way home the child asked, "Grandma, what are you going to make with the cloth you bought?" My mother answered, "The fresh, unused cloth is needed for a coffin." "For whom?" the child asked. "For me. On Tuesday I will die." The child wondered, "You must be sad, Grandma." "No, I am happy. Since my husband is gone I do not want to live any longer."

When Monday came, she was bed-ridden. The family and neighbors gathered, as they do in India, as her health began to rapidly decline. But my mother was in an ecstatic state, telling them that they should not worry, "It is blissful." On Tuesday she departed.

What kind of life my mother must have lived! A life free of consequences.

*   *   *

I was nineteen years old when my interest in education began. The teacher lived amidst a grove of trees about a half mile away from my village. He was a renowned musician originally from a faraway province in Bengal and had won acclaim for his rendering of the chaste Raga. The people of our village had built a little temple and a house for him to live in. Students came to him from all over India. He was also a sannyasi* who had renounced the world.

Guruji, as we called him, had come to Punjab to pay homage to the memory of an ancient sage whose anniversary was celebrated each year during the winter. Great musicians from all over the country gathered in the city of Jullundur about seventeen miles away from my village. The people of Jullundur were generous in their hospitality and thousands came to the auspicious festival of pure, classical music. Only master musicians could mount the dais. It was a free symposium, one of its kind in the whole world. Nothing was commercialized. An entrance fee would have been shocking.

---

*An ascetic who has renounced involvement with the world and turned his attention toward God. (Editor)

Guruji was walking through the pastoral landscape and villages of Punjab — the yellow mustard fields of winter — alone with his sitar. When he arrived in our village he sat to rest a while under a big bo tree beside the water pond. The villagers who saw him offered him respect and refreshments; passersby, seeing the poised sannyasi, stopped in reverence. Elders of the village coaxed him to stay and grace the village with his presence since he liked the refreshing water of the well. He consented to do so, but on his own terms, saying:

> "I will stay outside the village where we are now sitting. There will be no cooking where I live. For my food I will go once a day to the village, knock at no door, make no announcements, nor even enter any house. And from those who want to give me something to eat I will accept."

Thus he went with an open basket at noon, walked silently through the village, and made the contact. He got his food from those who were waiting for him, then returned to his sanctuary, birds fluttering around and about him with whom he shared his bounty. He often had enough food for a wayfarer or any student who came. I have never known anyone so independent.

It reminded me of the stories of Yudhisthira from the *Mahabharata*,* who would first renounce whatever came to him and then accept it on his own terms. The ancient sages of India lived by detachment and taught the Indian people that the greatest action of all was renunciation.

There was no money involved in anything Guruji did. Yet he always had something of his own to give. Daily, from

---

*The famous Hindu epic which tells the " . . . tale of heroic men and women, some of whom were divine. It is a whole literature in itself, containing a code of life, a philosophy of social and ethical relations and speculative thought on human problems . . . He who knows it not, knows not the heights and depths of the soul. . ." From "Kulapati's Preface" to *Mahabharata* by C. Rajagopalachari (Bharatiya Vidya Bhavan, Bombay, 1951), page 2. (Editor) about 4 A.M. until sunrise, he would practice sitar and singing — music the farmers felt would bless the earth. The villagers later discovered that he was a celebrated and well-known master musician.

Guruji was nearing fifty but he had a healthy body, well proportioned and coordinated. One evening, out of his joyous stillness — a state that related one with that which is not of time — he danced a dance that brought our minds to a quiet not known before. For a moment one saw how all things that are God-created express their joyous perfection. The graceful movements of his body were not only effortless, but impersonal. There was only the dance.

Such beings are often outside the range of choices. When he first came to the village he saw the reverence the people expressed and sensed their need for him, which he met by staying. Thus he completed the action. The ancients lived a lifestyle of compassion; they lived by the ethics of meeting the need of all those life brought into contact with them, be they animals, people, or students. Such beings are not ruled externally. If and when the reverence or the need diminished, they would depart. Incorruptibility cannot be commercialized.

The sages of India related with Divine Laws and valued man's relationship with God above all. Almost every art — architecture, sculpture, dance, music, even the social relationships of parents and children, and of marriage — were based upon man's relationship with Eternal Laws. The first step in degeneration was the shift from man/God relationship to man/woman relationship. Today, it has degenerated even further to a level of business-mindedness. Profiteering flourishes all over the world. And even though it promotes, exploits, and feeds on the wanting and desires that annihilate simplicity and wisdom, profiteering has gained status as if it were a virtue.

One day I stopped by the peaceful surroundings of Guruji's

abode. There were a few students singing and others practicing the tabla, the two drums which represent the ecstasy of mathematics. Music took over and my whole body became alive. I sat a good while. It did not seem that I was on the earth; it seemed like a celestial place. I asked Guruji if I may learn from him and he said, "Of course, it is open to all."

Classical Indian music is perhaps the most evolved music in the world. It has a direct relationship with Creation and Eternal Laws since its primary purpose is the offering of man's joy to his Creator. The master musician does not teach an instrument, or voice, he teaches music itself. A flutist may teach a student violin; a vocalist may teach a student tabla.

Guruji explained to us that you do not have to have any inborn musical talent to learn it; each one can learn and there are no exceptions. One may have a good voice, a bad voice, or no aptitude. It does not matter. Music represents more than vocal cords. More important than the quality of voice is the atmosphere the voice carries. It relates one with the spiritual centers of the body that produce peace and serenity, the holy offering of your gladness to your Creator. It is the quality of a virtuous life that awakens the musician's holy faculties.

My interest became my teacher and I practiced day and night. I learned the sacredness that accompanies Indian music.

*   *   *

I was twenty-four when I met my second teacher, on a train. Giani Kartar Singh, a genius and Gandhi-like person of noble life, lofty mind, and pure spirit, was a man of renunciation and religious outlook who never had a bank account. He was vulnerable and always had something of his own to give. Gianiji, who had the makings of a Socrates, raised politics to humanism and spiritual life.

Gianiji awakened me to an awareness that extends beyond nationality and personal interest. He taught me statesmanship, self-honesty, love of friendship, unworldliness, and self-giving. The force of Gianiji's love transformed my life and in his atmosphere I blossomed. He offered an intimate relationship through which I became a friend of Prime Minister Nehru and other eminent leaders of incorruptible lives. Under Gianiji's tutelage I was prepared to be an industrialist and to revolutionize the economy of Punjab. He wanted me to integrate the ethical and moral foundation of India and relate it with the industrial age and the technology of the twentieth century. He had said when people asked him, "What do you see in Tara Singh?"

"The word *impossible* does not apply to him. He will not accept second best and this will make him or break him."

*   *   *

In New York, in 1953, I met Mr. J. Krishnamurti.[2] He invoked in me the dawn of True Knowledge. With him the duality of relative thought came to an end. He remained and remains my Teacher for life and beyond. His teachings continue to unfold in all that I do, for relationship with him is not of time. Mr. Krishnamurti is a life-giver, comparable to Lord Buddha. In his presence one grew a century in a moment.

Mr. Krishnamurti imparted the energy to move from fact to fact in those who had the capacity to receive. Once a fact was realized, its vitality silenced the verbal chatter of the brain. He insisted that if the fact was made into an idea it was devoid of Truth. Mr. Krishnamurti also emphasized that there was but one decision in life — to end the bondage of limitation. This decision was not of choice. Mr. Krishnamurti,

*The complete story of my relationship with Mr. Krishnamurti is included in the autobiography chapter of *Our Story*, soon to be published.

Jesus, and *A Course In Miracles* extend Absolute, True Knowledge, not the relative knowledge of the clergy.

*   *   *

Driven by loneliness in New York, I was compelled to educate myself. I read from eight in the evening until two in the morning every night. When I travelled I read the classic books of each country I visited. In Navajo country I read books like *Touch the Earth;* in Iran I read Hafiz, Rumi, and Sadi; in Europe I read Rilke's *Letters To A Young Poet;* in Russia, Dostoevsky inspired me with his moments of "mystic light." Education in schools is compulsory and the classes are crowded. One is carried on by the current of tradition. You learn about names and forms, function, and cause and effect, but nothing about who you actually are. Wherein lies the wisdom in *not* knowing the truth about yourself? The manmade knowledge of experience is what the student learns. But of the unchangeable Reality that supports the world of appearances and of which we are a part, we learn nothing.

*   *   *

In 1955 I met my fourth teacher. I was staying for a while in Ojai, California, so as to occasionally meet and go for walks with Mr. Krishnamurti, and to attend his Talks in the Oak Grove. After the first Talk I sat transfixed for hours on the ground under the trees, silenced by the impact of Absolute Knowledge. When I finally got up I saw a sophisticated lady sitting in the grove as well. I had no idea anyone else was there, for it was late. She spread the mat she was sitting on and I sat by her. There were no words. Later we stood up and walked through the trees and a large meadow where the horses came running toward us.

The lady, Miss T., whose name I have chosen not to mention, had come to the Talks from New York City. Miss T. was very sensitive, well bred, and highly educated. She had studied music with Madame Boulanger in Paris for ten years and in all things her taste was exquisite and classic. Being refined, she dressed well. Miss T. knew literature, art, and theatre, and taught me the best of America. She was highly moral, deeply religious, and lived a life of simplicity. In addition, she was a great admirer of Mr. Krishnamurti. Our relationship continued for years and I learned a great deal from her.

I would never meet Miss T. without being dressed in a suit and tie. We would go for walks in Central Park or to the Cloisters and sit for a long time in silence. For her silence came naturally and she drank deeply of it. I would always walk her home to her apartment. Reverence for the wise and the elderly came naturally to me.

These were not casual relationships. For me relationship is one that affords the opportunity of self-giving and I always valued those that made the utmost demand of me. I could not have found a relationship more unnecessarily demanding or less uplifting than the one with Miss T.

Once Miss T. had gotten sick and I took care of her. I did not even have five minutes to myself. I would cook breakfast for her at my apartment a half mile away in Greenwich Village and take it to her. Then I would go pick up her mail and return with the lunch that I had made. At times Miss T. would falsely accuse me of things. It never bothered me. I was elated when one accusation was true because it gave me the opportunity to correct.

Often in the evening, at midnight, I would go and open the window on the ground floor where the landlady lived so that Miss T. would get heat in her third floor apartment. At six in the morning I would have to go back to close the window so the landlady would not know. Even though I had no time for myself, I discovered the joy of being wholehearted in one's undertaking. No money in the world could have introduced me to a state that had no thoughts of alternatives in it.

Miss T. had chosen to live a non-pretentious life, but her background and stature were contrary to the lifestyle she imposed upon herself. She lived in inexpensive apartments and had an ordinary job.

Miss T. lived alone and living alone takes great wisdom, for an idea may enter the brain and keep resounding until its vibration takes over and compels one to do things over which one has no control. Peculiar conclusions would take charge of her and one could never deter her from them. Unless aloneness is natural and inwardly productive with its ever unfolding newness, it has consequences of imbalance. Silence is the most precious and powerful state a human being can ever know, but the brain has to be free of all deception. It is not something achieved but more the given Action of Grace.

Miss T. remained unproductive and therefore deprived the world of what she had to give. When silence becomes self-centered, it is to be questioned.

Every encounter with the wise, indeed, every event in one's life, is an opportunity to learn. It is like finding a gold mine within yourself. Miss T. was a teacher and a great influence on my life. She had so much to give and yet had no ability whatsoever to learn. In truth, she never knew me even though she revolutionized my life.

It is from relationship that one learns. It teaches one more, at times, than the human teacher. Every incident has the potential to impart freedom from it, if the student has the capacity to be with the living moment. Whether the situation is good or bad is irrelevant. For me it was this relationship with the moment that inspired me and not the idiosyncracies of the mortal. With the exception of Miss T., all of my Teachers were non-commercial and unworldly — they lived by grace.

*　　*　　*

The Honorable Dilawa Hokuhutu, the Teacher of the Dalai Lama, was my next mentor. Miss T. had introduced me to him. Dilawa, the head lama of a monastery in Mongolia, was a remarkable being. He was revered by the Chinese government, and it was said, as well, that he had a standing invitation from the Emperor of Japan to be the honored guest of that country.

However, a strange phenomena had taken place. The Dilawa became enlightened. This is unusual for professional clergy. Having outgrown conventional religion he could no longer play the role. Quietly he departed, became anonymous, and went to China as a layman. From China, he went to India and eventually came to America.

When I met the Dilawa in 1958 he was living all by himself on the ground floor in an old tenement house on East 32nd Street in New York City. He had the majesty of an emperor, poised and self-reliant, wanting nothing. Having made contact with Mr. J. Krishnamurti, I was no longer in need of a Teacher. Some of what I had already learned I had yet to bring into application and organized religion had no meaning for me. But Dilawa was a state of being.

My visits to him became frequent. Now I could learn how he related with the world of laymen and women. But even more than this I observed how worldly people related with him. I became a witness. It was one of the most rewarding and inspiring periods of my life. Such learning I had not anticipated.

Dilawa was in his seventies, a quiet man without the pressure of thought upon his mind, and I remained silent for the most part. The love grew and often I felt as one with him. A new kind of learning began. It invoked an internal thoughtfulness in me. An awareness of "what is" brought about a spontaneous interest and action in me. Before I knew it I started to take care of some of his needs.

There was a small group of people who visited with him. Now and then someone would stop by, sit a while, talk a little, and before leaving ask the Dilawa if he needed anything. He would invariably say, ''All is good. No need.'' Then he would ask if all was good with them. ''Good'' was the one word that was often repeated. These were friendly people, not students. They would inquire if he needed food, clothes, or laundry done. His answer was always, ''No. All is good.''

On my part, I began to wonder if it was at all necessary to ask him about his needs. So I started to discover the needs without making it obvious. I saw to it that they were met. ''Givingness'' is a force that extends itself without words.

I discovered there were cockroaches in the apartment because the building was old. Tibetans, I learned, did not kill, but they ate meat due to their home being in the mountainous regions of high altitude. I saw no contradiction in this. It is so good to give space and not make everything mental. When the Dilawa was away on one of his frequent trips to a Tibetan colony in New Jersey, I would brush turpentine wherever the cockroaches were and on the floorboards. I also took care of any other need at that time.

(Several years prior I had learned the joy of self-giving devotion in the Himalayas. Every summer Sant Gurbaksh Singh came to Simla. He would walk along a narrow footpath to a spring two miles from his residence. I would go before his arrival and remove the pebbles and sticks from the path. Every evening all through the summer I would boil milk for his evening meal and walk up 2,000 feet to take it to him, often on pitch dark, rainy nights. Such a commitment becomes a law that defies every other interest or engagement.)

What I learned by being true to one relationship and never putting it in the second place fascinated me. It seemed to make life impersonal and introduced me to an inner strength and order in life that I never would have known — that one can live amidst the hustle and bustle of New York without being controlled by circumstances. What a gift to give yourself!

There were times when I did not have money for my own food or rent — for I would not settle for having a job and being a mercenary — but an aesthetic feeling touched me when I would quietly meet Dilawa's needs instead of my own. What a blessing to overcome calculation.

In the East the simple needs of such holy and lofty men — conduits of heavenly energy — are graciously provided for by the householders. And the holy ones, who had left their homes and outgrown the comforts of family attachments, in turn, inspired the householders out of their domestic preoccupations and unfulfillment. Thus there was a relationship. For centuries, in India, a culture of friendship and hospitality existed without restaurants and hotels. In contrast, the commercialized existence of modern man seems like an insult.

The Dilawa did not want to be patronized by any one person or family. We tried to find ten appropriate people and arouse interest in them to donate $10 a month to meet Dilawa's primary needs: $50 for rent and the remainder for food and expenses.

When I first heard of this plan, I thought I could present the situation as a fact to the affluent and elite friends I knew and, by sundown, I would have the ten people. Here one learned what it is to be a student, and to learn from each situation. You grow in wisdom only heavens could impart.

Not one single person in New York found it necessary to respond. So preoccupied are our lives, so set the ways, that we cannot make the space for anything original, simple, and direct. We are confused by the unknown and our process of investigation and reasoning is inhuman, illogical, and stupid.

Each one had suggested the same solution, for in modern society you must provide a solution and guide people towards it. This usually serves as self-giving. They wanted to know what would bring such a man to New York, to such a hopeless situation? I would say, "First of all, he is not helpless. And secondly, here is where he is needed most, where everyone else is inwardly helpless."

After reviewing the situation, my sophisticated, affluent friends suggested that the best thing was for Dilawa to go back to India where he was respected. One learns what the world is like when one is dealing with a situation of eternal value, blessed with rightness.

There were two ladies who lived in a manor house beside the Hudson River next door to me in Nyack, New York, where I was living at that time. They got interested but they first wanted to investigate the saint. Now we had to display the Dilawa, incorporate their input, and make him saleable. They welcomed the opportunity of his coming. When they saw him, skin and bones, they were impressed by his holiness. They returned home and started preparing for him to come and live with them. They announced it to all their friends, by telephone and by letter. "The Teacher of the Dalai Lama is coming to stay with us."

In the midst of it all, a second thought occurred to them: "But what if he dies here?" Now the problem arose and therein ended the interest. "The saint should go back to India where he is respected," was their solution.

I recall the words of Jesus:

"VERILY, VERILY, I SAY UNTO THEE,
WE SPEAK THAT WE DO KNOW,
AND TESTIFY THAT WE HAVE SEEN;
AND YE RECEIVE NOT OUR WITNESS."[3]

*   *   *

I had lived in New York with no money, refusing to get a job. To work for another seemed so degrading, nor did I have any skills. I knew many eminent people at the United Nations and the heads of philanthropic foundations, and was a frequent guest of Mrs. Eleanor Roosevelt at Hyde Park. Relying on my own resources, I worked in consultation with the State Department, Senators, Chief Justice Douglas, and others, in the interest of bettering the relationship between the people of the underdeveloped areas and the highly industrialized world.

After a year or two back in India, where I was able to exchange the Indian currency which I had there, I returned to New York with ample money. Dilawa was not well. The same small group of friends visited with him occasionally. He had been admitted to a hospital connected with Yale University, since he had done some work for their Tibetan Studies Department. I went to visit him several times. When he returned to New York he was still not well. I had learned not to interfere but to be a witness and meet the needs.

Since I had sufficient money from the sale of my art collection, and knew of several displaced Tibetan disciples of the Dilawa living in India in desperate need, I asked the Dilawa if we could send them some money. He consented to my sending a small amount to some of his disciples, although I pleaded with him to send more.

Slowly the Dilawa was getting worse. Friends would come and urge him to see a doctor to which he would not agree. He would say, "It is not serious. No need to make a fuss." Their sympathy was overwhelming, and with enthusiasm they insisted he see a variety of doctors and healers — family doctors, homeopathic doctors, and "good Chinese doctors." But their authority was of hearsay and the enthusiasm a substitute for direct experience. The result was always no improvement. His life was in their hands but their own personal feelings prevented them from heeding. More and more doctors came against Dilawa's wishes and his health continued to decline.

While the Dilawa was in the hospital he was fond of his attending physician, a Dr. Ford. Later, when Dilawa became very weak, Dr. Ford was the only doctor he would consent to see. But he did not make house calls. Many people asked Dr. Ford to come to see the Dilawa, but with no success. Nevertheless, I went to his office on Fifth Avenue because the Dilawa had consented to see him. The nurse asked me if I had an appointment. I said, "No. I just want to see Dr. Ford for a few minutes whenever he has the time. Tell him not to hurry. I had a big breakfast and I will not be hungry for months."

Immediately on being given the message he came out to the waiting room. Dr. Ford seemed to have recognized me. I said, "Dr. Ford, I know that you do not make house calls, but I would do all the ground work, have a taxi ready to pick you up and take you wherever you need to go after the visit, if you would be kind enough to come and see our beloved Dilawa."

He agreed without hesitation and said he had his own car and would be very happy to come to Dilawa's apartment on East 32nd Street that evening. And so it was. Everyone was surprised. When someone asked Dr. Ford what made him come, he said, "Mr. Singh's sincerity." I had seen that when there is no other option or alternative in your mind and your intent is impeccable, all things work.

The student learns to heed the vulnerable voice of such a stately man. He is like a divine child entrusted to the care of humanity. But hardly anybody heard what the Dilawa wanted, nor could they give the space. Doing good was not good and yet the devotees persisted.

The Dilawa became very weak and eventually had to be admitted into the hospital for a major operation. People came to visit him from far away — a Mongolian professor at one of the universities in Indiana, the brother of the Dalai Lama, and people from Yale University, as well as his New York friends.

The student can learn from Life. School is not the only

place and certainly not the best. What you learn from your own initiative awakens sensitivity within you. It is of your own conviction and integrity.

I asked the Dilawa if he would permit me to pay the hospital bill. The all-wise Dilawa said, "Let us wait and see." People made gestures but gestures are never action. However, they raised about half the money needed to pay the bill.

There was nothing sentimental about the Dilawa. He was who he was — a law. The day of his release from the hospital, many limousines came to get him, but Dilawa would only go with the person he chose. As the end was approaching he would not even see people whose lives were not consistent with: "MAKE STRAIGHT THE WAY OF THE LORD."[4] His action put every life into right perspective.

I had art exhibits in a major gallery in Los Angeles as well as at the La Jolla Museum. Dilawa urged me to go and attend to them. I had been away for several months when a friend called and told me that I must return to New York because Dilawa was severely ill and had asked for me.

How does one respond to urgency? What kind of wisdom would it require? What would you learn about yourself? Now, within a matter of hours, I had to take care of practical matters.

The student, valuing honesty, would want to learn of "know thyself." I learned that urgency imparts its vitality and a competence that "play it safe" will never know. Within a few hours I had vacated my apartment in La Jolla, carefully packing all the valuable art and other belongings in the car. I went to see my friends with whom I could leave the packed car. They asked me how long I would be gone. I said that one does not go to see a saint with a return ticket or with any loose ends hanging. Action is always complete. I took the first plane, arrived at the East Side Terminal in New York, put my luggage in a locker, picked up some flowers, and walked to Dilawa's apartment, arriving sooner than if I took a taxi.

It was about seven in the evening when I arrived. Our eyes met and I stood stunned to see the Dilawa a mere skeleton. I must have stood there for over two hours. I could not move. Someone pulled a chair up and had me sit. I sat until midnight without any distraction or word.

It was late when I left the apartment with a friend and I did not know where I was. As I collected myself I recalled that my luggage was at the terminal. I went to get the luggage and then to a dilapidated hotel near the terminal.

Although the hotel room was appalling and the atmosphere malevolent, I slept some hours. I took my bags down and left them at the desk to be picked up later and went again to see the Dilawa. Not until midnight did I leave. So, I returned to the same hotel and paid for a room for the night. I did the same thing for three nights in a row but never had the time to move to a better hotel. On the fourth day, in the early hours of the morning, Dilawa breathed his last. The sky thundered as the Tibetan monks started their chanting.

What I had learned about vulnerability, non-defensiveness, "RESIST NOT EVIL,"[5] not to interfere, and the impersonal action beyond feelings, remains incomparable. This was in 1964.

*   *   *

My life then took a turn and I returned to the source of life, my roots in India, to make contact with internal life and the vitality of the spirit. Having extricated myself from all obligations and family ties, I felt blessed by the spacious aloneness of my life. A sense of freedom overwhelmed me. It was as if I was uplifted by being my own man. Wanting and unfulfillment were fading away and the dawn of having something of my own to give was upon me.

It was during my solitary existence in South India that I
had several encounters with Shankaracharya of Kanchipuram
in the state of Madras, now known as Tamil Nadu. From
Shankaracharya I learned much that is not earth-born.

The Adi, the original Shankaracharya, born in 788 A.D.,
was an enlightened being. He wrote commentaries on the
Vedas, Shastras, Upanishads — the sacred Sanskrit scriptures.
Even at a very young age he was lucid and formidable; his
words were realized. His renowned name is chiseled in the
memory of Hinduism. It is he who had said:

> "Knowledge is not brought about by any means
> other than enquiry, just as an object is nowhere
> perceived without the help of light."

> "Everything is produced by ignorance and dissolves
> in the wake of knowledge."

> "When the mind becomes purified like a mirror,
> Knowledge is revealed in it. Care should therefore
> be taken to purify the mind."[6]

Tradition has it that he passed his power on and the lineage
continues. But this was not my own direct experience.

While in Madras, since the south of India is known for
holy men, I asked a friend if he knew of a God-lit saint. My
religiously inclined engineer friend said, "Yes, Shankaracharya
is unquestionably the holiest."

Some weeks later the engineer came to lunch. There was
the first rain of the season the day before and the earth was
impregnated and alive. The purity of air was infused with
pranic energy. Overhead the Krishna-colored sky had clouds
of dramatic forms. We went for a drive with five friends. The
countryside surrounding Madras is unforgettably beautiful.
Centuries upon centuries of man's holy thought has produced

a benediction upon the land and a peace rarely encountered elsewhere. The silent feet of men, women, and children of the Dravidian race had walked there for untold centuries. It may well be the oldest land on the earth, perhaps having survived even the deluge of Noah's time.

It has been a vegetarian civilization, free of slaughterhouses, from time immemorial. Out of this land, the sensitive, pious-minded Dravidians of dark complexion and classic features, built temples of great magnificence. Amidst the wooden wheels of the bullock cart and pastoral landscape it produced the greatest of the God-lit men ever known in the 19th and 20th centuries — Sri Ramana Maharshi of Tiruvannamalai and Mr. J. Krishnamurti. And out of the neighboring Bengal emerged the incarnation Sri Ramakrishna Paramahamsa.

It was pleasant and we drove for about thirty miles. The engineer recalled that I had wanted to meet a saint. He suggested that we inquire to see if the saint he knew about was there. We discovered where he was in the outskirts of Kanchipuram, a short distance away.

When we arrived we were asked at the entrance to the compound, which consisted of several acres with trees and a hut, to remove our shoes and shirts. No sooner had I stepped into the compound than my mind, stimulated by the chatter in the car, instantly came to stillness. I don't even remember being amazed. It was not the kind of experience I had known before.

In the twilight blue of the evening we walked toward a group of four or five people sitting some distance away. My companions, in the manner of the south, prostrated themselves, laying fully flat on the ground in reverence. I stood, charged with the stillness that knew no lack. My friends urged me to ask questions but I was in a state that had no questions and needed no answers. After awhile another friend whispered in a loving tone that I could ask the Saint for his blessing. But

I felt blessed already. There was not a thought in my mind and I was not even curious or interested to know which one out of the group was the Saint.

I stood transfixed and it seemed as if I could remain that way forever. But householders have their tomorrows. As much as they were stunned by what had happened to me — something so auspicious — they had to attend to their duties. After a few hours they gently took me by the arm and walked me back to the car. I could hardly speak on the way home and very little for days afterward. For the first time I had understood what the word *darshan* — the vision of the holy — means beyond the word.

A week passed and, with a friend, I went again to see the Saint. It was a Sunday and there were hundreds of men and women in a long queue holding flowers and coconuts for offering. Each one in turn prostrated himself.

When our turn came we bowed respectfully. I felt too shy to prostrate but I made my offering of fruit and flowers. It was a hot day and we went and sat under a tree and watched until all those who had come had made their pranams.*

The Saint then went to his hut. Part of the crowd clustered around the cottage while others departed. Perhaps over an hour passed and, to my great surprise, I saw the Saint in his saffron dhoti emerge from the crowd like a flame. Gently and deliberately he walked toward the tree where I was sitting.

As he came closer I stood up and walked toward him. Our eyes met and the presence of goodness engulfed me. Every cell of my body became alive. We stood awhile and then he walked backwards away from me, like a Bharat Natyam dancer impersonating Lord Krishna or Lord Shiva. He handed his attendant the rosary he was wearing to give to me.

---

*Offerings. (Editor)

On my third visit he was at the temple surrounded by hundreds of devotees and pilgrims. I stood in the long line of people with my offering. A young monk with dark, clear eyes and unworldly countenance recognized me and told the Saint that I had come again. The Saint told the boy to fetch me. I went, bowed in my unconventional way, and the Saint asked me to sit near him while others came, made their offerings, prostrated, and left. Shankaracharya surrounded everyone who approached him with his pure energy. As each one came he would say, "All will be well." To the next, "All is well." To the next, "All is good." With his outstretched hand he blessed everyone with the gesture of reassurance.

After a while I politely took my leave so that I would not interfere with others who had come. The boy came running after me with a message from the Saint asking if I would like to meet him alone to talk? I said that would be nice. The Saint told the boy to tell me to return in two hours at four o'clock.

We met. There were not many intricate questions or problems. In his presence one was overcome by a sense of wholeness. He did ask me what I did and where I was from. I told him I was studying the Vedic and Upanishad way of life.

Being a Sikh, he said I was of Nanak, the great Sikh prophet. He also said that I was meant to live abroad — that it was blessed. We stayed a long time together and words were not half as good as the purity of silence.

I learned a great deal. My life was affected by every encounter with him. To recount and to measure seems futile. I met him on two other occasions. The last time was when I went with a group of friends, foreign and Indian, to receive his *darshan.*

When we arrived at Kanchipuram we learned that Sri Shankaracharya was in silence for the day. Kanchipuram is a city of temples and my foreign friends, with their cameras, became consumed by sightseeing. Before they dispersed they asked me to come with them to see the temples. I said, "No, I have come to see the Saint." "But he is in silence." I insisted, "I came to see the Saint. I do not know options, so I prefer to stay here." Who knows the power of desirelessness?

Some hours passed and quietly the Saint appeared from out of the temple. He came and sat near where I was. I could see my French friend in the distance preoccupied with photographing the temple.

That is all I remember about the external scene. I asked the Saint that if he were to be in Kanchipuram, could I stay with him for a month and meditate before I left India. He nodded, "Yes." There is much I learned in these brief encounters. I hope the reader does too.

*　　*　　*

A saint is one whose pure spirit has renounced and outgrown the world and possessions. His holiness is his treasure. The poet had said, "The heart of a king trembles before a man who wants nothing." You cannot go to see a saint with other plans and options, for then it is distractions that regulate you. The power of your own wholeness is a law. Quietness has its own sanity and wisdom. To be desireless is a way also of knowing the saint within yourself. If you could have no alternatives, then, in actuality, you came to see the saint. How could he refuse darshan to the one who could receive it?

Learning and teaching, giving and receiving, are infathomable. They cannot be limited to a small fraction of cells in the brain. Little knowings and beliefs are more a distraction and detrimental. Pretense is dangerous because it sustains separation. To learn through silence is supreme and meditation is the greatest of blessings. Heed these words of

Mr. J. Krishnamurti and you will know what I am saying:

"Wisdom has no direction."

Having no alternatives is perhaps more arduous for most people to achieve than a masters degree, and yet it is having no alternatives that is the ground for the human being to flower.

*   *   *

My next and last teacher, I was privileged to meet in 1977. She had probably a greater impact on my life than anyone except Mr. Krishnamurti.

In Virginia Beach, in 1976, I heard Judy Skutch speak on *A Course In Miracles* — how it came into being and about the Scribe. Judy was so articulate and brilliant in her presentation; I was moved and thanked her. Some months later we met again and walked together awhile. I wondered if it was possible to make contact with the Scribe of *A Course In Miracles* who refused to gather people around her and was not all that accessible. Judy said that she had spoken to the Lady about me and that it may be possible.

On July 27, 1977, Judy invited me to stay the night with her and her husband, Bob Skutch, in New York where I was to meet Helen Schucman, the Scribe of *A Course In Miracles*. When I arrived at Judy's spacious apartment facing Central Park, I was introduced to Helen Schucman. She abruptly asked me, "Are you a holy man?" This caught me off guard and brought me to attention. It was a difficult question because it demanded nothing less than self-honesty. I did not know what to say, but one thing was certain, I could not be casual in her presence. Sentimentality and politeness vanished.

I said, "In times past, in ancient India, there was a sage who had a temper. When the students could not respond adequately he would throw stones at them. There was one student who would gather the stones and place them in a pile before the teacher prior to the next lesson. I am that student."

On the surface, Helen Schucman appeared to be preoccupied with earrings that Judy was to get for her. But you cannot hide the sun by placing a sheet before it. Bill Thetford, Bob Skutch, and Ken Wapnick were also present and we spent time together. The next day, when I left the Skutches, I flew to San Francisco where Jerry Jampolsky met me at the airport and took me to Tiburon as his guest.

My second meeting with Helen Schucman took place at her home in October, 1978, on Yom Kippur, the holiest of the holy days. Since that time, it seems as if we have never parted.

In India I knew a Sikh saint. On an auspicious day, in the early hours of the dawn, a group of devotees quietly went to his room and asked him if he would like to come to bow at the Temple. After a long pause, the saint said, "I bowed my head once and I have never lifted it since."*

My relationship with the Scribe of *A Course In Miracles* transcends learning. Since then this life has become part of the action of *A Course In Miracles* and I am blessed to be alive. The Course is for the very serious student. It would transform coming generations and bring the light of heaven to earth.

*   *   *

THESE ARE NOT STORIES

My Teachers, Guruji, Gianiji, Shankaracharyaji, Krishnaji,

---

*For a complete account of this incident, see *A Course In Miracles — A Gift For All Mankind* by Tara Singh (Foundation for Life Action, 1986), pages 74-76. (Editor)

and the Scribe of *A Course In Miracles* were limitless —
treasures of humanity. Their lives remain the permanent light
upon the planet. The *Manual for Teachers* of *A Course In
Miracles* says of the Teachers of God:

> *And then they are seen no more, although their thoughts
> remain a source of strength and truth forever.* [7]

How few understood the loftiness of the Scribe of *A Course
In Miracles*, who remained anonymous and would not accept
helplessness as a part of life or indulge personality issues, the
opinions that most people regard as absolute.

We learn from the Dilawa of his holiness, set in the most
adverse circumstances. If the reader does not appreciate the
vulnerability of the Dilawa, he misses out on a man who lived:

> *By grace I live. By grace I am released.*
> *By grace I give. By grace I will release.* [8]

The Dilawa allowed others to do what they wanted with
his body — to teach them the consequences of irresponsibility
and trust in false enthusiasm. From the Dilawa we learn, *In
my defenselessness my safety lies.* [9]

And from Guruji, too, we learn:

> "AND WHY TAKE YE THOUGHT FOR RAIMENT?
> CONSIDER THE LILIES OF THE FIELD,
> HOW THEY GROW;
> THEY TOIL NOT, NEITHER DO THEY SPIN. . ." [10]

What have skyscrapers, shopping centers, or houses of
entertainment to give? It is the boredom of a false lifestyle that
sustains them. To be related with such beings is to witness the
glory of man as God created Him.

I am not a body. I am free.
For I am still as God created me. [11]

From Miss T.'s conclusion to live an unpretentious life, we learn that it is totally out of place in a city. Living in an apartment where you share the kitchen with others and riding back and forth in a subway every day for hours to a meaningless job makes one calculating and always concerned about money. To impose upon oneself the most austere discipline usually results in the crystallized and harsh tendencies of a narrow, routine existence.

It is not that one should withdraw from the city. Most people are doomed if they do, for small towns are gossip-ridden, dull, and ugly, with ordinary people of TV minds who know only cliches. Perhaps few, if any, are close to the dawn or the twilight, to the stars, or the morning dew, nor do they know the creative spirit of man's expression.

Guruji, Krishnaji, and the Scribe of *A Course In Miracles* were liberated beings, therefore, the most productive individuals I had ever known. They were extensions of what man calls Love and Wisdom, bearers of the *eternal good*. None of my Teachers charged fees or lived off their students. The fact is that they were not teachers in the conventional sense.

Rarer even than a Teacher is the student who recognizes the vertical Teacher of life, whose life is non-commercial, and who has the capacity to learn from each encounter rather than from books.

Once you are awakened you learn much more than any school or university can impart. But where would you go to be awakened? All the institutions of learning, universities, and so-called teachers — all those who are out in the open — are mere interpreters of knowledge. True Knowledge is nowhere to be found by those who have lost discrimination. And extremely rare is the student who needs it. There are those who want to be students, but very few who really *are* students. All the Teacher has is for the student if he will but receive it. A true Teacher dispels all doubt and purifies the mind. He has an intrinsic power to transmit. You meet such Teachers only if you value wisdom and virtue in your life and will not live by man's conventions.

Direct knowledge is what the Enlightened Being transmits. The sages in India and China related the student with the very source of his being. To them the brain had a different function than preoccupation with learning and self-improvement.

My Teachers are still alive in the work I do. They are all part of the dawn of the Non-Commercialized Action in America which flowered with the Foundation for Life Action. It represents wholeness, the totality of One Life, the humane perspective that is religious because it is of the spirit, not dogma. When religion becomes dogma, it is limited. The fact is that love, spirit, and truth are unlimited.

God's Plan for Salvation — the curriculum of *A Course In Miracles* — provides an opportunity for those of strong mind and pure heart to come to flowering and to transform life. The Foundation for Life Action fully realizes the significance of God's Plan for Salvation. The place is blessed where the opportunity of self-transformation is made possible. In times to come the transformation of one person will revolutionize life upon the planet and Absolute Knowledge will awaken a new age.

The Foundation for Life Action started on the principle of the one-to-one relationship and, for us, it is the human being who comes first. We endeavor to lead a life of ethics and virtue and live by Eternal Laws.

The Foundation for Life Action, a federally approved, nonprofit, educational foundation, has evolved into a School dedicated to training teachers to bring *A Course In Miracles* into application. It does not accept charity or seek donations, nor does it own a community. Because the Name of God cannot be commercialized and ill-earned money begets other vices, the School charges no tuition. It has its own integrity of bringing the student to:

— being self-reliant and productive,

— extending his own intrinsic work
   and not working for another,

— having something of his own to give
   and never taking advantage of another.

The work of the Foundation is to be consistent with the Call to Wisdom of the Founding Fathers and "In God We Trust."[12] Its timelessness will affect all that is of time. It is an action of wholeness that has something to share, something to give.

Truth is not learned, but realized. Whenever it is realized, you see you are not a separate entity from that which is God-created and eternal. There are no nationalistic boundaries, no political or economic divisions, nor organized, religious dogmas in it. To heed the true words of Jesus is to know the Absolute and to take it beyond verbal, intellectual understanding. It is application that ends duality and conflict within man. *A Course In Miracles* tells us man is . . . *under no laws but God's.*[13]

Religious beliefs make people small-minded, as do political concepts, economic theories, and military defense systems. Institutions of education have done little to free man from national prejudice and friction. Instead, they have kept the past alive. Parents will find it difficult to keep the child's mind free from beliefs and dogma. And because of that, the need is greater to awaken oneself in order to protect the child. There is only so much the professional teacher at school can do. Much may have to be undone. But you, as a parent, can introduce your child to the lives of men and women of ethics like Emerson, Thoreau, and John Muir. There is a lot of goodness in America to share with the child.

The function of education is to awaken man to the Call to Wisdom and Freedom and to his own God-created, eternal Self. Instead, by imparting skills and not Knowledge, education has served only as a means of survival. It enslaves man to the body and the brain; it does not introduce him to his free spirit. It bolsters a culture of irresponsibility and promotes not life, but death. Education is to awaken you to who you are; then you will know all there is. The Mind of man, lit with the light of heaven, can have no sense of lack. It sees only what God created.

To bear and rear children of strong mind and pure heart will right all wrongs in your life. The parents are blessed by the light the child brings to them. It is through the child we learn of this awakened love within us. And parents are under an obligation to introduce the child to his God-given potentials.

There is a growing awareness in America, perhaps everywhere, that one need not be subject to limitations of conventional schooling, which trains people to be wage earners. Families can get together and start their own school. Experiments were made by teachers who went to the child's home to teach as opposed to teaching them in a classroom setting. It was found that one hour of instruction, one-to-one at home, was worth days in the classroom. Home schooling is on the rise, but one must be aware of the pitfalls as well. Mr. Krishnamurti has warned that if you limit your children to your own world, you merely condition them with your prejudices and beliefs. Children need children for play, laughters, friction, and exercise.

There are resources to help the parents who want to educate their child at home. Holt Associates, 729 Boylston Street, Boston, MA 02116, publishes a newsletter and provides resource information to anyone interested in alternatives to public education.

In addition, the Foundation for Life Action offers a service of one hour consultation free of charge to anyone in need.

CHAPTER ONE

1

THE LAWS OF PARENTING ACCORDING TO THE DIVINE PERSPECTIVE

A child comes to birth, to earth, for his own divine function and he needs love's protection, the atmosphere that sustains life. Involuntarily, love wells up in the parents for their offspring. This love is effortless and natural, an energetic gift of God to the parents who instantly become co-creators. This is the ever-renewing divine Action of Life. In reality there is no difference between the child and the parents. It is the One Life ever extending its manifestation. We are all its children.

The parents are blessed with an awakening of care which calls upon deeper levels and potentials within them. If their caring is not intense they deprive themselves of their own wholeness. When the perspective is right, however, the child's presence can bring a rebirth in the parents themselves. Jesus spoke of this spiritual rebirth when He told Nicodemus:

"VERILY, VERILY, I SAY UNTO THEE,
EXCEPT A MAN BE BORN OF WATER AND OF THE SPIRIT,
HE CANNOT ENTER INTO THE KINGDOM OF GOD.

THAT WHICH IS BORN OF THE FLESH IS FLESH;
AND THAT WHICH IS BORN OF THE SPIRIT IS SPIRIT."[1]

As life on the planet becomes more fragmented and pressured, the growing child needs much greater protection from the stimulation of the manmade world which surrounds him. It is quite a responsibility to keep the child's vulnerable mind free from the images of fear and ambition. The question is, will the parent change and impart the newness of the moment to the child and thus, from the very outset, be consistent with the Action of Grace? Is it possible to raise a child responsibly without also awakening awareness within ourselves?

There is no dependence in Creation, only relationship, for Life is one. That is the Law. Everything in the universe exists to bring man to perfection. Thus Life has provided the parent and the child with all that they need. The milk comes to the mother's breast prior to the birth of the child; the teeth appear when the child is ready for solid food. Knowing the fact that all needs are met protects you from insecurity, for it relates you to the holiness of Life.

There is a new way of looking at responsibility. Few have known its benediction or how it focuses the universal forces and gets things done effortlessly. Generally, the world perceives responsibility as a burden while the contrary is, in fact, true. Responsibility frees us from our own limitations.

The things a child needs to learn are not necessarily taught in school. School is where his external faculties are trained and skills acquired to make a living in the world. Real education, on the other hand, would relate the child to his divine nature.

Parents must see the false as the false to provide the child with the right atmosphere. And as we will see, a parent need not feel inadequate in facing the challenge.

A Course In Miracles states:

> *Do not despair, then, because of limitations. It is your function to escape from them, but not to be without them. . . . All the help you can accept will be provided, and not one need you have will not be met.* [2]

This truth establishes its own strength and space upon which nothing external can intrude.

Thus we begin with the parents' need to realize a new conviction, a new vitality that neither draws conclusions nor imposes weaknesses upon them. Now that they realize they are raising a child of God their whole perspective changes. With the child comes the grace that surrounds him as well as his parents. They are no longer limited to their own resources. All the forces of the universe are focused in the child. He is not isolated from the Action of Creation and so the parent is not alone in his upbringing. Helplessness is only an indication of our belief in separation from totality.

The demands of the external world, including the educational system, will change as you, the parent, put your alternatives away. Take the approach of one who wants to learn. Make it your need to know Truth and the action of wisdom. Wisdom is a plea of goodness that finds a common ground. Because wisdom never underestimates the potential of goodness in another, it carries with it human warmth which even the most threatened mind would heed.

In actuality there is only one mind — the Mind of God. It remains ever impeccable, for it is guarded by His Grace which extends to every human being. It is the brain, limited to the physical senses, that can be conditioned, prejudiced, and trained to hate and fear. Indoctrinated by limitations, man is preoccupied with survival; conditioned into a narrow existence of routine and habit, he rarely ever attains his full potential.

The parent must see that the child came to be awakened. Thus a process begins in which the parent himself becomes his own teacher and pupil. He learns to be free of dependence — a self-sufficiency that is essential to discover what relationship means.

It is time we realized the consequences of not bringing the child up as God intended. What man identifies with he becomes. Limiting the child to physicality denies his Reality. Thoughts of fear and negativity will make the child susceptible to the vested interests of society. If from a very young age the child's vulnerability is invaded upon by our fear and discontent, he soon becomes defensive.

Let us instead introduce the child to the awareness of:

In my defenselessness my safety lies.[3]

And,

My present happiness is all I see.[4]

How rare is the person who is in the present, the only reality. Past and future are the projections by which we normally live but the limitless reality of the present dispels the illusions of past and future. The present is free from the belief system of man. Consciousness, freed of its limited content, is holy and boundless.

Because the parent is the co-creator the strength of rightness can protect him from limiting himself. An individual affects all of humanity whenever his action is consistent with Eternal Laws.

Let us not limit the child to his physical consciousness. If we do survival will become his preoccupation. This dissipation of energy deprives the child of the vitality of passion which can discover its own vast potential and the simplicity of self-sufficiency. Teach the child to renew himself with the energy of silence and it will provide the passion for him to outgrow the limitations of man's material preoccupations.

It is trust that frees the mind, not education.

*   *   *

Blessed the birth of a human being
who dies to all things of the world
before he dies.

Blessed the parents who give the world a child
who would be honest to his words
and responsible for his deeds
all the days of his life —
a child who sees only the One Indivisible Life
behind differentiation.

This is the supreme goal of parents and society —
to align with Universal Intelligence
and raise a child of God,
independent of all belief, lack, and limitation.

Surely wholeness will not be divided.
Though society will not change its abstract values,
Awakened Vision is still possible.

All is already perfect and complete.
The resources are intact
— in the midst of brain activity —
to be with the Peace of God.

CHAPTER TWO

2

THE CHILD TEACHES ONE TO LOVE

To raise a child of God changes must begin in the parents and the prospective parents. What kind of life would they have to live to raise a child responsibly? What kind of child do they want to bring into the world? Do they have virtue and truth to share with him? The child comes with the light of heaven, but it is difficult — though not impossible — for us to change as parents.

There is a natural urge to want to have a child. But the responsibility that goes with it is demanding. We want to fit the child into our lifestyle of job, activity, stimulation, and outlets, and we are reluctant to question our values and change our habits. What kind of atmosphere would you provide for a child?

One of the most important factors in raising a child is the character of the parents. Is the wife inspired by the noble seed of the man whose child she wants to bear? Does she have that discrimination? Is the husband responsible for his seed, for the quality of it and what he will extend to the world? Or is he always unfulfilled, lacking, and therefore, continually manipulating to get something? If so, that too will be in his seed.

Once a child is conceived the wife must become a mother; she can no longer only be a wife, can no longer be pleasure-seeking and competitive. She has to have peace within; the quality of her blood must change because the child will be sustained in her womb and later by her milk. What kind of vibration does she carry? Is she insecure? Frightened? Opinionated? Aggressive? What *is* the quality of her blood? All of these factors must be considered and changes made to provide a wholesome atmosphere in which the child can grow. The opportunity the child brings is one of renewal for both parents.

Society has never been as externalized, nationalistic, and money-bound as it is today. And it has the least internal security and space. Without the protection of the parents the child will be compelled to follow its dictates. The tragedy is that most parents, being part of society, are not even aware of how conditioned they are.

Can you afford to give your child extra years in which he can be free of the pressure of abstract learning, free to play and laugh and be with his own serenity? The space the child needs to protect his innocence is totally invaded upon when, at such a young age, we send him to school. Because we over-rate the value of education his freedom and his atmosphere are taken away and conformity begins. If, during the impressionable years, you could protect what the child was born with, the child may never know the insanity of externalized life, may never be bound by nationalistic prejudice, or be limited by abstract ideas.

The parents have to be responsible to safeguard and heed their own natural wisdom. They must have the courage to stand up against the external rules the world made up. If we were responsible for the entry of a child into the physical plane, it could help us to rise above reactions and even prevent many divorces from taking place. We need to discover that the child brings something unique into being which *we* must learn to receive.

The parents have the responsibility not just to educate the child in the ways of the world but to make him aware of the boundless spirit alive within him. Once in a while parents have succeeded in giving the world a child who remains related to his wholeness. Such a child could never be false. Every parent is blessed with the potentials to succeed in this; therefore, his faith in the love that is born in stillness need never fail.

The child comes fresh like the dawn, clean and innocent, and then he does a wondrous thing. He introduces the mother to real love and shows her how to give. So if she missed out the first time — if with her husband she was too young or too excited or too selfish — now she has another opportunity to know love directly and learn to give. Her trust in the love within her would give her the strength to heed her own innate wisdom and not merely comply with standards the culture has set. It would prevent her from seeking baby sitters or putting the child in a crib in a room by himself.

The child teaches one involuntarily to love. Could you ever thank him enough for introducing you to your own real nature? That real nature is precisely what he needs to be surrounded with. How self-sufficient the child is, if we are willing to learn!

When we are not willing to learn, we evade the awakening of love within us and justify expediences. Mothers justify going to the office, putting infants and children of one, two, and three years of age in day care or school. It is unlikely that these over-schooled children will ever discover their own natural abilities. When we do not give the child the love and bonding —

the atmosphere and space he needs — the child grows up knowing fragmentation, not wholeness. He will always be plagued by a sense of unfulfillment, but will not know why.

Since the child is part of eternal life, he can teach us something that is not time-bound. But when we are unwilling to learn we teach him things of time. The entry of a child into the family can correct the factors in our own lives which bring about fragmentation. Possessions, achievements, outlets, and stimulation cannot take the place of human warmth which the birth of a child fulfills. Man was not meant to lose his sense of wholeness or relationship with his God-nature.

This raises deep questions. We tend to blame our irresponsibility on circumstances and conclude that what is virtuous, ethical, and right is impractical. In a simple way the parents must ask themselves, ''Do I want my child to fit into society or do I want to protect him from its mediocrity, violence, and insanity?'' Mr. J. Krishnamurti has said that there are very few people who are really aware of the insanity in which the present world is caught. Look around you.

Your love for your child would make you particular about what kind of education you provide for him. By meeting this responsibility the parents themselves would be guided. Real education would not teach but awaken the child to his eternal Self. Society does not encourage that. But anyone who ever amounted to anything was a person who could stand independent of society.

Unfortunately, today almost nothing can prevent a child from growing up to be a mercenary of the system. You think your child is your child? He does not belong to you; he belongs to the nation, the corporation, the economic and military forces. He belongs to the Pentagon. Once the child is exposed to the media he will want to emulate its prepackaged heroes and be an astronaut, a pilot, a policeman. He is not exposed to lofty beings like Sir Thomas More, Socrates, Lao Tzu, or Mother

Teresa; to Saint John, Saint Paul, or Mohammed. And even if he were exposed to them it would be difficult for him to aspire to their values because there is no thrill in it. Children today are accustomed to externalization and are not even aware of an inner life.

In modern society corporations run everything — transportation, media, agriculture, food distribution, fashion, news. They have the resources and exert their influence. They want you to like football; therefore, they pay football stars millions of dollars. Mediocre people are made important and after decades, the nation gets used to such heroes at every level. But it is all programmed. We have experts telling us what to do. Look at the hairstyles women are sold, the way people dress, the food they eat, their lifestyles — there is hardly any individuality left.

As we gradually become more inadequate, reliance on other people to tell us what to do becomes more common. Our own intelligence is not awakened, it is trained with skills. You hear people say, "I like my job," but the opposite of it is equally true. If you look deeply into it the job does not offer any challenge, just a paycheck with which to buy things. And the money you earn goes right back into the hands of the corporation. If corporation heads decide you should not get certain information, you do not. And whatever is presented is done so with a bias. You do not have to think anymore. Somebody else does the thinking for you as natural intelligence is being invaded out of existence.

A person with his own intelligence, the intelligence of self-reliance, can cope with any occurrence, physical or mental. He would be a unique person. He would not worship skills or the belief that somebody else knows. Is such a person being produced by our culture or the educational system today?

The human brain is like a field in which you sow seeds and grow food. What is being sown in the human brain is what the companies want that brain to do in order to harness its energy. Human energy is far superior to earth energy.* When earth energy and human energy are combined, it results in corporations.

In the absence of wisdom there is hardly a man who is capable of ending self-destructive patterns, either individually or collectively. Wisdom is incorruptible. The brain, the most sensitive organ of the body, the greatest miracle of creation, is subject to the externals. But the mind is not a physical organ; it bears the indivisible light of love. Only when it extends itself through the faculties of the brain is there peace, harmony, and holiness.

Because the child is of God, inherent in the parents is the capacity to raise the child without conformity and the fear of consequences. There would be changes the parents have to make, but every challenge is an opportunity. If we plead helplessness then we produce an exhausted, helpless generation, more advanced in violence and horror stories, more fanatic and distorted. What are we doing to our children? Children who have never had a pet are given teddy bears, Mickey Mouse, and Donald Duck. They have not seen a fawn or a running stream, nor have they known the laughter of their own feet running through the grass wet with dew. A child is as soft as dawn and his spirit is as invisible — something so gentle and tender in the midst of our noises, knowings, and bondage.

The law is that love extends itself. For a child to grow and extend his reality, you and I must grow also. Could we make sure that every answer we give him is noble and of eternal value, not something earth-born?

---

*For further clarification of "earth energies," see *The Future Of Mankind — The Branching Of The Road* by Tara Singh (Foundation for Life Action, 1986), pages 25-40. (Editor)

PARENT: I have never heard what you are sharing about children approached in this way and I see that women especially have lost touch with their real nature. We are getting so distorted, moving further away from anything real inside, from the ability to give. When a child is born there is the natural instinct to protect and nurture this being that has come, and yet very quickly we begin to violate these instincts because of ambition and unfulfillment. Is it possible to regain that purity of what a woman is? It seems we have harmed something basic.

Yes. We are so convinced of our littleness, of our lack of resources, or that the circumstances do not allow us to live differently. And we say, "I want to do this for my child but I can't." These assumptions need to be questioned.

If you love your child you will never be subject to circumstances, because he brings with him potentials that man has not yet discovered. All that you need is already provided, for perfection, being part of creation, is ever present. It is our own sense of lack that projects problems and blinds us to the compassion of Life. If you were to be honest and to trust, you would see that the life in the child is part of all Life. And Life has its own order, its own holiness.

Refuse to accept limitation as a fact. Love gives strength. It is not helpless. When we underestimate love and overvalue expedience, we betray ourselves. But if you said you would not compromise you would discover your own strength and the truth that Life preserves life.

We don't have reverence for Life; we just know how limited and weak we are. But the actuality is that man's life is a blessing upon this planet and we need have no options to love. Your reverence for everything that lives is the peace you can give the child. If you had reverence for Life you would not waste food, money, water, time, or your own life. It took only one Moses to free the slaves, part the sea, and start a new civilization; one Socrates to influence the course of thought for centuries. Your child is no less than they were. It is relationship with Eternal Laws that makes a man virtuous and that is what we have to share with our children.

Who do you think is going to bring the Kingdom of God to earth? Man. There may not be many — but what do you think Jesus did? Mohammed? Moses, Elijah, Guru Nanak, Lord Rama? Did they not bring the Kingdom of God to earth? What makes you think your child will not?

So even before conception, and certainly from conception onward, prepare for your child. Just as the birds build their nests, you need to find out how to relate with Eternal Laws. Are you going to take the child away from the whole of which he is a part and make him into a citizen? What will you teach him?

> PARENT: The standard you present for the parent is inspiring but shows me how far short of it I have fallen, and how I have, for the most part, merely transmitted my conditioning to my child. One cannot help but feel guilty.

We only feel guilty if we are not going to change. Would you be guilty if you changed? No, you would be delighted. Why not change and come to newness? If a transformation takes place within the parents, then what I have shared has served a good purpose. We believe in guilt, in punishment, and in sin. But if you read A Course In Miracles, it removes these notions. The Course says:

I am under no laws but God's.[1]

And,

I will not value what is valueless. [2]

This is what parents need to know. Don't educate the child, educate yourself. Undo your misperceptions, narrow-mindedness, bigotry, and helplessness. And then your child will not know them. In that sense the Course is the best mother and father to the parents. It takes away all fear, all guilt and sin. It doesn't believe in attack thoughts nor in punishment. In a profound way it brings to one's attention:

I am sustained by the love of God. [3]

and provides a different atmosphere in which to live. You cannot free your child from being conformed by society if you are conformed.

The wise has said that wisdom is only wisdom when it is in application in your life. If a person were wise, how would he relate to the child? Would he not teach the child a fact? And then another fact, and then another fact? This would revolutionize your life because when you are dealing with fact, opinion and assumption are gone. You have to find out what a fact is and what opinion is. A fact is independent of time. And so is a child independent of time if you would introduce him to a fact rather than your assumptions, prejudices, and fears. A fact is never afraid. What a gift you would give yourself to give the child! Teach him a fact.

Introduce silence into your life. Your stillness would take all your child's fears away and bring him to peace instantly. It is the stillness the parents impart to the child that affects his whole life. That is how bonds are established. When we live under the pressure of time, we should question its insanity.

If you love the child you will know what to do; it will come naturally. Love has wisdom and insight. Once you love your child, you love every child because love cannot be divided. The child is entrusted to you and how you bring him up will show you who you are. The child brings all the resources he needs from the day he is born to his last breath on the planet. The child comes to liberate *you*, for he is the child of God. Let us surround him with love and blessing — every child you see, everywhere — for each child is our child, not just the parents' child.

CHAPTER THREE

3

MARRIAGE

Marriage, in its essence, signifies the love of one for another, the joining of two opposites in order to give birth to a child. The eternal perspective sees marriage as two people looking in the same direction — toward God, not at each other. The whole foundation of the marriage is based on something eternal as each one becomes a strength to the other. It becomes the action of two people who would change their way of life from the horizontal to the vertical in order to make it whole. To such a couple, eternal resources are available. It is the beginning of a relationship within the One Life. New wisdom blesses the individual lives when the marriage is consistent with higher laws. The eternal acknowledges only relationship, not dependence. If the couple become absorbed in each other, then personality, which engenders weakness and indulgence, is given the strength rather than the Divine.

Marriage is a bond in which separation is no longer acknowledged; problems cannot affect it. It is the action of two people who take a stand and say, "We will not be regulated by what is external. We agree to find the resources within ourselves." How will they cope with the problems apt to emerge out of the changing circumstances in marriage? Whenever there are problems, they would question themselves: "Where have I deviated from what is right? Why am I reacting?" In this way, the real action of marriage always leads to freedom from misperception and blaming. Strength comes by being related to the eternal and valuing something beyond pleasure and personality.

This is the path of virtue and harmony. It is a pledge to live consistently with the Will of God, for God's blessing is what marriage seeks. It is a real action — one of stepping out of the personality and its activities in order to create a harmonious atmosphere in which two people can grow together and welcome a child.

In marriage, one is no longer the same. A sense of responsibility and caring for another begins to awaken; you can no longer be merely physical. Another tenderness comes in that you never knew existed. It is not sexual; it is a feeling of sacredness for another human being by whom you are completed.

Both the man and woman become noble through giving and tenderness. Every act speaks as love and respect grow. Today, most people only know common passion. Seldom do they grow in this way, where each person gives the space and recognizes the noble goodness in the other. That is a marriage.

The relationship between man and woman is physical and sexual, but it is also something else because the human being is an extension of the Divine. He can recognize his eternity, his holiness, while the animal cannot. And so the relationship between man and woman, at a higher level, is beyond desire and pleasure. It can introduce them to an action that is purely of love. How tragic it is if in a marriage this has not been discovered!

In the attraction between male and female, there are a few cases where the union produces a child that is a gift of God — a child who is not born out of pleasure. It is a three-way marriage; God is there, and the male and female are there. But the main action is of the spirit. The entity that is born would also be very evolved, one who is not so limited to the body, but who came to express something eternal *through* the body. And the parents who bring such a child have been responsible — by providing a purity of atmosphere and taking sex beyond pleasure.

For many couples today, whose children are born only of pleasure, marriage does not change or uplift them so that they are totally different beings. Having had a wrong start, the marriage often ends in divorce and the children end up having only one parent. And because most of our "friendships" are based on self-centeredness and not on higher values, we don't really have relationship with anyone. We walk around in isolation. The deterioration in society is like a landslide. Everything one sees is in decline. Even gentleness is disappearing from our relationships with one another. We don't have the time; we are too accelerated, too unsure, too uncertain. We don't even know who we are.

There are so few people who can see a thing through to the end. Who can dare to say his words are valid, that nothing of time can affect them? Marriage is for life. It must be based not only on attraction for another but on wanting to build a life together based on ethics. If we are motivated merely by physical forces, sensation, and pleasure, there is the sorrow of not discovering what a real marriage is. Sorrow should always alert us to question, "Where have I gone wrong?"

What makes life meaningful and happy is having something of one's own to give. One finds fulfillment only in giving. This is a law one has to heed. To find someone to whom you can give is the real search in life, even though the impression is that we always *want* from another. This is only partially true. The fact is, there is no greater joy than when you have found someone to whom you can give. Givingness is what makes marriage possible. It brings relaxation, peace, and sharing of the deepest part of one's being. It opens the heart.

We know so little about the heart. We have analyzed and probed into it, but of its essence, we know very little. We associate it with feeling because feeling and experience is all our bodies know. Experience automatically becomes memory; and memory is always of the past. Most of mankind is controlled by the routine and habit of memory and the repetition of experience.

But the heart, in truth, is of another realm. It does not fall into these categories. There is a subtle heart on the right side of the chest that few know about. It is barely physical, but is the core of impeccable life. It can never be contaminated. Its action is Divine.

Men and women who are inspired by God are moved by this universal heart. The love between husband and wife, in particular, must move towards the spiritual heart. Marriage, with its shift to givingness, is the appropriate atmosphere in which to reach, to touch, that which is non-physical in life, and non-physical in sex. Relaxation and the serenity that slows down thought provide the energy for that which is not of words or time to come into being.

It is not easy to come to such harmony. The key is when you yearn to give rather than to have. Then you are moving in the right direction. Only when one's life extends rightness is it free of consequences. Such a life is boundless in its freedom, for it has learned to give. It makes sex secondary.

Givingness will not fit into time limitations. It is a step out of time which requires space and a brain unpressured by thought. Once a man and a woman have found the joy of giving, they have discovered the purity of innocence. They are vulnerable and defenseless.

A man at peace with himself loves simplicity. When he is not controlled by his appetites, his will is strong and pious — a compassionate light surrounds his life. Appetites can become ambitious and ruthless, for they have the lust of wanting. But the will has the power of heaven and extends virtue.

Let us learn from the outset to be calm. It is a challenge to weed out reactions. But where there is affection, reactions subside. It is best not to shape one another according to the way it should be. Watch out for unfulfillments. Marriage is an opportunity to outgrow them.

Givingness silences most of the restless, inner chatter and brings one to a calm that is not lonely. Life is in the present, but the brain constantly evades it in its preoccupation with the past and future. Thus, it constantly wants. But the heart knows and yearns to give because it is more connected to the present. You will see the present is free of time and therefore never pressured. True marriage brings one out of time into the endless present where the two become one.

How is the husband or the wife going to have the space to give to the other? Space has been taken away from man. He is pressured and his need for outlets controls him. What he needs is space, for space is required to share your real self. What you give to another is born of the space you have within yourself. But today there is no time to empty the brain and renew oneself. We live in a society that is so stimulated it limits man more and more to the body senses. We are owned. The externals make a claim upon us — the monetary system, working at a job, not having one's own land, home, or water, not being part of things that grow.

Yet marriage is based on renewal because it allows the

giving. The love of a husband and wife is where an individual action is still possible, where affection and compassion are still possible, from which another value system, another lifestyle, can evolve. Simplicity and wisdom go together but neither are possible without relaxation. How you would find the boundless space within yourself in the present circumstances will take conviction and the discrimination to see the false as the false.

This book is written for those who see the need to awaken and be true to themselves; therefore, they need not conform to the pressures of society. Neither react, nor accept, but be responsible for your life, for what you say, what you do. This is meaningful and productive. When you have learned to give in your own family, to one another, you will have something of your own to give to mankind. It is a different lifestyle. In your having something to give, all your problems are solved. There would not be a single need that would remain unfulfilled.

There has always been and will continue to be friction, tension, and wars between individuals and nations. Marriage offers the joyous opportunity to discover that the one person you love, to whom you learn to give, has civilized you and transformed your life. Thus givingness breaks the bond of time and self-centeredness, and continues to extend itself onward in the child. Each needs the other to end the separation. That is the primary function of a marriage blessed by God. A child born out of non-separation grows up with the awareness of inherent wholeness.

The fact is that we exist as potential. It is man's potential that has the capacity to receive. But in this mundane world, receiving has become difficult, unnatural, and nearly impossible. How can receiving really be difficult? How can gratefulness for *what is* be difficult? We are surrounded by two worlds. The God-created world that sustains life is perfect, ever giving, and beautiful. It is independent of manmade rules. The manmade world in which we live is based on human appetites, survival, and educated ignorance. In it there is neither the space to give nor to receive. It has become highly commercialized. It spends more money on fear than everything else put together. Man's life without ethics and responsibility produces problems and pressures.

To develop the capacity to receive, the woman must only give and serve in every way. She would receive many, many-fold more than she could ever give. The heavens would shower blessings upon a woman who serves her husband and her family. By so doing she gives strength, confidence, virtue, peace, nobleness, and dignity to her husband, which he needs in order to know who he is.

The woman brings peace and harmony into the family. It is a warm house where the woman is at peace. But if she loses patience and becomes competitive, justifies her frustrations and makes demands, it drains the male energy, haggling starts, and the forces of divorce and discontent begin their voodoo dance. The woman's internal disorder would affect the house. It would be devoid of warmth, like a house without a light, a lamp without a wick. And her children would not have integration.

As a mother, as a wife, her main function is integration. She is the shelter for each one in the family. When she is true to her own Divine nature and to her God-given function — the feminine polarity — she is happy and blessings are upon the family.

> "LET THE HUSBAND RENDER UNTO THE WIFE DUE BENEVOLENCE: AND LIKEWISE ALSO THE WIFE UNTO THE HUSBAND."[1]

> "BUT I WOULD HAVE YOU KNOW, THAT THE HEAD OF EVERY MAN IS CHRIST; AND THE HEAD OF THE WOMAN IS THE MAN; AND THE HEAD OF CHRIST IS GOD."[2]

The minute she becomes assertive, she has lost her own nature and is not at peace with herself. The answer is not that she must subordinate herself to man; no one needs to have authority over another. There are differences of polarity, temperament, and psychology. The answer is that she must be true to her own nature.

It is the woman that is entrusted with a womb, of which the home is an extension — that womb where the family lives. Man is more the strength of nobleness, daring, fearlessness. She is not to know insecurity and she will never know scarcity. He is not to know weakness which corrupts his nobility, the very poise of his life. It is the discovery of who you are that brings about something sublime in relationship. Relationship is not limited to gratification or dependence. It is looking in the same direction, each being true to his God-nature.

I am as God created me.[3]

This is the aim, the goal, the aspiration, and those few who have realized it are the Lights of the world. It is not a man's monopoly, or a woman's monopoly, it is each one's responsibility.

*　　*　　*

PEACE

It is amazing how strong one little weakness is. Its impurity can defy and undermine the whole life of a person — his virtue, strength, holiness, perfection. To one such trait everything else is subordinate. You *want* to correct it but it takes your attention away. Then you discover, if you are lucky, the pursuit of correction is the very life of the weakness. Constantly you are preoccupied with it under the illusion that you are improving, and for a lifetime you are misled without knowing.

This is the story of mankind. Every generation believes in peace, searches for peace, while giving its energy to war. War is ever there, ever destructive, cruel and painful, while we are busy with the illusion of seeking peace. The very seeking is the promotion of war.

Peace within and peace on earth are indivisible, a wholeness so spacious it caresses everything it sees and touches. It is our lack of inner peace that expresses its anguish and externalizes life. Ever dissipated, it seeks energy from sources without. It exploits nature and becomes subservient to money and other factors, and now there are thousands of artificial barriers between man and man, man and woman, and even parents and children. And because we are unable to outgrow, make internal correction, and change, we make *ideals* of virtue, rightness, and ethics. But an ideal is never real; our internal conflict is real. How many deceptions one has to overcome to come to self-honesty!

Competition between the genders is a violation which prevents wholeness. Without wholeness we dissipate the life force within. And for this pure and impeccable life force we are responsible. It already *is*; it is not something you have to achieve. It is something you retain, protecting it and guarding it against your lower nature. The law is that nothing can intrude upon your own purity and holiness. But when we blame the externals for our difficulties, misperception has already taken place, and we are lost from the outset.

One cannot externalize a problem, for there are no problems externally. The root and the source of every problem is internal misperception. Correction is only possible at the internal level. Wisdom starts with self-knowing. The relative knowledge by which man lives, and is so thoroughly educated by society and the school system, may pretend to know the solution, but it doesn't know what the *problem* is.

"Know thyself" is the maxim.

Mr. J. Krishnamurti points out that man only lives in relationship. Relationship is the mirror through which you discover who you are. Who you are is jealousy, fear, loneliness, sorrow, the compelling need for distractions. Are you willing to see this, to be a witness to it without self-condemnation, without creating conflict within yourself? Could you just observe?

Seeing a fact as a fact undoes it. It is not difficult to awaken yourself from the ''sleep of forgetfulness''[4] of who you really are.

*   *   *

LOVE

Love is that which does not change and is not subject to change. It is eternal.

If a marriage ends in divorce then it was not based on love but attachment. Love is not subject to interpretations. Having heard this will you make sure — is it love or is it attachment? We are reluctant to take things to a deeper level and make a demand upon ourselves. It is easier to just use the word ''love,'' and bring it down. But love is sacred.

That is the discrimination each individual must have. To be honest and truthful with one single relationship is all that you need. It brings order in life and has the ability to awaken.

Where there is disorder, there is confusion and a sense of despair and helplessness. When you are in that state, you call sex love for it is the only outlet you have ever known. But pleasure is not happiness. Anything that is of emotion is physical and personal. It is not dependable. Love contains all — the spiritual, the physical, and the emotional. But emotion is not all encompassing. By its very nature, because it is of time, it subsides.

The man who is fully evolved loves. Whether the person is male or female, a child or an adult, he just sees the life and not the gender. That is real love.

But we want "my darling so and so." Question it. It may be very good for a while but it doesn't last. That which is true can weather all crises, all circumstances, for it doesn't change. It loves every life and doesn't have preferences.

Have you ever loved someone just because you are full of love and you want nothing? When you love, it ends all "wanting." When you "want," it is not of love. Sensation and pleasure are not of love. You may say you like a person, or even that you love him, but then there is the *you* liking and the *you* loving — always the you. The *you* can never love.

When you love, you can heal a person just by looking at him, or thinking about him, even from a distance. The other person may never even know it. You can walk around the busy streets of New York and impart your stillness. Something takes place because when you are still you can bless. When you bless another, somehow you are blessed too. If you didn't have the blessing in you, how could you bless? By giving, you receive — but not from another person. It is a receiving from heaven because you feel the need of a brother and you want to give. And you are given what you need to give. It is so swift. Every time you see a need, you are given what you need to impart. You and God become one in that moment. You are surrounded by the compassion of God, lifted and purified, as your giving becomes your laughter and your song.

This world needs "LOVE YE ONE ANOTHER."[5] Whether we think we are great or not, if we love, we *are* great, for then we become an extension of God. Thoreau had said that the finest gift a man can confer upon his fellow man is to rise to the height of his own being. But we will never know what love is as long as we have vested interests. We will never discover our own eternal life as long as we are conditioned by concepts of time.

When we begin to see that our likes and dislikes are conditioned, we can question our thoughts and not live so much under their authority. Certainly, at times, they will still get the better of us, but somewhere something has happened. The first step in freeing oneself of conditioning is to become aware of it. From then on, you can refuse to accept anything of thought without first questioning it. This brings you to self-honesty. This is true learning. You would be more relaxed and calm no matter what you are doing. And you would have a different atmosphere around you because you are coming to self-honesty.

When I begin to free myself from the opinion that I have about you, I am becoming more open. I might find it easier to forgive you for whatever I hold against you, seeing that it is just my opinion. To the degree that I succeed in doing this, I am more at peace with myself.

We must start with forgiveness because it helps us see how conditioned we have become by our opinions. By reversing this process we begin to know ourselves, break the cycle, and become responsible. Then we can forgive anyone we think has done wrong to us. Perhaps if we were put in that spot we would have done the same thing. At the relative level, there is no such thing as a perfect situation. If you think your neighbor is bad, the next one would be worse — especially if you are of that mind. But if you have overcome your opinion of the one that you think is bad, then it doesn't matter where you are or who your neighbor is.

Unless we forgive everything that we think someone else has done wrong, we will not know peace. Without forgiving the other, we will never forgive ourselves.

*   *   *

THE TRANSFORMATION OF MARRIAGE
CONVERSATIONS WITH A HUSBAND AND WIFE

Kris, something is happening in your husband's life — he is dedicating his life to God. For him to come to the purity of giving his life to God, wholly and totally, he needs your help and support. That is the real function of the wife. Can you strengthen him to always look towards God — not towards you and not towards the world? By doing that you are also being prepared. He would be grateful, for he needs a wife who has the same ideal — to realize the Self, to know God. Can you totally dedicate yourself to making that possible for him? Then you are his strength and he can say, "I am so blessed to have a wife who is not competitive or selfish, wanting things of the world all the time. I really have a wife."

In this way growth takes place in both people. Once we come to that, the little frictions, little irritations, don't have as much meaning. They only become important when one doesn't have a clear direction or when one's priorities are not right.

In the end you will discover that every challenge you have is an asset. If the challenge, the weakness, were not there, you would learn nothing of humility, nothing about patience with others. You would become arrogant. This weakness — I call it the one-percent in each person — is what controls the life. One issue. Any single person you see today may have many extraordinary characteristics but one weakness is the controlling factor. It may be jealousy, attachment to money, reaction, selfishness, or casualness. Most people do not want to overcome it, they want to ignore it, they want to justify it, they want to brood over it and condemn themselves with it. But its real purpose is to bring other energies into being so as to constantly overcome it — because it is constantly there.

Once it becomes present in your awareness, then by giving it attention in the present it is dissolved. Then you are so grateful to have dealt with something that could have destroyed you and your marriage — that one aspect that was immature or self-centered. You can see that this weakness was also the source of the help you received. Because the weakness is there, the help is given for you to overcome it.

This action of inner correction is true to the marriage. Marriage is not for pleasure. It is to bring the two polarities to one, two people looking in the same direction. But it is important to go past the idea of this. Will you dedicate your life to making things work for your husband? He needs your strength.

If it is the other way around, that you are superior and that you can get him to do this or that, then you have started your own action and the marriage will not work. One day he will find out that you have been manipulating him and separation would come into being. The one-percent that is already there would take over.

You should feel that you have no other life, that your life and his life are no longer separated. To that degree you will have fewer demands. You are solely there to make it work for him. And then it will work for you too.

The weaker the man becomes, the more he needs a woman for strength, and the more he uses her for pleasure. She also starts using him: ''I need this. I need that.'' Shaw had said that a woman's constant demand for distraction is worse than twenty children. You see that it is true in one way or another.

Make your home simple, your life simple. Live with the total dedication that you came this time to make things work for your husband and consider it a joy. That is why God granted you this marriage. You were born a woman to help your husband, so you are being true to your nature. And do you think if he makes it you are going to be left out? There is no separation in life. The whole culture is falling apart because it does not believe in cooperation; it believes in competition and ambition.

There is a story of a young man who became a Sufi saint of the highest order. When he was young, his mother inspired him to yearn to know God and as he grew older, he left home and went into the forest to meditate with the sages who lived there. The mother told him to come back when he was enlightened to awaken them.

While he was practicing austerities in the forest, he made some experiments with the powers he had achieved. He saw some sparrows and said, ''Sparrows. Die!'' When they died, he was horrified. Immediately he said, ''Sparrows. Live!'' And they came to life. Now he thought he was developed enough to go back to see his mother.

While passing through a certain village along the way, he stopped at a well where a woman was drawing water. The custom is that when someone is standing at a well, it is only courtesy to immediately draw water for him. But this woman did not serve him; she just filled her own pitcher. He watched, and thought, ''She must not have seen me, she will probably serve me the next time.''

Again it happened that she put the water into her own pitcher without offering him any. He was beginning to think (his one-percent reaction is starting to surface): ''How arrogant this woman is not to serve me. No courtesy.''

Just then the woman looked directly at him and said, ''Sparrows die. Sparrows live.''

He was shocked. ''How did you know?'' He fell to his knees before her. (Notice it is a different culture. There is humility.) He said, ''How did you become all-knowing? I have been meditating in the forest with the sages for sixteen years and I have not yet come to that state.''

"I serve my husband."

What a beautiful thing, that by taking care of her husband the woman had come to realization. Not "me and mine," not competition, not separation — marriage means coming to One Life in which both of you as personalities die.

The wife must keep the home absolutely at peace. Whenever your husband does something you think is wrong, you are not going to see it as wrong, you are going to see that reaction is still alive in you. It is not your department to correct him; your department is to correct yourself. It gives purpose to life. Marriage is an opportunity to give, and you will find your joy in giving. A casual lifestyle of "me and mine" can never be happy. But to perfect what marriage is, not what is more advantageous to you, brings deep happiness. Wrong and right should not affect it. All our knowing is poisonous because there is no *love* in it.

There is no ideal marriage. Friction is inevitable. But if each of you wants to overcome dependence and come to relationship, God would help you find the strength within. Thus, marriage becomes the perfect tool to undo the "me and mine" notion which destroys relationship. It serves the purpose for which it came into being — to awaken awareness of the man/God relationship. Yours is a marriage where that experiment is taking place, where the relationship is with God, not with "me and mine."

The real wife should have faith and trust in her husband because she is satisfied; she is fulfilled. If one wants to overcome the thought process of "me and mine" and live with the nobleness of the spirit, that is what marriage offers. Women today, however, tend to be unfulfilled and always in doubt. A real marriage has not even taken place.

Richleigh, you, as the husband, must find the strength to always be consistent. Your life is no longer your own. When you are consistent, your wife will feel the peace and the joy of serving and being your strength. But if you are not, then she will not have it. You and she are no longer separate. If she becomes distracted, you won't have the strength either. It is essential to live by higher laws.

> WIFE: I see that marriage must come to that because the way of competition, ambition, and worldly values does not work.

The world says, "You are the wife, you must do this. You are the husband, you should do that." But it doesn't work. What does the wise do? He brings God into the picture and lifts us out of you and me. Thus a special relationship has become a holy relationship because there is the Presence of God. Both of you have given your life to Christ. Those who get married and live according to Eternal Laws have His strength for all times.

The deeper meaning of marriage is the ending of separation with God. By meeting this function, you need never be insecure, for you are doing that which is essential. You are taking the marriage from the time level, the changeable level, and bringing it to that which does not change. Then there is harmony. We think harmony can be at the time level but it is not possible. Harmony does not exist at the level of "me and mine."

It is a gigantic step not to allow the body senses, as stimulating as they are, to interfere with your decision to live by holy relationship. Your values change and you can say:

I am under no laws but God's. [6]

The minute the relationship becomes one-percent special, that one-percent poisons the whole and it is not holy relationship. As long as there is special relationship, there is insecurity; as long as there is special relationship, there is pleasure. And there is no way of evading the law that where there is pleasure there is sorrow. One gets taken over by needs and projections. Rightness does not seem to matter and your life becomes a series of consequences. Holy relationship has no consequences; it has something else to impart.

Can you imagine how much time and energy we would have if we were freed from consequences? What wisdom would you impart to the world? To live a life free of consequences is to know a life that has no lack. That is holy relationship. We have to get away from learning through experience because there is no urgency in it.

Why have we forgotten to live by Eternal Laws? We are the beloved Son of God. When we know that we are sustained by His love, we know what love is. When we don't know the reality of the love of God, we need sensation and we give it a lot of good names. But sensation is sensation. Only love is of God.

> *HUSBAND:* Some of what you are saying makes me feel remorseful for my actions in the past.

That may occur in a swift, passing moment, and it is helpful to realize: ''I can't be part of that anymore.'' If it has helped you to change, then it's good.

We have to impart strength to one another and come to nobleness. If it has brought you to nobleness, or to a burning in you to live by Eternal Laws, then whatever you have done is all right. It has made it possible. Don't ever feel like a sinner or let guilt touch you, for your spirit is protected by God. It is untouched. We are children of the spirit. Don't underestimate yourself or feel that you are damaged. It is best not to give authority to that kind of thinking.

When you have met the girl you love in that eternal way,

there is no other girl but her. When she has met the man, everybody else ceases to exist for her.

When two people get together in this way, their marriage is blessed. And out of their intent they produce a child. Once the child comes, the intent is no longer the same. Now something *else* has happened. The woman is no longer just a wife; she now becomes a mother. Her whole responsibility changes. There is no longer just a husband and a wife, she must include the child who is born from her. Then, as the milk dries and the child grows up to older age, she cannot be limited to being a mother. She has to take another step. As a woman her life is one of continual outgrowing — girlhood, adolescence, being a wife, being a mother. But in the outgrowing she includes more, rather than excludes. She adds other dimensions to her life until she comes to old age when she can outgrow physicality itself and become whole. From that point on it is an Action of Life, the Action of Grace. In the Indian system, renunciation is the final step — overcoming the world and the flesh itself. Then you bring the Kingdom of God to earth because you are not physical anymore. You are enlightened.

*　　*　　*

TWILIGHT

Twilight comes like the wisdom of the age,
having outgrown the commotion of the day,
to the serenity of the evening.

The flaming colors of sunset
greet it with triumph over activity
and the commotion of the day.

The twilight in its atmosphere of blue
dissolves shadows — ends the duality in man.

The solitary man stands vertical,
his head high in heaven and feet on the ground,
for he is whole, taller than the sun and moon.

The twilight comes with its intensity of blue,
and there is serenity upon the earth.

In relaxation, all things are complete at last.
Tensions disappear.

Peace upon the land is the vibration of twilight.
What a benediction, the calm holiness of each evening.

In the sky appear the stars
and in the carefree man
a new sensitivity and its appreciation
that surrounds him with gratefulness.

Twilight is an inspiring call
to become one with the rhythm of life and day.

It bestows relaxation
and prepares man for the miracle of sleep.
At night the senses gather themselves.

In sleep all distractions end,
and God caresses His child.
The Father caresses His child,
shares the ecstasy of His moments with you
and makes you Himself.

Again the awareness is renewed that you are He.

As the soft light of dawn spreads upon the land,
you awaken to your awareness
and bless the whole world all day long.[7]

*   *   *

QUESTIONS AND ANSWERS

QUESTION: What is the relationship between
man and woman? What is its source?

One is always being given intimations but we are
preoccupied and ignore them until we are no longer aware of
what is real. Since reality is there, it is always intimating the
truth of itself.

Can we begin to see that at the level of the spirit there are
no genders, there is no polarity? There is only the One and that
is whole. It doesn't need the body. The body is an afterthought.
If you perceive this as a fact it begins to unfold and extend its
reality in you. It is a most joyous experience. It cleanses you of
all knowings and preoccupations of the brain and brings you
to silence.

In ancient times, especially in the Vedic Age and in ancient
China, man was always referred to as the lord of the woman.
This continued even as late as the Christian culture. She felt
completed when she met her lord. And he introduced her to the
oneness of creation and to her womanhood. Inspired by his
strength, his justice, and his love, she was totally at peace.

When woman competes, she is betraying her own sublime
and gentle nature. She will not be happy for she is not related
with man or God. When she takes on attributes of masculinity,
she will change her physicality.

Today very few people know what the relationship between
man and woman is in its essence. Woman finds her completion
in man and he introduces her to her real nature which is giving,
trusting, and receiving. He finds his fulfillment in knowing God
and she finds fulfillment in him who, in turn, introduces her to
God. That doesn't mean that she can't have a direct relationship
with God. But it is as if she has to fulfill the very function for
which she was created — to give the world a child in which both
have participated.

QUESTION: It is striking how far we have strayed from that. There is not even any idea of that relationship anymore. All there is is fragmentation, competition, and disharmony which certainly do not provide an atmosphere of love and affection.

Yes. When a woman's nature changes from being creative to becoming assertive and aggressive, she is no longer related to fulfillment in any form or fashion. But when a woman comes to fulfillment, the action in her is born of life that aligns itself to express: "THY WILL BE DONE IN EARTH AS IT IS IN HEAVEN."[8]

The purpose of man is to introduce the woman to God-consciousness. Because she is his wife, she respects her husband and he must merit her respect. She is the gentler, tenderer side. Even if he wants to do something harsh, she discourages it and civilizes him. According to the *I Ching:*

"The correct place of a woman is within."[9]

It is not to be equal. That is external and political. We have to come back to our own honesty. Women wanted equality and now they don't have husbands. By becoming irresponsible, both women and men have betrayed their real nature.

QUESTION: I am having a reaction to what you are saying about the role of men and women. It seems archaic, not related to what is happening today.

Before I gave my life to spirituality, when I was living in New York, I met a girl whom I loved. When we began to live together she wanted to divide up the household duties. "You do this. I'll do that." I told her I wanted to make it very clear from the very beginning that I would not do anything, that she was to do everything. She said, "That's not fair." I said,

"I don't care whether it is fair or not. It's a man's world. You will clean, cook, do the laundry." She said, "No, you do some things and I'll do some things."

I said, "You people are so primitive. All you want is competition, barter. I don't barter and I don't compete. I am who I am and I am not going to do anything on terms." She was in a fix. Either she becomes a doormat or she would have to leave. She asked, "But don't you love me?" I said, "Yes. When I say something I mean it. I love you." What a bind to be in! You become nothing, or weak. It seems harsh, brutal, uncompromising — like throwing you in the desert and saying fight the rattlesnakes.

She was quiet for a long time. Slowly it began to affect her. She came and asked, "Why won't you agree that I'll do this, and you'll do that?" I said, "Because it doesn't allow me to love you. You don't know what love is yet. Very few people know what it is. When there is love, love gives. If we make an agreement, then it deprives me of loving you, it deprives me of giving. I am a man in love and I have something to give to you. It can't be fit into a barter or into competition. Those are too base, too low. Love knows to give. It is something you would never know your whole life if you are going to barter."

Immediately she saw it and was at peace. Everything got settled. Then if I was inspired to help in any way, I would do it. But it was not going to be a barter. That's the American way of life — a contract. When you have something real to give, something else takes place. It was a joy to see the givingness on both sides.

Have you known anyone who has a voice of his own, who can say something that is his own discovery, something he can stand on, some principle? There are very few.

> QUESTION: Is yoga compatible with married life and raising children?

Yoga, in its pure spirit, is compatible for someone who is married, compatible for someone who would like to have children. In the highest sense, it is not only compatible, but for someone who is serious and wishes to live a life of virtue and purity, dedicated to that which is eternal, it becomes a necessity. One would probably bear children that are different. And there would be a blessing on the marriage because your values are vertical.

Yoga helps in all things that are natural: to be married is natural, to have children is natural. Yoga is an aide to bring one to a different consciousness. Then you have an independent relationship with God.

When you have met your calling, which becomes a way of life, productive and therefore meaningful, it enriches your life and makes it possible for the marriage to work in this culture. If you have something of your own, a light within you, your husband will be drawn to you. If you haven't, then you will be weak.

When you have an independent relationship with something that is eternal, the possibility of success in your marriage is more real. Without it, the outer relationship is undependable. No matter how cozy it seems now, fantasies change.

> QUESTION: It has always been difficult for me to see how one can lead a religious life and be married. It seems that if my dedication to religious life were sincere, I would be able to give up all those things.

Life begins when seeking ends. Once the seeking has ended and you have found what you want to give your life to, things would start to unfold and you would be able to cope with everything. Once you have given your life, however, you cannot change your mind. Whatever it is — whether it be marriage, yoga, being a student — it has its own means of bringing one to truth. One must be receptive and welcome it.

In the West, or in any overly stimulated, externalized society, there is very little reverence. Reverence must be there for that which is true. If we do not have reverence, we will not find truth.

> *QUESTION:* I have a very rebellious nature. I have seen it all through my life. Even though I think I have respect for someone, when something doesn't quite go my way, I just want to walk out. I have not figured out how to deal with it. It seems involuntary but I don't think it actually is. I think it probably is culturally based. It starts with an irritation and then one wants to go away. Would vigilance take care of it?

I don't think that what you call rebelliousness is altogether bad. Any person who is not going to compromise has to have passion. *A Course In Miracles'* emphasis on forgiveness would add conviction to the non-conformity. It would transform your relationships. Then you would not be conventional. But it would not be a reaction; it would be an outgrowing. It is important to see, from the very beginning, that you would be moving toward outgrowing, toward God.

There is a lesson in the Course which begins:

I let forgiveness rest upon all things.[10]

Let forgiveness rest upon all things — on your relationship with your father, your husband, people who come to work with you. Just let forgiveness rest upon them.

QUESTION: What does that mean?

It means you will have no thought, no opinion about anybody. You remain impeccable.

For thus forgiveness will be given me. [11]

Then you will receive the gift of forgiveness which is boundless, which is not of personality, not of this world. It outgrows the world.

When I did this lesson, I saw that forgiveness is instantaneous. The minute I let forgiveness rest upon the world, immediately I have the benefit of forgiveness for myself. No time is needed. The minute I forgive an individual I know the actuality of forgiveness. Every lesson of *A Course In Miracles* imparts truth. It is not a matter of time to learn it. You can learn it instantly.

But non-forgiveness is the only "knowing" we have. All "knowing" about a person is non-forgiveness. You can say you love your husband but when you look at everything you "know" about him you will find that each is a limitation, each is of non-forgiveness. When you no longer want that "knowing," you can come to forgiveness and the words will have ceased.

The only knowledge that is valid is the knowledge which relates us with the eternal, with God. Nothing else is knowledge. One year spent with *A Course In Miracles* could awaken you.

A Course In Miracles is not a book; it is the Thoughts of God. Inherent in every single lesson is the potential to awaken us to application. We know a lot but we cannot bring anything to application. That's our difficulty. We have heard "LOVE YE ONE ANOTHER," that we must care, that we shouldn't cheat another — but we cannot bring anything into application. Now, for the first time that humanity has ever known, there is a systematic, divine order of bringing a person to awakening. It is not just another book.

There are some people who are highly evolved. How do we know that? Because their process of outgrowing is very rapid. What would take a normal person fifty years to outgrow, they outgrow in ten. For most people, during fifty years they become more entrenched, more involved. Thus it takes a longer time to undo and to outgrow. What this process of postponement has done to the personality! Finally, when they come to urgency, they see how much burden they carry — their mental attics and cellars are crowded and need to be cleansed. Great people do not accumulate; they can quickly see the essence, the fact, the principle, the law, and outgrow.

When Sri Ramakrishna's wife, Sarada Devi,[12] came to him, he told her that although he was her husband, his mind was not on the physical, marital relationship, but that she had a say in the matter and if a physical relationship was what she wanted with him, he would abide. She, being a very highly evolved person, said that she was not interested in the physical relationship either.

If it was asked of you, or me, we would tend to be heroic. We would say, ''I can do without it too.'' But we are born liars. Our words have no meaning. We have never outgrown anything — neither our desires nor our own phraseology. What we say is absolutely meaningless.

The wiser thing would be to ask: ''Sir, is it possible not to experience something and feel independent of it? Will it not linger in the mind — that I have been denied? Will my saying I can do without the physical relationship leave a little seed, a little residue, a feeling I am being denied and, therefore, make me idealize spiritual life that much more? Would you please tell me what is involved in my totally outgrowing it?''

Then you would become a student. We are seldom ever students. If we don't become a student we would know nothing of outgrowing. We would not know what integrity is, what seriousness is, what honesty is. It starts by being a student.

The student is one who is responsible for his words. He would not want to be heroic, idealistic, or shy. He would have very basic questions to ask, questions that demand clarity. And then he would find a teacher who has the ability to *impart*. But the mundane person settles for good answers. And all good answers are conventional. There are no answers. There is only the dissolving of the question, which brings clarity.

I let forgiveness rest upon all things.[13]

You have to be in a state where you are innocent and vulnerable, where you no longer know or judge.

For thus forgiveness will be given me.[14]

Then you receive and what you receive is a state of *being*.

CHAPTER FOUR

4

CONCEPTION

Spirit is in a state of grace forever.
Your reality is only spirit.
Therefore you are in a state of grace forever.[1]

The Law of Creation is outside the realm of time, for in creation there is no beginning and no end. At conception, spirit steps into the level of time and physicality; yet inherent in that moment is the timeless present — free from past and future. It is an action of eternity upon time. This creative action of Life takes place within the body but it is of the spirit, not the body.

At the level of the body, limited to time, there is ignorance of the Mind of God, of which the spirit is part. Spirit is not physical; it is neither in the body nor in the womb. Its action is multi-dimensional, beyond the comprehension of the brain.

Conception is a holy instant in which the pure energy that transcends past, future, and memory invokes an action not known to the present thought system of man. Something "else" takes place. The "else," the other, is the Given. In conception, the woman's purity receives the seed of the man she loves and in this receiving she learns to give. As they come closer to this union, which may not be voiced or even thought of, it brings about, when it is in its purest form, the flowering of givingness in both the man and the woman. Rather than wanting to receive, one wants to give. Giving emerges out of fulfillment. It is the end of self-centeredness.

Conception is a creative action. Whatever is created is of the intelligence of Life, independent of personality. When the child is conceived, his conception is part of the action of the universe. All the planets are in a particular place and it is that instant which continues to extend its reality in the life of the child. How decisive and precise are the Laws of Creation, for nothing is outside of their wholeness.

The union between man and woman can bring one to a state free of time and pressure. The influence of the external world begins to recede and thought interferes less and less as givingness comes into being. There is an overwhelming force, a vital atmosphere. You approach each other with gentleness; the look in the eyes is the look of innocence, the highest of refinements. Something of the spirit has come into being. This entrance of the spirit is related to the seed and to conception — a feeling of great warmth, real gratefulness, the joy of life. It introduces the two people to a deep caring for one another, a deep need for each other, and a sense of completion. Their separation ends and they come to wholeness. In that instant the involuntary, creative action of conception can take place which is not of bodies. Both have been blessed by it and in their giving, they have received the gift of God to man.

> In the holy instant we share our faith in God's Son because
> we recognize, together, that he is wholly worthy of it, and
> in our appreciation of his worth we cannot doubt his
> holiness. And so we love him.[2]

The presence between the man and woman who care for one another becomes the child's real home. This tenderness awakens other levels within the parents; it slows down the brain and the pulse and can totally relax the body. But our thought and our culture have made so much of the sexual act that there is not the necessary relaxation to free us from self-consciousness.

In most things, the personality looks out for itself. But when the feelings are real, a different spirit enters into lovemaking — a spirit of reverence. This new spirit awakens the centers of the endocrine system, known as *chakras*. In Sanskrit, chakra means wheel. Chakras are vortexes of energy that are not solely physical. One can visualize them as a flattened orange, cut in half. When these two halves, male and female, are joined together they become whole. This is an involuntary action of creation and yet the quality of your being and the purity of your intent are part of it. You could limit this direct experience to personal pleasure, or expand into an awareness that is impersonal — the glory of the action of Life.

Seeds are eternal. Time does not affect them because they are not of the earth. For instance, the seeds of wheat and rice found in the Egyptian tombs were untouched by time even though the metal that encased them had rusted away. This is a wondrous thing. The seed originates the action of evolution, bringing everything into time, tangibility, and growth.

Directly related to the human seed is the quality of blood. We are all familiar with the types of blood, but little attention is paid, especially in the West, to its quality. The quality of your blood is who you really are. It even reflects the abilities your spirit brought with it to earth. The quality of blood determines the strength of the seed the parents produce to create the body of the child. Their heredity, diet, and consciousness are all related to it. It has nothing to do with one's race or color.

The child will grow from the seed, weak or strong, that the parents produce. The milk he drinks, the food he eats, will turn into blood to nourish his cells as they multiply. And in his blood will be his purity.

When the blood and the seed of both parents are very pure, they can create an impeccable child. But conservation of the same seed could recreate each of them into new dimensions. That is the true meaning of celibacy. Celibacy has a dignity born of ethics. In celibacy, newness flowers; it is not a denial. Truth that ends duality relates one with the eternal and purifies the blood.

To live according to the path of virtue and ethics changes the quality of the blood. It regenerates the seed within. Thus one is not limited to heredity or to the consequences of weak seed, for these can be altered. In reality, man is not a victim of the flesh. His perfection is eternally protected by the Divine Forces that created him.

> *In peace I was created. And in peace do I remain. It is not given me to change my Self. How merciful is God my Father, that when He created me He gave me peace forever. Now I ask but to be what I am. And can this be denied me, when it is forever true?*
>
> *Father, I seek the peace You gave as mine in my creation. What was given then must be here now, for my creation was apart from time, and still remains beyond all change. The peace in which Your Son was born into Your Mind is shining there unchanged. I am as You created me. I need but call on You to find the peace You gave. It is Your Will that gave it to Your Son.*[3]

The first thing a person has to discover is that he has something to give. The pressures of the external world cease as givingness comes into being. It harmonizes man's relationship with the external world as a sacred atmosphere is invoked within him. It breaks through all the barriers of selfishness and self-centeredness. This transformation has to take place to provide the right atmosphere for the child. When we merely use each other's bodies for the needs of the senses — for pleasure and the release of tension — the blood is affected and the seed of man is weakened.

The child's life begins when conception takes place, not when the child is born. Therefore both parents have the responsibility of being in harmony with one another from the origin of life in the womb. Their serenity and the laughter of harmony will be transmitted to the child.

The child is God's gift to the parents. What is crucial then is that we understand what prevents us from being aware of what is of God. What is your approach to the arrival of this child? Parents can give the growing child space if they have been introduced to the wonder of creation. They would then have reverence and would prepare for the birth of the child with the same tenderness with which nature surrounded conception.

What joy the child has to offer! The very house changes as if a light has entered it. The child can revolutionize the parents' life and make it intrinsic if the parents realize that they can no longer be false. One right action has taken place in the family, between the parents and the spirit, and this action makes one grateful for a new order in life. Gratefulness transcends personality; it is fully alive.

Whenever the woman discovers that she is pregnant, her joy is unlimited as new levels awaken with their own potentials. It is the mother's gladness that will provide nourishment for the child, both physically and spiritually. Her spirit will have its impact. Is there virtue in her daily life? Is she eating good food? What does she read? What kind of air does she breathe? And what about relaxation? Is she surrounded by laughter? Is she somewhat in harmony with the dawn, noon, and twilight?

All of these considerations would awaken the child to things that are important and he would be stronger when facing the pressures and influences of the external world. The time in the womb is a period of preparing the child to cope with the earth forces* and the physical nature of the body.

Life is a great responsibility. If you assume that responsibility it will bring you to rightness of action. If you give your best to the conception of the child, you would give your best to the child when he is born. You would know you are capable because you *love*. And there is never lack of strength. Love is never touched by doubt. Love knows no fear, no limitations, no justifications. It just *is*. It has enormous vitality to create, to renew, and to cleanse.

The room where the baby is born should be very clean and simple. There should not be one unnecessary item in the room. Cleanliness and orderliness are synonymous. Where there is disorder, angels would never be. It is one's cleanliness and order, one's authentic quality, that establishes a pure atmosphere. The parents should put their love into the room. There should always be fresh flowers and a sense of aesthetic beauty where the child is. It is good to play low, whisper-like music — Bach, Vivaldi, flute, or classical harp — hardly audible, but providing an atmosphere of gentle welcoming. Everything should be mild, quiet.

In ancient times, they knew the truth that the child enshrines the eternal spirit. Thus the place of birth held spiritual significance. Most families had a room in their home — a sanctum of consecrated atmosphere where a person entered with reverence and silenced his mind. The order, flowers, and sounds in the room were an extension of the perfection within man. Childbirth, on many occasions, took place in this sacred room where the child remained with the mother for ten to eleven days. Only close members of the family and saintly people were allowed to visit.

---

*For further discussion of "earth forces," see *The Future Of Mankind — The Branching Of The Road* by Tara Singh (Foundation for Life Action, 1986), pages 25-40. (Editor)

The family valued holiness and they related differently to the entry of the child. As the outgoing senses awakened, the child first made contact with those of pure intent and loving hearts because the first contact made the deepest impression. The spirit in the child is awakened by others in the family. Thus, the parents, who had been preparing for the child all through the pregnancy, made sure only those who had the peace within themselves could come to greet the child and awaken him to his God nature.

Often the child was surrounded with songs, prayers, and chants of holy origin — True Knowledge — prior to joining the rest of the family. The child heard only the melodious voices of people not caught in the pressures of time. When they sat, the stillness that surrounded them communicated its peace and gladness to the child. The gentleness of the baby introduced the adult to the tenderness within.

If the child is greeted as if he is of Divine origin, it will help him to grow up consistent with who he is. His own first awareness of holiness becomes his protection.

There may be some significance that Jesus was born in a manger rather than in the rooms of questionable vibration in the inn, and that the three wise men, with respect and adoration in their hearts, were amongst the first to come to greet the Child of God.

According to True Knowledge man is part of a cosmic process, perfect in the image of God. Man's spirit is perfect and outside the range of evolution. But the body — the earth-born gift of creation — is confined to the laws of time, goes through evolution, and is changeable, subject to its environment, heredity, and circumstances. The spirit, at the physical level of manifestation, needs the body, but when the physical dies, the spirit is unaffected. The Spirit, ever in a state of Grace, is unchangeable.

Commonly, the spirit that would manifest in materiality has past ties and involvements which bring about the repeated cycle of birth. There may be karmic* relationships between the parents and the entity of the child. Or, the entity may be attracted by the parents' virtuous qualities. High souls have been, and can be, attracted by parents wholly deserving such an entity. To attract the impeccable spirit of a lofty soul, parents in ancient times were known to prepare themselves by living a life of purity. Their lives, being virtuous, had few consequences.

Immaculate conception is even possible, as recorded in the lives of Jesus and Sri Ramakrishna. It is the purity of the silent mind that is the home of peace with which the Ishwarakoti[4] harmonizes his entry into physicality. The real function of parents is to provide birth for these beings. Guru Nanak[5] said the householder is also a saint because he can bring the being of purity to earth.

In the Vedic and Upanishad age of Satyayuga[6] — the Golden Age, the pre-historic era of wisdom — the child was considered to be of Divine origin. In that age, work was not the goal of life, salvation was.

> "Men lived upon the earth, but were not confined to body senses, thus they were not in a state of cause and effect. They sensed no lack in themselves or in creation. . . They were masters of the natural world. Creation existed for the sages of this state and they commanded it what to do. Their needs were met by the blessing they conferred upon nature.
>
> "They were not limited to thought. Having nothing to achieve, their lives were not confined to

---

*"The law that governs all action and its inevitable consequences on the doer." From *The Ramayana* by C. Rajagopalachari (Bharatiya Vidya Bhavan, Bombay, 1951), page 317. (Editor)

the body. Each remained an altar of heaven reaching beyond the universe. They were consistent with the Will of God and had but one choice, not to deviate into alternatives. Thus they were ever with the justice of love and forgiveness.''[7]

A child is conceived in fulfillment. The parent's responsibility is to see that the child remains fulfilled and knows that God provides. Being aware that the action of conception was involuntary and creative, the parents realize the child is of God and they prepare him to be part of creation and bring the Will of God to earth. The parents and later, the teacher, must help the child become aware of the action of Grace and not limit him to his body senses. This reversal is the most essential gift you can give to your child. By so doing, you also develop your own capacity to receive. The birth of a child, as well as the rearing of a child, makes us all co-creators.

It is quite a challenge to be with the eternal in the midst of external changes. Whenever you forget, just look at the child and his very innocence can bring you to that purity. The parents need never feel inadequate. Their new learning undoes the old and makes the space for the growth of the awakening child. The child comes with heaven's love in him; he is not alone.

The guide for the parents to maintain their equilibrium is to learn what forgiveness is and that:

God is the Strength in which I trust.[8]

The parents must, before the child is born, attempt to outgrow the misperceptions of society's values. The reading of each day's Lesson in *A Course In Miracles*, together when possible, and with the space of reverence, would help them in their own growth.

It is whatever you are doing that spiritualizes your life and changes the atmosphere of your whole being. The energy of rightness corrects future events yet unknown. By personalizing your life you not only isolate yourself, but subject yourself to problems yet to manifest. The quality of what you do in the moment perpetuates itself; therefore, the correction begins here and now — and what it corrects is all your tomorrows. If your intent is not right, what you are now doing will invoke all kinds of hardships, anxieties, and problems, and would open up the Pandora's box of ''wrongness.'' But the power of inner correction can heal relationships continents away and centuries ahead. Never limit yourself to personal life. Be gracious and God-like. Your love and goodness makes all things possible.

''LOVE YE ONE ANOTHER'' is the only thing the child needs to know. Clear the way, ''MAKE STRAIGHT THE WAY OF THE LORD,'' for the child of God is on the way. Blessed is the womb and the home where he enters with angels surrounding him.

CHAPTER FIVE

5

TO BE A MOTHER

In a young girl's life there are certain years of childhood and adolescence, and then there comes a time when she is totally free — free from dependence on parents, childhood, education — when she is really free to make her first choice in life. It is her first "self-expression" and it can start with the discovery of a man who becomes dearer to her than her own being.

This is such a powerful experience that it frees her from all her past ties with parents and dependencies and totally opens a new dimension in her. She is so full of love for this person that she gives herself to him.

In so doing, she loses her freedom because she has started a new cycle with its own cause, its own effect, and its consequences. It is an enormous responsibility and requires the utmost discrimination. A woman is born once, she dies once; and she gives away her freedom once.

Then a wonderful time begins with this new life that the man and the woman start to build together. Out of that atmosphere she bears a child and now she is not just a wife, she is a mother. When she becomes a mother she has the blessing of Life upon her because she is consistent with the forces of the universe — of procreation and of giving the world a child.

The child needs two polarities — the male energy and the female energy. In awareness the two become one. But the world today, with acceleration and artificial stimulation and its mania for pleasure, has deviated far from what is actual. Split families abound today and so many children grow up without a father in the house.

If only men and women would respect the bond they have formed. People who are irresponsible say: "What is marriage, only a paper?" Why do we have the tendency to bring everything down to that casual level? A bond takes place that invokes higher forces. We can find the strength and the integrity to be responsible and respectful of that bond. Then we would be able to cope with the differences that take place between us as husband and wife, and with our children.

But if that respect of reverence is not there, "I do as I please" is the dominant attitude. Separation and a lawyer result. We cannot correct wrong with the overdoing of wrong, for within each moment of relationship we create the atmosphere the child lives in.

The child is born with his own space and with his own resources. He is an expression of God-Action, a creative action of life and an action of innocence. It is the responsibility of parents not to intrude on that innocence by putting their own frustrations and knowings upon the child. He is born with space. Let his space be. Let it expand more and more so that he can grow.

The child can lead the parents to God, for he is born out of love. This action of life starts a new vibration in the mother. She might have been distorted and selfish before, but after the child is born a change takes place. The mother learns to care for the child. She is blessed to have one. The child is a gift entrusted to her. And her whole life changes. She never thinks it is her child. She tries to bring him up as God's Child and she can learn from her Father how to do so. Therefore, a direct relationship gets established between the mother and the Creator. She discovers she has created a child too. And everything is created for the child already — there is milk in her breast. First it is an intimation, then the intimation leads to fact, to a truth. "There is milk in my breast for this child. What intelligence in my body that could have done that!"

First it is just the slightest intimation, and then it turns to be the truth and she is silenced. Then when the child is a few months old, out of nowhere, the teeth appear and the earth provides the food. That child would never know lack or insecurity if the parents have introduced him to the mystery of creation that is ever looking after him.

A mother once asked me:

"I heard you say that a person makes a choice between creating a child or recreating himself/herself. Does that mean if one creates a child one is not able to recreate himself/herself because the energy is devoted to the child? Or is there more?"

If you want to produce children, you have sex. But if, with that energy, you want to reproduce yourself and come to a rebirth, you contain those energies. The same energy that can produce the likeness of you can also recreate you into another state. That was the principle of celibacy. So there is responsibility in whatever you do.

Nature is very wise. First of all, the child is entrusted to a woman. Why would it entrust the child to a woman and not a man? There is much more of a givingness in a woman which starts with the act of giving herself to a man. Then she can also give herself to a child.

In her giving she comes to a rebirth in herself. First she gives birth to a child, and then she keeps giving the child her energies. Not only does the child flower differently in this atmosphere of sharing but so does the mother. In giving, she receives. That is so beautiful, isn't it?

A Course In Miracles says:

> *To give and to receive are one in truth.*
> *I will receive what I am giving now.*[1]

Thus they can both grow to a rebirth. She makes sure that the child has the space, so as his cells change he becomes impeccable and strong. She educates him not to be conditioned by external values. A woman can come to a rebirth within herself by using the same energy of life, and she can come to rebirth by having a child.

The mother watches over and cares for her child just like the doe protects the fawn from mountain lions and coyotes. In this world the mother has to protect the child from belief systems, from fear and reactions. But how does she protect him? She cannot isolate him, for children need other children.

If children do not have children to play with they follow your habits. A child is not happy alone. One season at Lake Como in Italy, while the adults went about the business of recreation, I watched a solitary, young boy lay in the sun by himself. He was Swiss and spoke no Italian. After several days another family arrived with two boys about the same age. The newcomers found a volleyball and tossed it back and forth, while the Swiss boy watched from a distance. After a time one of the boys threw the ball playfully at the one lying down by himself. He was instantly energized. He threw it back and joined them. From that moment on the three were inseparable although they did not even speak the same language. The Swiss boy became so joyous. That was his Italy — the friendship he had found. There are myriad little challenges which impart confidence and awaken the child's faculties within such relationships. Without this friendship and play, children fall into their parents' habits or into isolation.

A child needs a great deal of affection. He is not only the child of his parents but the child of everyone in the world. He inspires a feeling of love because he is defenseless, because he is harmless. Those are the qualities we have to learn. If we would consider the child as everybody's child, we would have a different society altogether.

What do we introduce our children to? Cartoons? Why not to something of God? Children, when they are not distorted, respond to beauty. Discover and explore with them silence and prayer, but not in a sentimental way, for there may be no need to say anything. Love is not an expression of sentimentality. It is the love you feel within yourself. The child knows it without explanation. Children, being more innocent, have another kind of sensitivity, an inherent response to love.

It would be so good if you could take your children to a prayer or meditation room in your house — a spacious little room, uncluttered, with a few cushions, a bowl of water, a plant, and a picture or two of Divine Beings. Let it be peaceful in its very simplicity, something not of the world. A room, like the mind, emptied of objects, can become alive with the purity of space. The child would grow knowing that there is a place, a sanctuary, in his own home. With all our affluence, rarely do we have a place to sit quiet, to pray, to meditate. Why can we not afford something so simple that would bring stillness and beauty into our lives?

Take your child into this room every day and come to peace with yourself. Conflict ceases and time ends. You will see how precious it can become, a room that is not part of circumstances, a place to establish a relationship with the infinite Self. Ask for a blessing to be upon you both and your husband so that you may come to the right relationship with the child, as God would want it, to learn and to receive.

Your prayer could be:

"THE LORD BLESS THEE, AND KEEP THEE:
THE LORD MAKE HIS FACE SHINE UPON THEE,
AND BE GRACIOUS UNTO THEE:
THE LORD LIFT UP HIS COUNTENANCE UPON THEE,
AND GIVE THEE PEACE."[2]

If you do not continue growing in love, the child, not having been nourished by your love, will become insecure. Soon he will start stamping his foot and saying, "I do as I please." Somewhere, some irresponsibility took place for that kind of reaction to come into being. The minute we put the child in a secondary place the conflict begins. The mother is the one who has the energy to bring harmony to the family and to give strength to the children.

If the love in the relationship continues, the Lord will provide. The child has his own destiny. If you don't trust that, then you are believing in your own insecurity. What do you think is going to come out of insecurity? What do you think insecurity is going to breed? What kind of atmosphere would there be but self-survival and competition?

But if one really had reverence for Life, the child would have it too. And one would inspire society to change. Unfortunately, we have become so confused and so dependent we cannot trust the truth — that the child is entrusted to the parent and the reward is the growth of the parents. He grows physically and you grow spiritually. As you grow you have more to give to the child. How else could it be? For Life is Supreme Intelligence and is always related.

When we violate these laws, there is no relationship between parents and children. Wars increase. A child brought up with love could never go out and kill another. He just could not do it; he would have a conscience.

The mother is the first teacher for the child. As the child is exposed to more and more of the external, conditioning is going to take place. So, the mother has to establish a rapport with the child and explain to him in a very loving way what anger, frustration, and possessiveness are. As the child is exposed to these things there awakens a discrimination which undoes the negative influences and he becomes capable of seeing the world without fear.

A new responsibility is placed before the mother of today as the world enters a crisis of false values. This new responsibility is what brings her to rebirth. If she accepts the responsibility she will need more energy and greater wisdom. But God loves the child and He will provide. Therefore, as the child grows physically, the mother grows in wisdom to cope with the pressures and the invasions of the external. There are more ways than one in which the child brings a parent to rebirth. If it were not for the child the adult might be casual and not realize how much kindness is needed. Because there is love between a mother and child, kindness and compassion are natural.

In the end the parents must grow so high spiritually that they are no longer attached to the child, so there is no dependence, no crippling effect. The parents have made the child independent in a healthy sense and he can become an extension of God.

The parents now grow gracefully to older age, a period of serenity. Having made the child independent, they are very close to ending their own duality too. Parents cannot give freedom to another if they are still caught in conflict. But if they have understood attachment, they have then imparted freedom to the child and they age beautifully. The world needs wise elders who have grown spiritually because of their relationship with their children.

As the parents get older, there is the child to take care of them with the same love he had received. And the cycle of love and creation completes itself. Otherwise, it is the old folks' home and isolation. There is very great loneliness in America. Mother Teresa once said to an American lady:

> "Tell your American friends they do not have to go around the world to find people who suffer. In America there are many needs. People are lonely. They feel alienated. Some people are so lonely they want to die. They need love. Loneliness is amongst the worst human pain."

If we have heard these words, we can reverse the current trend. We can value the blessings which our children bring us, for it is their need to grow in a harmonious atmosphere. As a parent you are the custodian who brings the child to the awareness that he is an extension of God on earth.

*　　*　　*

Mother of the World

Peace is a woman, mother to the world,
Whom God has sent to lay a gentle hand
Across a thousand children's fevered brows.
In its cool certainty there is no fear,
And from her breasts there comes a quietness
For them to lean against and to be still.

She brings a message to their frightened hearts
From Him who sent her. Listen now to her

Who is your mother in your Father's Name:
"Do not attend the voices of the world.
Do not attempt to crucify again
My first-born Son, and brother still to you."

Heaven is in her eyes, because she looked
Upon this Son who was the first. And now
She looks to you to find him once again.
Do not deny the mother of the world
The only thing she ever wants to see,
For it is all you ever want to find.[3]

CHAPTER SIX

6

DIVINE LEISURE —
BIRTH THROUGH PUBERTY

When a child is born he is innocent. And for a period of time he has Divine Leisure. He doesn't have to think about food or survival. It is the most wonderful period. Divine Leisure. From the child's birth, or possibly even from the onset of pregnancy, there has been another awakening in the mother of caring for the child. The child is fully protected and Life helps. Discover how everything is part of a perfection! It is very interesting where Life has placed the breast. The distance between the child's face and the mother's eyes might be governed by other laws. The sound of the heartbeat that the child heard in the womb is there and when he is held close, he doesn't feel totally a stranger.

And then, slowly, the child's senses begin to awaken. How would you discover and comprehend these senses that gradually extend themselves? The child's brain is still and innocent; it is also in a state of peace. But innocence is very energetic. It is itself. It doesn't burn in duality and dissipate itself. It grows an enormous amount in a short period of time. And in the process of opening-up, the child is very impressionable. Everything is new. It is the first time he hears a sound, the first time he sees light, the first time he tastes something. His senses have no interpretation in them. They are direct.

How nice it would be for the parents to be gentle with the child, to speak lovingly to him so that that is what he would know. If the parents' tone of voice is harsh, that becomes the impression. It leaves an imprint. If the parents are quarreling, the child senses the tension. How will the child ever know fear and insecurity if the parents don't communicate them to him? When we are insecure our thoughts have a different vibration. The child, at this time of Divine Leisure, is going to become acquainted with vibrations. He will take them in and be shaped by them because the brain is shaped by its environment.

> PARENT: When you say the child would sense the tension, if he is not judging or forming an opinion, how can he make the distinction that there is tension?

Yes, because the quality of the human voice is expressive. It vibrates. Gradually, the child would discover: "When I was caressed, the vibration was this way." It is a language that is not verbal but has enormous discernment. The way you feel about the child has a way of communicating because "what is" is. The child is very sensitive because he is not translating, he is just becoming whatever surrounds him. In nature, we see how animals and flowers have camouflage, how the lioness has taken on the color of the grass in which she lies. In a similar way, as the senses of the child awaken, they begin to make contact with "what is" and take on those qualities.

During this period from birth to three or four years, the child has his own stillness and peace within; he does not know lack.

> PARENT: Where does the quality that the child had in his previous life show up? As you said, we don't end a life and then start again; it

is a continuous thing. Doesn't that color the child's life?

Well, this can become a "teaching," which I would like to avoid. But let me just give something of a background.

The spirit is our reality and, obviously, it is not a body. But when the spirit is in the body, the body becomes a temple of God. This spirit, the entity, changes bodies many, many times. And every time it is not a body, when the body dies, it thinks very differently; it has different kinds of images because it is free from physicality and the thinking of the brain. But it may have something we could call memory — memory of the concept that it has died, or a recognition that another form exists. And then it takes birth again with the intention of freeing itself from the bondage of flesh and blood and the lifestyle of the body which is narrow, limited, insecure, and selfish.

With the right parents, the spirit could make a different start. How much the parents help by providing the right environment! It is the foundation of the child's life. If the child has been provided with Divine Leisure until the age of five, he will retain it all his life.

> "WHOSOEVER SHALL RECEIVE ONE OF SUCH CHILDREN IN MY NAME, RECEIVETH ME: AND WHOSOEVER SHALL RECEIVE ME, RECEIVETH NOT ME, BUT HIM THAT SENT ME."[1]

If parents want to give birth to a child who is Christ-like, they must prepare for it. If they would raise their child as if he is the Christ, they will be blessed as parents who did not limit themselves but prepared their child for salvation. Salvation is of True Knowledge. Lack and limitation are of one's own projection; they are not of God. When the child is born, the parents must begin shedding old values in themselves rather than accumulating more.

How the parents protect and nurture the child's Divine Leisure is the issue. It is important for the young child to have time to be alone with nature so that he retains what is natural within him. Aloneness can introduce one to Divine Leisure and heal anything. The leisure we are talking about is not daydreaming; it is a space where something else takes place within that makes direct contact.

Is it not our responsibility how we meet the child's innocence and vulnerability? What if you had stillness and peace when you held the child? We can strengthen and extend his Divine Leisure or we can violate it. Usually, we are in haste; we have so much going on inside we are rarely present with "what is." Don't we all feel it is difficult for us to be responsible? We would like to be — we would like to end the violence in South Africa, we don't like what is happening in Central America — but then there is the opposite: "What can I do?" "We would like to raise our child responsibly, but we have other things to do." The brain is ever helpless, and out of that helplessness it creates a monstrous, chaotic world.

When the child is born, he has certain notions, certain tendencies, certain abilities, certain handicaps — all built in. One child might love music; another couldn't care less. One is very passionate; for another, that is not a strong force. One is courageous; another quick; another slow. There are other forces within the child of which we know little. Those forces are going to bring into play the laws of cause and effect.

During the first seven years, a child could outgrow the whole pattern of cause and effect if you provide the space the child needs without psychological conditioning — without the prejudices, fears, and insecurities. He would become strong in conviction and be free of deception because you have provided the right atmosphere and made sure he doesn't learn things he will later need to undo. Probably *not* teaching him would be the greater gift. But you have to learn to undo things in your own life so as to not pressure his brain.

As the parents start to undo in themselves, they give more space and teach the child only facts, nothing psychological.

> *PARENT:* This other force that you speak of that the child brings or expresses — like one would be slow, one would be fast — does that other force have in it the psychological aspect as well?

Yes, some.

> *PARENT:* So they don't get everything from the parents?

No. But we must see that if the parents do not produce the atmosphere whereby the child can recognize his personality trait and become strengthened in it, he will outgrow it more quickly. When you *recognize* something, it has an effect.

> *PARENT:* So the child, even as a baby, would have these psychological traits?

Yes, somewhat. The tendencies may be there. To be fearful, for example.

> *PARENT:* And the parents have to undo it somehow, even at that age?

Yes. The parents must provide an environment where that trait is not strengthened but rather diminished. If the parents value undoing rather than teaching, it brings a transformation.

> *PARENT:* So the potential is there for the child to outgrow it even though they have been born with it?

Yes. But usually in addition to the tendencies which are already present, the parents further condition the child with their prejudices and beliefs. Therefore, during the seven years when he can outgrow things, the undoing never takes place. We pile more onto him.

We must realize that children are receptive. When you cook food, if you are totally attentive and your hands move slowly, the child will be affected. When the child is nursing, if you are at peace and pass your hand over the child's head, you can change the atmosphere. Suppose the child has never seen a harsh movement, haste, or tension in you, would he not also imbibe that peace? Can you imagine what space and freedom it would give the child to sit between two parents who are desireless?

But today, children's brains are trained at a younger and younger age and they are pressured as they have never been before. Can one see the criminality of forcing abstract learning on a young child in order to *improve* him? The child needs to *learn* nothing because he is learning directly every minute. He sees color and responds to it. Did you ever wonder what color does to a child? You could probably heal a sick child by putting the right colors around him because the child can absorb the vibration of colors.

> *PARENT:* I see that the child is innocent and therefore, responds to what is there. How then is thought introduced to the child?

We think and we teach the child to think. Thought is of the earth; its roots are of fear and survival. What would it be if our thoughts were Thoughts of God? Would the child not learn that? He need never know relative knowledge — "this" versus "that." If the parents, having understood this, attempt to greet the child with thought that has no duality in it, then the Force that protects the child's Divine Leisure would be assisting them as well. They will have called upon It. That same Divine Force that assures that the child's needs are met, is at their disposal too, if they became receptive.

Schooling should be started slowly after the age of five or six, for teaching can become a form of conformity. Formal schooling activates the brain which makes the child adult-like. The parents have to be very selective in choosing a school for the child. They must spend time with the teacher and know how many students are in the class. Twelve to fifteen students should be the limit for one teacher. If these are the needs of the parents they will be met.

In need there is no dependence; dependence is only when you want. The parent could become the teacher and meet the needs of other children as well. In fact, a parent who has learned to raise a child of God would be the best teacher.

What is most important, however, is the period prior to school. It is during the years from birth to five that the child needs to learn ethics and wisdom in the home. The school does not have these to give. It is at home that the child learns love, goodness, charity, and stories of noble lives. Harmony in the family is a very important factor because children learn without being taught. They learn insecurity from disharmony. But in harmony, the trust that is naturally there remains intact and grows in strength.

I recall my mother being unassertive and ever spacious. Her goodness nourished me and stilled my mind. She took away the desires that possessed me. I was thankful without knowing why, as if the irritation of a sense of lack had disappeared. Her presence was always healing. She had a way of staying away from "me and mine," "you and I," desires, and memory.

Could we awaken in ourselves, and by so doing, in the child:

> an awareness of universal and earth forces,
> an awareness of God's love and eternal life,
> an awareness of beauty, goodness,
> and compassion amongst men,

an awareness of a saintly life free of fear,
gratefulness for all that is?

*   *   *

PARENT: What is gratefulness?

Gratefulness always precedes wanting and therefore it is
ever present. Gratefulness is for "what is," not for what you
want. Where there is gratefulness, there is hardly any desire or
memory. Needs are spontaneously met. You cannot separate
yourself from gratefulness anymore than you can separate
yourself from compassion. Love in its gladness is what you are.
Once this is realized there is no lack. Abundance manifests itself
and keeps the mind ever free of anxiety.

PARENT: What is prayer?

Prayer is a link, a living link between man and God.

To understand prayer we have to know the Divine Laws of
creation and the relationship between man and God. Even
though we are in a body and forgetful of our real nature of love,
God made sure that the memory of who we are is never lost.
The Holy Spirit accompanies us and is ever in contact with the
Source of creation. God and His Son are inseparable.

Though in a state of illusion, the Son can call upon God. This
calling is the prayer that unifies. One does not pray for things;
one prays to be true to who one is by invoking one's true Self.
All that is is yours in unity and wholeness. "Separation"
praying for things intensifies the misperception of separation.
Let your prayers be for correction of wrong-mindedness. Prayer
teaches one to forgive and not to judge. Freed from these, you
are unlimited.

*   *   *

Begin by educating yourself and then transmit the awareness of the world of goodness, so vast and abundant, to your child. Learn the ways of self-transformation. Teach the child what *you* want to learn. *A Course In Miracles* tells us: *The purpose of the course might be said to provide you with a means of choosing what you want to teach on the basis of what you want to learn.*[2]

This book is for exceptional parents who want to give their whole lives to raising a child of God. This requires deep study and a highly moral life. There is a need for this kind of preparation of parents. It is an auspicious undertaking, a whole life action, beyond the scope of the individual.

You, the parents, the bearers of the new generation, have but one responsibility: to reverse the process of self-destruction and live by internal values. Because you have seen the need to awaken yourself, you will know how to awaken the potential in your child as well. You will have the wisdom to impart to the child whereby he can renew himself from within. There have been children that never left God-consciousness throughout their lives. The age of the Vedas and Upanishads produced great beings because there was right relationship between parent and child, teacher and student.

When the Divine Leisure is protected, the entity that the child is can make a decision as to how it wants to express itself. The parents can awaken the child so that, maybe in this lifetime, he will not prolong the past. Thus a new beginning can take place. The right intent and deliberate decision not to do the wrong thing will not only strengthen the child but will transform the parents' lives as well.

> *PARENT:* Do the parents have a direct affect on the child's making that decision as to how he wants to express himself? My understanding is that when the child is in that vulnerable state, the entity would make a choice. Is that regulated by the parents?

Partly. I think once having understood what the child is, that understanding would make the parents responsible and not helpless. If it is merely an idea, however, they will not receive the strength. Somehow, we merely learn ideas. Bringing them into application is quite another issue. Without application, violence continues and we don't have the peace to impart. Can you imagine what a large percentage of children are fed by bottles or spend their young years with baby sitters while their mothers are working? Just see what we are doing — the violence and artificiality of it. We deny our own sensitivity as we rely upon ''experts'' to tell us what to do.

In understanding that the child is surrounded by Divine Leisure and is impressionable — you no longer have to worry about *him*. The change has to come in you. We want to learn more about the child because learning is abstract. Anytime it is suggested that you, as a parent, have to change, that's when the difficulties arise. You say, ''I can't do that.'' All through your life, you are going to be saying those words. ''I can't do anything about the hunger in the world. I can't do anything about my neighbor. I can't do anything about the child of my own flesh and blood. I cannot love. And I will not love.''

But as you read this, is it not beginning to undo what you have learned — your illusions and deceptions? Similarly, *A Course In Miracles* has come with miracles to undo, to reveal the limitations of thought and awaken discrimination. With discrimination comes the awareness of that which is not real. Awareness, in itself, undoes deception effortlessly. Awareness knows no fear. Every line in the Course has a miracle to impart. Could we read it like the child — without translation, judgment, interpretation? Could we hear it directly? When I first met him in New York, Mr. J. Krishnamurti told me:

''There are no problems apart from the mind.''

Knowing this, could you ever have a problem?

There are no problems in life. Try to make a problem, come to a moment of awareness, and the problem with all its nightmares vanishes because it is not real.

Forgive us our illusions, Father,
and help us to accept
our true relationship with You,
in which there are no illusions,
and where none can ever enter.[3]

*****

A baby, for months and months, does not know who you are. At first his eyes do not focus, and then after some time he looks at you. How honored you feel. You have been around him and one day the child looks at you with some recognition and smiles. What happens to you?

For the rest of your life you would take care of that child, you would love that child more than any flower of heaven. You would make sure that the child is totally protected from the wickedness of motivations, from everything that is not of God. And you would never tell a lie to the child, nor speak of a lie before the child, nor would your voice ever change its tone of soft lovingness. You would begin to mature and you would become a father to the whole human race, a mother to all human beings because you had a child.

What gifts a child gives. Just that smile! What would you give to that child? Something that is yours beyond clothes and toys.

You would give that child a voice that is a song. You would sing to the child in a very low voice. You would sing a song that is True Knowledge. Something from Jesus' words in the Bible — one sentence, or a few words only. You could find some beautiful things out of the Prophet Mohammed, or Guru Nanak, Lord Buddha, or Lao Tzu. True Knowledge. Because you are honest, you would find that which is honest to give to your child — not vulgar love songs or songs of unfulfillment, but songs which introduce him to fulfillment and to what is already perfect.

Where would you kiss the child? You would find out how clumsy you are once you have to find out where to kiss him. You would find that you are not original, that you don't really know anything. You would realize, "I don't know to give. I can imitate. All I know is what somebody told me. I am not myself."

The whole house would change when you sang to the child, or when you held him. Can you put your problems away? For how long can the child never know unfulfillment, never know a problem, never know the sound of a harsh voice or word? That child would grow up as an extension of fulfillment and joy, ethics, beauty, virtue, wisdom, and tenderness.

This has to take place in the home before the child goes to school. If the parents who love the child cannot do it, one cannot expect the school to do it.

The function of the parent is to awaken the child to his own eternity, to his own holiness, to the perfection of what God created — not to phony books, crayons, and waste. We only do that when we don't have anything to give. Thank God there is milk in the breast. How few mothers today have even that to give.

When your child gets to know you and smiles,
you will know the power of the purity of innocence.
It will give you life.
Sing holy songs to the child,
gently, softly, lovingly,
in a caressive voice —
"*sotto voce.*"*

---

*"Literally 'under the voice.' In either vocal or instrumental performance, in an 'undertone,' i.e., with subdued sound." *Harvard Dictionary of Music.* (Editor)

Anyone who can make his voice soft and loving
knows how to sing.
Holy songs are like flowers and stars in the sky.
Kiss the child lightly and sing.
The child will listen.
A light will shine in his eyes
and love, out of your heart,
will bring the mind to peace and serenity.
Make sure the songs are of True Knowledge
and your thoughts and your values will change.

The smile of a child liberates man. Just his unrestrained smile. It is a most perfect moment in creation, cleansing anyone who sees it. First the child is impressionable, and now the child begins to give. And what a giving — his own joy of being a child.

The primary need of the child in childhood is love that protects him from external forces. His need is of protection, not of education. A child needs to play. Mental faculties must awaken in their own internal way and should never be forced. Play and laughters are his nourishment and in that there is a natural learning, without conformity, because he is not being imposed upon. If he is protected from being imposed upon, he will have the discrimination of his own conviction and will not violate what is true within himself.

It is possible for the child to grow without schooling and yet be educated in a most sane manner. Do not be afraid of the new or you will bind yourself to the past and never enter the energetic reality of the present. The present is forever whole and heaven and earth are within its range.

There is the need for extraordinary parents, but all parents have the potential to be extraordinary if they do not undermine themselves. The parents who are delighted to learn how important Divine Leisure is — that it shapes and molds the child's whole life and character — are strengthened to be co-creators with the Eternal Laws of growth. Consistency with the law itself becomes the parents' strength. The whole of society could be wrong and you could still afford to be right.

Know that rebirth is possible now that birth has taken place. This is the Divine Law. Would you deny your child the awakening of his potential to be liberated? Would you subject him to the limitation of the physical world when he is of the spirit as God created him? Do not stop short and limit the child to his body.

As the child's faculties begin to awaken and he becomes curious about the things he sees, hears, feels, and tastes, his span of interest will increase. The parents are obliged not to abandon him to the mere world of appearances. His purpose for being in the physical world is much greater.

To introduce him to that which is eternal, to that which never changes in the midst of the outer world that is ever changing, is the parents' responsibility. The wonder and mystery of the timeless, the Unchangeable and Unnameable, is far greater than the physical world of appearances, for it is the very Source of creation. To the degree the parents are inspired by it, to that degree they will be able to transmit the wonder to the child. Emerson knew:

> ''The world of senses is a world of shows. It does not exist for itself, but has a symbolic character which shows the co-presence of other laws . . .''

Everything that is timeless touches one with the intensity of silence. The purity of silence is the greatest gift the adult can impart to a child.

> *My brother, peace and joy I offer you,*
> *That I may have God's peace and joy as mine.*[4]

The years from five to the approach of puberty are important for awakening the child's internal faculties. Unless a balance is kept between the internal and the external, the child will not have the moral strength of virtue and nobleness, the dignified aspects of the spirit, to contain the impulses of the body as he enters puberty. As his reproductive glands are activated, he will be drawn to pleasure if he is ignorant of the happiness and contentment naturally within him.

Pleasure is not something to be sought. Pleasure exists in the way one sees the world.

God is in everything I see
because God is in my mind.[5]

God goes with me wherever I go.[6]

God is the Light in which I see.[7]

I am sustained by the Love of God.[8]

During the years from five to twelve, the parents must prepare the child not to get taken over by the externals. This is done by nurturing the child's inner life and by the stillness the parents impart through their wisdom and their love.

*   *   *

PUBERTY

After the period of puberty begins, usually around the age of twelve, a child whose childhood has not been invaded upon with adulthood, stimulation, knowings, and concerns, has learned how to think objectively and creatively. He is capable of coming to total attention and values order in life. He has the ability to comprehend or to recognize the wholeness of "what is." Such a child, at the approach of puberty, is mentally mature, capable of being responsible, and in charge of physical urges. He is now ready to use that energy for his greater potentials, to make contact with God whose Son he is.

The parents have played their part in helping him to overcome limitations and have prepared him for that reunion. They have introduced him to Divine Leisure which is creative — a space within him that is never pressured. In the worst of turmoil, he remains intact. The responsibility of the parent and the teacher is to bring the child to a space where he will . . .*not value what is valueless.*[9]

From puberty on, his purpose in life and his direction is to come to Atonement, to bring the separation to an end. Two growths take place simultaneously. One is the natural, internal growth of joyous self-awareness. The other is the awakening of the external, physical world of the body senses. Today, children tend to mature too quickly mentally because they have been deprived of Divine Leisure. The accentuation on the body senses is very detrimental to the inner awakening. If the inner life of the child is given the space to mature up to adolescence, he will be able to cope with the forces of puberty, the body's need for sensation, and the abstract, mental sense of insecurity and fear.

His maturity and sense of responsibility would make right use of his life energy without having to deny, suppress, or impose. Now that he is capable of learning directly, the energies for self-creation and rebirth are rightly directed. Such a person, having his own clarity, is under no external influence. Without clarity, ideals, projections, and religious dogmas often become the authority.

There are three uses of this energy of puberty:

— gratification,
— procreation, or
— rebirth.

It is wise to direct the attention and the energy to rebirth in order to develop awareness and character.

Today, we live in a society that promotes free ''love'' and free sex. But parents have to teach their children not to be taken over by someone who tries to entice them externally. If a young lady has self-respect, she will not degrade herself, for then it will be difficult for her to know what love is. It is a question of self-respect, honesty, and discrimination. A girl with integrity and dignity is exceptional. With dignity, there is also purity. Then, when she falls in love, she has something to give to a man who didn't stimulate her outwardly. It is a meeting, not merely at the physical level, but at all levels of her being. The Divine Hand is in it. She would know it without any doubt when it takes place, if she can wait that long. When we are impatient, we lose discrimination. There is something innocence can know that experience cannot know, and there is something purity can know that impurity cannot know.

How important it is to prepare the child to contain his own physical nature as the expansive force of youth imparts enormous vitality to physicality. If contained, youth has an integrity, a passion that can become a source of moral strength and conviction. Ultimately, it will provide the discrimination the young person needs to discover the one with whom he will build a life.

In clarity, one knows directly. This is what is behind ''love at first sight.'' What is essential is always given. If you try to find it, you will blunder into errors because the physical senses cannot be trusted. Once you limit yourself to the physical senses you limit yourself to preferences and prevent the eternal action of creation from taking place.

The involuntary, creative action is always there. It is always of love. Love alone creates and love brings two people together. The one with whom you are going to share your life is for you, and no other. Seeing this, one would be inspired by the goodness of life, by the compassion of creation. One would be surrounded from head to toe with the glow of gratefulness for the Source of all things. When we limit ourselves to physicality we are tormented by what we project and assume.

It is seldom the child who is responsible for his problems. Until puberty, the parents are largely responsible and therefore, the correction must lie with them. It may seem arduous, as changing a lifestyle always appears to be, but if transformation is what you want, you will discover it has its own resources. Inherent in each person is a strength that can cope with all alternatives. It requires total dedication and the right priorities. Only when one doesn't have an alternative is it possible to raise the child of God.

Childhood outgrows infancy, adolescence outgrows childhood, youth outgrows adolescence, and adulthood outgrows youth. Each stage has its very definite characteristics, development, and awakening. Each stage has tremendous potentials. Very seldom has any one stage been fully explored or the potentials of it realized. Anyone who would realize these potentials would be unique in the world and have the capacity to affect the whole of humanity.

Our present society does not produce great and noble beings. Early education desecrates the space of innocence and invades upon contentment. The child is deprived of the natural space to be a child. Even his toys and his ''wantings'' are no longer natural. When childhood is cut short and puberty awakens prematurely, it plays havoc in the child's life. If children are exposed to what is not natural to their age, we do great harm and awaken them to sensations that distract them with their need for gratification.

Love is so important in the early years prior to puberty because love stabilizes a life. When human warmth is rationed, innocence is shortened and the child becomes overly concerned with himself. He feels alienated as a sense of ''strangerness'' begins to take place in his nervous system and psyche. Part of him becomes unstable, panicky, unsure and unprotected, as the opposites become real due to the lack of love.

What the child would do during adolescence is determined largely by his childhood. Has he grown too fast in his awareness of lack? Has the awakening of insecurity taken place too early in him? For how long did innocence endure? What was the span of his total carefreeness and trust? All of these will determine his behavior in adolescence — how gentle, thoughtful, responsible, loving, moral, virtuous he will be. What kind of self-expression and self-honesty he will give to this new phase is almost predetermined. Will he be motivated by body needs or will he extend what is of the spirit and the noblest of intelligence?

The child's early years are most important for they affect and determine his whole life. If the child is put in the second place during his early years, he will mature faster than nature intended. His brain will become too activated and the things of the world will crowd his mind. Once that space is lost, the child is weak of character and willingly accepts the conformity and prejudices of the external world that surrounds him.

Either the child gets to know his boundless Self or he knows the distractions of society. The healthy, balanced child would question society and a child lacking strength due to misdirection would submit to it.

The wisdom it takes to retain a balance in body, mind, and spirit is the parents' privilege to discover. In protecting the child from external stimulation, the parents reawaken in themselves the leisure and the love that make everything external secondary. Love is in the sharing. If you can share it with your child, nothing of the world seems of much importance.

A Course In Miracles points out the Law of Completion — the

Father God gives His love to His Son and the Son responds with his love.

> Today accept God's peace and joy as yours. Let Him complete Himself as He defines completion. You will understand that what completes Him must complete His Son as well. He cannot give through loss. No more can you. Receive His gift of joy and peace today, and He will thank you for your gift to Him.[10]

The child will respond to the love you give to him with his love to you. If this sharing of love between parent and child is extended through adolescence, you will give a child to humanity that will shake the foundation of the world.

Today, with all of the pressures on man, we often have more than one thing to do at a time and it is difficult not to become confused and disoriented. The next generation will not be able to make decisions because the computer will control the mind of man. By the time this generation matures, man will know nothing beyond what he is told. He will not be able to think for himself. People who can think for themselves would be a minority, for there would be enormous pressure to think like the clan. There may not be the moral strength to stand alone.

It is horrifying to observe what is happening to mankind and what the next ten or fifteen years hold for us. Now with the advent of subliminal tapes, man will be even more controlled. Our children will no longer be our children. They will be children of the state. The corporation will own them, educate them, mold their minds, condition them totally. And the parents would say, "They died for their country." In a life without wisdom, in a life that thinks there is an enemy, that thinks there is fear, concepts become important, not ethics.

Business can persuade you that subliminal tapes can help the child to remember his lessons and improve his mathematics and his algebra. But why is external learning so important? Is it not always fragmented and unrelated to the whole?

The child is a creature of all eternity. He is related to Mars, to Jupiter, to the Sun, the Moon, the stars, to the earth that feeds him, the air that he breathes. But we invalidate these. Only what is manmade has meaning and the child has to fit into that.

I can see that subliminal tapes would start with helping the public. Such things always start with helping man. Communism started with helping man; capitalism started with helping man; wars started with helping man. Everything "helps" man. Are the constant accounts of murder on the television, radio, and in the newspapers — accidents, bloodshed, and violence — "helping" man? We have degenerated into insanity. If you can live without God, without Eternal Laws, without virtue, without wisdom, then fear, violence, and exploitation are the natural result.

And now the child can learn all kinds of things merely by putting a tape on. But it is shaping the child's mind! Lincoln only went to school for a year and this country has not produced a man of his caliber since. He still had the space of Divine Leisure and he spoke of Eternal Laws.

If you want to help your child, you have to give him your life. If you always make decisions for him, you will deprive him of the ability to make decisions when he grows up. There is an allotted period of time for correction after which correction is no longer possible and the bind of consequences can go on for eons. Life is a great responsibility.

The period of puberty will determine the child's manhood and his Christhood. Heaven dwells in the child. Mold him, not into a citizen, but into a human being. Never would you be helpless again. The parent need never limit himself, for love is not bought and sold. Let your child awaken it within you.

CHAPTER SEVEN

7

LOVE, LAW, AND CHILDREN

Because there is a notion that the child needs education we start off by giving him "knowledge" based upon our limited concept of the physical world around us — art, history, geography, grammar. Why do we do this? Partly because we have names for everything. Very quickly we pass our belief in separation and division on to the child. What a terrible thing to do. It is as artificial as giving him canned food.

Somehow the child is not important enough to us to give him something true. So we give him ideas, beliefs, things. We shower him with "goodies" — war toys, computer games, and all kinds of factory-made gadgets — but we never see that in doing this we are denying the child his own inventive, playful capacity.

What if there were a parent who was unimpressed by "isms" and dogmas, who saw the Action of Life in the breath of the child, in the miracle of a seed, the song of the bird, in the mystery of the stars? Supposing there was a parent who saw the Action of Life as One. He would not be part of separation.

He would teach the child to come to the right perspective. It is only in the absence of right perspective that knowledge about things becomes more important than the awareness of Life itself.

Such a parent would teach the child Divine Laws, what is true and factual. He would teach what is God-created, not manmade. He would not give him concepts of America, Canada, Christian, or Jew. If one were to teach the child a Law of Life, then, in essence, one would have to know what non-separation is. In the absence of this direct knowing we have endless words, thoughts, and assumptions. How we limit the child to our world of unreality.

How long will it take the child to discover the hypocrisy of these teachings of unfulfillment? Probably we will make sure he never does; we will make him a hypocrite. But he will never be content in hypocrisy. Therefore, in the relationship between parent and child, the seeds of disharmony are sown.

The wise parent introduces the child to the creative and eternal Law of Love. In a society driven by ambition and desire it is vitally necessary to impart the strength of love to the child in order to protect him from unessential involvements. The law is born out of love; thus, it cannot be harsh or binding.

The real education of the child is to introduce him to what he already *is*. If you want to bring the child to Eternal Laws, then Love and the Law will help you. First of all, the parent should discover what is unessential. He may never know what the essential is, but he can start by discovering what it isn't. Energy for this discovery comes from simplicity and the benediction of the Law of Love. Love cannot be contaminated; it ever purifies itself like a self-renewing spring. It is the sustaining force in life.

Can we give the child an essential fact, one that will take care of all other issues? The child's own perfection is such a fact.

Impart to him that he is created perfect and you have introduced him to the Kingdom of God. It can be done with or without formal education. Most of us are oblivious to our perfection.

The child will recognize love because the memory of truth is still intact in his mind. We need never underestimate the child, for the miracle of love inherent in him is divinely protected. Nothing can take it away. It is ever there, as the present is ever there despite our preoccupation with past and future.

Once you have introduced the child to the Truth, every flower will remind him of it; the evening sky will introduce him to it; every song of a bird will awaken him to it — because all are part of the same one Truth. The child would see that the flower and the bird are joyously expressing their participation in creation, sharing the perfection of their being.

A few years ago, I saw a seven-year-old boy playing with a toy gun. "Gabriel," I said. "That is ugly." But I understood that to the child it was quite a thrill to have something like that. "I know you think it is fun," I said, "but it is something that kills. It represents anger, bitterness, and hate. You are of love. You do not want to kill anything — it is like stepping on a flower. Do you want to do that?"

"No," he said, and dropped the gun. Then he pointed at his playmate. "The gun is his."

"Jonathan can introduce you to the gun," I told him, "and you can introduce him to the flower."

Jonathan was listening attentively. "It is only a toy," he said. "It is also only a gun," I said. There was a pause, and in that pause my first contact with Jonathan was made. "Why not play with a ball?" I asked him. "I have a ball," he said. And he left with the gun and soon returned with a ball.

I started to bounce the ball against a wall and catch it. I had only to do it a few times before they, too, were interested. They quickly forgot everything else and were absorbed by the game. Later I saw them climbing trees and laughing.

It is not enough to tell a child: "You cannot do that." You have to bridge the no-man's land, that moment when the child does not know what to do. You have to introduce him to something new. That is what one extra step of being with him does. At every moment the question is can *you* give something up? You want the child to give something up, but can you, the adult, also give the child your space and the energy of attention?

The parent must be very loving, though not heavy with advice. If the very sight of the child does not bring you to exuberance, you will not have the gladness of friendship. It is not always necessary to "do" something with the child. What is crucial, however, is the spirit of the relationship. You can run with the child, wrestle with him, and help him outgrow so many toys. It is your own interest in and love for nature that will awaken him to appreciation. Learning and teaching take place irrespective of conscious effort. All you need is honesty; you cannot fake who you are.

Introducing the child to an Eternal Law is introducing him to an area of non-conflict within himself. Unless we bring the child to this point of certainty he will become dependent and manipulative. And then as he grows up his relationship with other children will be similarly affected. At the first sign of trouble he would want to run away or be arrogant. Because you have not given him your whole attention you have helped take away his strength. The question is, do you have within yourself the space necessary to nurture the growing child? It is most important to make the child aware of the causes of his inner conflict and the sources of disharmony without. This requires the parent to change his lifestyle of expedience.

Expedience is an oversimplified conclusion. It often evades

the real issue. Born out of the pressure of time, it makes the child secondary to your own plans. When you lack the space to give the child you resort to imparting conclusions rather than leading him to discovery. When a child asks, "Why?" is your answer designed to make him be quiet and not ask any more questions, or do you encourage him to find his own clarity? Even a sincere, "I don't know," is better than a lecture. Because we don't have reverence for clarity ourselves, our answers are usually influence or prejudice.

Clarity cannot be given by another. It takes place in the child when you, the parent, love Truth more than expedience. When you love Truth, how can you feel helpless?

Truth introduces the child to his own vitality. By explaining, exploring, getting past conclusions and opinions, parents bring the child to the energy that silences the mind with the light of clarity. That is the blessing of creation that the child needs to know. Love is not time-bound. It does not divert to the duality of choices. Whenever the child is not important, the insanity begins.

To avoid making a child dependent takes enormous discrimination: What is dependence and what is a need? What is essential and what is not essential? Everything can become an opportunity for the parent, as he enters the realm of the present, to be with the child. Thus the parent-child relationship is enriching because it leads to the discovery of one's own inner resources. What is essential imparts strength, not dependence or sentimentality.

How does a mother make a child dependent on her? Today when there are so many broken families, a child may not have a father, grandmother, cousins, uncles, or aunts around. The mother is also alone. The unnatural setting of modern life fosters loneliness. As long as she is lonely, she will impart the gloom of loneliness to the child no matter what she teaches him. A weak parent involves the child in external things. Because the parent lacks his own inner resources to deal with the child, he buys things for him, thus externalizing his life beyond necessity.

What does it take to become at once a teacher, student, and friend to a child? You can listen together to the sounds of trees, for every tree has a different sound and you do not have to buy anything to hear it. You can ask him to close his eyes and explore the bark. The rough feel of strong bark or the cool refreshing touch of a smooth trunk enliven the whole hand. You can awaken a sensitivity and discrimination in this way. What greater blessing can you impart to the child than his own awakening?

Be gentle with the child so that he remains innocent to harshness and reactions. It is best not to put too much emphasis on teaching. In the early years he need know only the gladness of love. Let him grow in strength rather than doubt, not clinging to self-consciousness. If he were really loved, a sense of self-preservation would not even occur to him.

It is your interest and awareness that will communicate to him the joy of the tree or the wind playing like laughter in the sky. At night, the sky is full of silence; and as the day opens its blue eye, the hum of scattered sounds begins and multiplies until there is a sky full of noises. And yet the child who has been introduced to silence is at peace within. This will grow in strength until the ever-renewing purity in his life is no longer affected, but instead affects the day with the stillness of his being.

Your gentleness is past all learning. It is the "given" that you share with the child who brings heaven with him. His vulnerability and harmlessness can melt your heart and teach you the joy of innocence. Your own peace is your greatest gift to the child. Let him blossom without knowing your anxieties. Become aware of how anxiety arises in you, in order to avoid its entry into the child's life. A child is sensitive. He absorbs everything. Being in the present he has a different way of knowing. He has not yet accumulated memories to lure him into the abstract. You, the parent, represent the world to him.

When you are relaxed you are also wise. Your pulse is steady and slow, and the gaps between your heartbeats have the space of eternity. The child will respond to the relaxed and loving touch of your hands. He is also very sensitive to tension in your face, your voice, your touch. Your words may lie but what you *are* can never deceive him. He has no motives or contradictions within him as yet. The child is the child of light, unaware of the pressure of time. He is direct. Your reverence for creation will enable him to see the holiness beyond appearances.

You can share with the child this reverence for every living thing, no matter what it is. Even a bell pepper placed lovingly in the child's hand would impart to him its quality, its vibration of greenness, smoothness, its smell. It can give more than nourishment. Let the child see its reality, so much more than its name.

The only real knowledge is of God. It is Absolute. Everything is an extension of It. Nothing even exists apart from its relationship with the whole. What peace this sense of wholeness could bring to man. This peace is what the child needs. You do not need to teach it to him; he will receive it, for his awareness is direct.

What a gift the child imparts. It civilizes us and makes us human, as pure as God created us. The child contributes to the lives of his parents. In his presence, the mother and father become closer and a glow surrounds their physicality. The child is certainly never a liability, for he has been given everything and he gives freely to his parents. In truth, the birth of a child brings the whole family to rebirth.

We talked about how all things originate in love — even the Eternal Laws. There must come a time in one's development when even the so-called *law* must be tested by the actuality of love.

The law becomes something you know. The child knows his parents love him. But this knowing is still incomplete if it is merely verbal. Since verbal knowledge retains the mental space for doubt, it is only more pretense. Knowing, in reality, is not only a function of the brain but is of the wholeness of Mind. The Mind is beyond appearance, situations, and concepts. In order to bring one to the actual state of awareness, life invariably creates a challenge.

In such a state, one's "knowing" no longer applies. There can be tremendous moments of doubt and insecurity. Only if there is real love can you help the child out of that depression and fear. Then love is no longer an expression; it *is*. This holy instant of Oneness eliminates doubt forever and completes the verbal knowing without sentimentality. It does not reassure; it is complete in itself. This relationship must come between parent and child, student and teacher, man and God.

No matter what you do on your own, the dependence will continue if you rely solely on abstract *knowing*: "This is my mother. She is good. She will do it for me." But one day the mother will not be there to do it. And unless the child really has love he will never understand, for only in love is there no demand for conformity, no need for compliance. Love is free of dependence and gives freedom. Its relationship is ever with Truth. The space it imparts is beyond judgment and the needs of personality.

An example of such love is seen in the Bible when Jesus said to Peter:

> "GET THEE BEHIND ME, SATAN: THOU ART AN OFFENCE UNTO ME: FOR THOU SAVOUREST NOT THE THINGS THAT BE OF GOD, BUT THOSE THAT BE OF MEN."[1]

Those were strong words, and yet they were not spoken out of anger. Because Peter knew Jesus loved him, he learned from it. Jesus was not angry. To know the truth of this is to know that Jesus never left God-consciousness, the state that is Christ.

Peter offers advice and expedience; he is identifying Jesus with the body, trying to save Him from going to Jerusalem where He will be killed. Peter's caring is sentimental. It is against the Will of God and the function of Christ, for Christ is not a body. Thus, Peter's suggestion, being of the thought system of man, is an interference. Jesus lives by the Thought of God that acknowledges nothing external as real. To Him sentimentality does not make the unreal real; it is superfluous.

Love will test everything that is of thought and belief. In so doing, it clarifies.

The parents' responsibility is not to introduce the child to human weakness but to his own Divine origin. They are responsible to life which is independent. This is a fact. How will you, the parents, realize the truth of it? What transformation will you have to go through to come upon the very state of truth that silences all the words? How often our priorities are not right. We lack both the space and the wisdom to know that truth is essential to life. The child will inherit what you value.

The parents must prepare the child with inner strength because one day the child will form new relationships where the right foundation of love will be needed. In these times, the tendency is to isolate rather than to expand in awareness and affection. This breeds dependence on the media and other distractions. So, it is important to establish within the child the relationship of love and law in order to provide him with strength of character and integrity.

Often the parent feels helpless. Know that this is unnatural and not what you want to impart to your child. You must first remove it in yourself. If you do not you will make the child dependent. Helplessness is not a fact. The situation, as it is, is perfect. And in that perfection is the strength to outgrow anything. Acceptance of limitations is the perpetuation of assumed imperfection. Realize that it is just as easy not to accept helplessness as a fact. For the true fact is the perfection that God created you.

*　　*　　*

APPLICATION

To bring the things we know into application is the difficulty. But we do not *know* anything in a basic way, even though we are always telling our children what to do. In order to survive, children only half hear what the parents are saying and, in the end, are absolutely uninterested.

Why doesn't the parent ever question himself? "Why are my words not effective?" What a change that would bring into the atmosphere! Parents have a lifestyle to which they want the child to conform. This is to be questioned. We have not created a world of harmony, love, and peace. We are split in our own minds and hearts and that is what we pass on to our children.

Those who know only ideas have nothing to say to children. Invariably they draw attention to themselves. How limiting this is because it produces dependence. We limit each new generation to the repeat of the same experience. Routine conditioning is the result. And we are totally unaware of the limitations *we* have imposed, and the harm we do in preventing newness and spontaneity in the life of the child. Each generation is limited by the poverty of the former, and generation after generation the deterioration into routine increases. Gradually the warmth of human relationship dries up.

The new generation is now oblivious to reverence for life, the values of humanism. They are taken over by the whirlwind of propaganda — nation against nation, the importance of the industrial economy. Parallel to this, with the stress that is imposed upon the brain, violence and reaction are increasing.

What would you teach your child beyond what you know? Who would teach the child not only to look, but to see that which is beyond appearance?

I can sympathize with parents because they are caught in the artificiality of life. Our parents didn't bring us up right either; we have inherited false values. But let us not desecrate the child's mind with a repeat of our own experiences. The child brings with him the space for his own growth. Better not to crowd him with our stress and pressure. Give the child the space and you will be consistent with the Law — the Law that never intrudes on what is of God. Would you learn of simplicity? Would you learn to relate the child with his simplicity?

The parents, and then the teachers, are the custodians of the child of God. Our responsibility is to awaken his divine faculties as well as our own. If this is not done, then we confine the child to our experience and make him time-bound.

At each age the child goes through a different phase. First the child is born and the mother nurses him; then when the teething begins, everything changes in the child. They are to be given different food and they are also capable of learning other things. Then comes phase after phase as other potentials are awakening within him. The parents must be aware that something new is taking place in the child. If the parents are aware they can be of greater assistance and love.

At every stage it is not just a body growing. There is an inner growth taking place; inner centers are opening. It is very difficult, particularly in this externalized society, to protect the child. The opening of other potentials is involuntary, but the child doesn't know how to communicate it to the parents nor to the teachers. The first thing for us to learn from a child is how *he* feels, not meet with him in order to teach something.

*   *   *

TEACHING RESPONSIBILITY

What a difficult task it is to bring up a child. We don't even know where to begin. He has his life ahead of him and we are bound to the body, bound to other pressures and circumstances, and we don't know what to do.

One has to teach the child responsibility. Just that. Not how he is going to make a living. You have to give him strength of character. Somehow this no longer seems to be required. Your loyalty must be to the flag, to your tribe, to your country. The child is no longer important. Mothers produce children and rear them so that they can go and work. We don't even know that there can be a different way. How would one teach the child responsibility and make it something very joyous?

The action must always start with oneself. If you have a schedule, a reverence for the rhythm in your life, you will see that the child has rhythm in his life. If you have your house in order, then you can teach the child how to have the house in order. Children love doing things. If you are gardening, they love to garden. Keep toys away. Children are very impressionable and much of the teaching has to be done knowing this law — that the child is impressionable.

We have to put the demand before us to build character in the child so that he can cope with loneliness and learn to trust Life itself. We should not make him dependent on things, but always point out something that does not change, something that is within.

All the time, *you* can be with gratefulness and thus give him a different awareness when anything upsets him. Can you always lift him out of problems and introduce him to a strength within himself? Can you lift him out of what you see, perceive, and hear, and expose him to a silent moment? Can you always show him that which does not change? These are the gifts the parent can give in a very loving way.

Often we are lonely or insecure ourselves and that is what gets transmitted — disharmony. What about strength, harmony, goodness? What about the joy of doing something with your child? This is the responsibility we need to assume.

Not until the child wants to learn should you teach him. It doesn't matter when he wants to learn. That freedom we must give. But we don't have the space. In earlier times, children didn't go to school until they were eight or nine. They had space to be themselves. God gives us the whole world; everything on the planet exists for man. In the Bible it says,

> "BE FRUITFUL, AND MULTIPLY, AND REPLENISH THE EARTH, AND SUBDUE IT: AND HAVE DOMINION OVER THE FISH OF THE SEA, AND OVER THE FOWL OF THE AIR, AND OVER EVERY LIVING THING THAT MOVETH UPON THE EARTH."[2]

Can we see that needs are met?

We must become a point of peace upon the earth — one person, one family, one group that is undisturbed amidst the roar and madness of a world caught in wantings. "Creation is of love, of God. I need not be concerned. My needs are met." Can we, individually or as a family, be that pure and calm point of silence? We have to live that way. Unless we come to that, we will not have the freedom and the holiness of self-reliance. Self-reliance, in itself, is a statement of being independent.

Wanting is a projection. It is unessential and false. Needs are met. Even before man arrived upon the planet, the earth prepared itself to welcome his spirit. As long as we don't have anything to give, we will be compelled to want.

With no "wanting,"
and knowing that needs are met,
each one becomes a point of stillness
in the midst of the waste

and madness of unfulfillment.
The populace is so externalized
and caught in the hysteria of activity
that neither peace nor order are in sight.

Our function is to be a focus of silence
and a point of calm
amidst the noise, haste, and chaos
of a world ruled by stimulation.

Hardly anyone today has peace to give.
Disquietude distorts life
and knows nothing of humanism — calm and serene.
To trust is to be the serenity of Heaven.
To trust is never to be disturbed by the externals.
And thus trust rests in the holy instant
and has something to GIVE. . .

Our lives are holy.
We are not of the earth but children of God.
All things are given to the one who is open
to receive from the holy instant.

*   *   *

IMPARTING CERTAINTY

When you tell a child, ''don't do this'' or ''don't do that,''
he becomes half deaf to your words. After a while, unless you
threaten or punish him, he won't hear you. If you were
responsible you would observe that your words are becoming
meaningless. You would then learn something that you didn't
know before: how to respond adequately to every issue. The
child is entrusted to you, and common sense and wisdom find
out. It is natural.

It is best not to say ''don't do that'' until it is absolutely
necessary. The action starts with you. You can become

responsible and change. You have to stop and think and assess before you blurt out, ''don't do that.'' Now you have become aware.

Then when ''don't do that'' is really necessary, make it absolute. No matter what it is, it is absolute. The child would try to use his techniques — cry for mommy, wear you down — because he is being confronted with something he doesn't like. It is predictable. But be very firm about it so the child knows it is irrevocable, you cannot be manipulated, and you are not going to change your mind.

Finally, the child would find out tantrums no longer apply. They don't work and they don't pay. He has to become convinced that your word is absolute. And then you have imparted certainty to the child. And that child, because of your certainty, will not be confused again. A child to whom certainty has been imparted learns there are authentic words, words that have meaning which cannot be manipulated. He doesn't have to understand it. He will know it. It is better than all the education he will receive in school.

Most children grow up without knowing certainty because the parents have conditioned them. See the damage that can be done. And then the parents become so frustrated and helpless they wind up beating or blaming the child.

If you have imparted certainty, when the child grows up he would have learned to say no to drugs, to sex — to anything that would externally try to take him over. When you tell him that he shouldn't smoke or take drugs or date at a young age, he would respect your words because he has a relationship with someone who is absolute. Thus, you begin to grow with the child because it is a love relationship — something that you share with the child. In the giving you are receiving. See the beauty of love. You are growing too. You were casual and now you are becoming responsible.

Once you have imparted certainty, the child will listen and that will protect him from many a consequence. No matter what anybody else says, that child will come and ask his parent. The child will listen if the parent is definite and clear.

See the wisdom of this clearly. Don't do it because I am saying so. Go into it in yourself. Don't become convinced and don't make it an idea. Bring it into effect. And it should remain in effect until the child is a young adult. It is a long range project that starts right now. That is real love. What a thing to give! Certainty. Having taken on the responsibility would impart something that senses cannot understand.

Once you are solid and have seen it, then you can talk to the child. Explain it to him and make it part of his life. Tell him, "We are going to work on this." You will see; he would cooperate. In the beginning he will find it difficult because *wanting* is easier, but you could sow the seed and he would start seeing it. Then you are working together. Otherwise the child gets confused. Work with him but don't give in. If you give in, you do great damage. It is best not to start something unless you are going to see it through all the way to the end.

CHAPTER EIGHT

8

WORKING WITH A CHILD — CRYSTAL
Part I

(Crystal is one of the children at the Foundation. Her father, John, first heard Tara Singh at the Mandala Holistic Health Conference in 1982. He subsequently attended the One Year Non-Commercialized Retreat in Los Angeles and then stayed on to become a student and an integral part of the work at the Foundation.

Part of being a student at the Foundation is the responsibility of bringing all relationships into harmony. John and his wife, Acacia, were divorced and Crystal would come from her home in Northern California to visit John from time to time. On one visit, Tara Singh met her and she was charmed from the very outset. Although at the time there seemed no possibility of harmony between John and Acacia, Taraji* persisted in encouraging John to see how detrimental it would be for Crystal to grow up without a wholesome family atmosphere, that

*In India, the addition of the syllable ''ji'' at the end of a person's name denotes respect, e.g., Gandhiji. This is similar to the use of ''Mr.'' or ''Mrs.'' in the West. (Editor)

because she is so bright and gifted, it would make her lose faith in life and result in cynicism and lack of any real relationship. Taraji explained that the child's function is to bring the two parents together and that the parents must be in harmony in relating to the child.

In April of 1985, when Crystal had just turned six years old, she visited the Foundation and Taraji asked her to sit quiet for twenty minutes every morning and evening. He telephoned her mother, Acacia, to explain to her the agreement that he and Crystal had made. Subsequently, he wrote a letter to her that solidified a contact that would eventually bring John and Acacia back together again. — Editor)

*   *   *

Dear Acacia,

Even though we have not met,
knowing Crystal has introduced you to me.
Anyone who could give birth to a child
of Crystal's sensitivity and love of honesty
is someone I would value getting to know.
The invitation to come and visit us
is not sentimental, nor impulsive.
It stands on real feeling.

The prayer we talked about is from the Bible:

"THE LORD BLESS THEE, AND KEEP THEE:
THE LORD MAKE HIS FACE TO SHINE UPON THEE,
AND BE GRACIOUS UNTO THEE:
THE LORD LIFT UP HIS COUNTENANCE UPON THEE,
AND GIVE THEE PEACE."[1]

Much love goes to you and Crystal.

She needs the twenty minutes in the morning and evening
to stay out of the stimulation.
Silence is the only protection we can offer
to children who are sensitive and vulnerable.
This may require some change of schedule in your life,
but there is rightness in it,
and that will give you the strength.

Crystal has a deep relationship with you
and what a blessing it would be
to share something
which you could do together each day.
It would strengthen the bond
and leave a lasting effect on Crystal's life.

These twenty minutes morning and evening
will become the foundation of Crystal's life
that will make her different from other children.
For silence would give her the strength
not to become so dependent on the externals.
Thus, she will be less apt to be exploitable
by the collective consciousness.

The parent gives the world the child and
one sees Mary holding Jesus in her arms —
not facing herself
but rather giving Him to the world.
And so you will be blessed for giving
to the world
a child who is intact and fortified
by the silence that you two shared.

And I assure you
where two or more gather, His presence is there.[2]
The child is of God and parents are the custodians.

I know how difficult it is to bring something
as simple as twenty minutes twice a day into application,

but the Divine forces would not have entrusted you
with a child like Crystal
if you did not have the resources within you.

I suggest that you do not ever underestimate yourself.

Much love goes to both of you.

"May the Lord bless thee and keep thee."

Affectionately,

Tara Singh

*   *   *

(The following sharings are based on the
numerous meetings Tara Singh has had with Crystal,
Acacia, and John about issues which they and many
children and parents must face. — Editor)

Crystal, at first there used to be just the Bible, and in the
Bible there are the words of Jesus. In some Bibles they are
printed in red, but there are not many pages of them. Before
Jesus came there were other saints and people who knew God.
First there was Moses and then came others who prepared the
people that the Christ was going to come — that He was just like
God, that He was the Son of God. These great prophets and
exceptional beings knew the Truth and they were trying to tell
everybody.

CRYSTAL: Did the people believe the saints
that He was coming?

That's such a nice question. Do you know, Crystal, not most
people. People don't believe. Oh they do in a superficial way,
but then they forget. If they could believe, it was unnecessary

for so many prophets or saints to come. In every generation there were always prophets of God who spoke the Truth and encouraged the people to live according to the way God would want them to. ''Treat your children nicely, treat your wife and husband nicely, the earth nicely — you must live a life that is honest and love one another.''

And it was said the Son of God would come and His Name would be the Christ. He would be born and would do this, and this, and that. Some people believed the saints and the prophets, but not everybody.

CRYSTAL: Why?

It's very difficult to say, Crystal. You see, for instance, there is spirit. And the spirit has no form, no shape — just like outside, in the day, there is light and it doesn't have any shape. The tree has shape, grass has shape, people have shape, cars have shape; but light doesn't have any shape. Spirit is like the light. Without the light, nothing would grow. Without the spirit, nothing would live. The spirit is like the light. The body has needs but the spirit doesn't have needs. The human body needs water and it needs food; it needs clothes and a house to live in. But the spirit doesn't have any needs.

CRYSTAL: Because it's everything?

Because it is the source of everything. We could say the light is the source of everything that grows but the light doesn't need anything. In the same way, the spirit has no needs because the spirit is the source of everything.

Jesus is all spirit.

CRYSTAL: Was He once a body?

Yes, once His spirit took a body. But Jesus had no desires, no fear, no ''wantings.'' So He ate good food and He did not want to own things. He did not want money. He was simple because inside He was not afraid, inside He was not lonely.

CRYSTAL: Other people who killed Him were afraid of Him?

Yes. They were afraid of Him because He would speak the truth and they loved money and they loved things of the body. Jesus took a body but His body never made any demands — "I want this and I want that."

You see, you and I, when we get stimulated, may not want to do the right thing for the body; we may ignore what the body wants. The body needs rest, but we don't want to sleep. And in the morning when it is time to go to school, the body says, "I want to sleep."

Maybe with Jesus it was never that way. The body probably did not interfere. It was always doing, or extending, that which was not of the body, but that which was of God. Jesus always loved because that's what the spirit is — it is always love. So, if you do something wrong, He still loves you.

CRYSTAL: Does He love you for doing that?

Well, He loves because of who you are, and the doing good and the doing bad doesn't affect Him. Like if I love you and you break this, I'd say, "Crystal, please don't do that." But my love will never get affected. But if I love that more than Crystal, then what?

CRYSTAL: Then it is not love.

Yes. Then you would get into trouble because I love this thing more than you. I would scold you, stand you on the bench, say I'm not going to give you money next time, and so forth. But this is not love. If I love you I can teach you: "Do it this way. It won't fall." We must love the human being because in the human being is the spirit of God.

CRYSTAL: If you love this more, it's not real love.

Yes. If it's real love, then it never gets affected; it never changes. And Jesus loved people no matter what they did. He never stopped loving because love is love, just like light is light, air is air.

For the spirit to come and teach other people, it needs a body. Jesus needed a body and the earth provided the body. But, you know, Jesus never ever was away from God in His thought. He never ever was dishonest. He was always honest and always loving. And if people did wrong, He always forgave them. It was not difficult for Him. Like flowers have perfume. It is not difficult for flowers to give perfume. The flower and the perfume are one and the same. The flower is not doing a difficult job — it just gives perfume because it is natural for it. It is natural for the moon to give moonlight. Only when we come to people is it something else.

Do you know what is natural for people? Their own interests. They want a better house, more money, more clothes. All the time they are busy.

CRYSTAL: No fun.

Crystal, I also wanted to talk to you about stimulation. I always want you to be a child and I want you to play. I also want you to listen and try to understand the things your parents and I share with you. But if you don't do it, that is all right too. As long as you understand it, I know that sometimes you will do it and sometimes you won't do it, but that is all right. Understanding it is good.

CRYSTAL: Yes, like what you said about my working?

Yes. I see that you like to work and you like to help. You

were standing there so alert helping to put the tapes in the cases. And then you came to me and said, ''I don't want to do that anymore.'' I said, ''That's all right because you like to work.'' Whenever you don't feel like it, then that's true and I must respect that. But if you were a lazy child and a selfish child and you said, ''I don't want to do it,'' then you are going to get into trouble. Because you can do it and like to do it, then you don't have to do it. And I would respect when you don't want to do it. No one is going to force you.

Then I was saying that when you get stimulated and you don't want to do something, I will never force you. But can you become aware when stimulation is getting the better of you? Then you can tell your mommy what is happening. You can cooperate with your mommy and she can cooperate with you.

Do you know how my mother brought me up? It's very nice. You know I come from India. People dress differently, they eat differently. Bedrooms are different. Everything. Glasses are different; plates are different; songs are different; trees are different; music is different. In India people love God a lot also. My father did. My mother did. And they would never tell lies.

One of the things they teach children in India is that if your teacher or your parents ask you to do something, you should never contradict. Do you know what that means, ''to contradict''?

CRYSTAL: Yes. Not do what they tell you to do.

Do you know I had never ever contradicted my teacher. Never. Even when the teacher was wrong. It gave me so much strength. That my body was not in control, my spirit was in control. When the spirit is shining in you, your body is not going to be in control. But if the body is in control, you are not going to like things of the spirit. One can't love Jesus if one doesn't love the spirit.

Most people like the body. The body likes to eat, the body likes to be lazy; it likes sensation, gets lonely, wants videos, all day long. But I want you to find a happiness inside of you that is of the spirit, and then the body won't be so demanding — wanting this and that all day long. The spirit is always happy. The body is not always happy.

I saw that no matter what my teacher said, whether wrong or right, if I didn't contradict him, then I had control and power over my body.

I was thinking, Crystal, that it is unavoidable for a child not to get stimulated. A child would be dull or ill if he didn't want to play and do some wrong things. I like children who sometimes do wrong things. It is natural for them. Why should they be afraid? You will see all the time I would be true to this. But if the parents say to you, "Come, Crystal, don't get so stimulated." And you can say, "Yes, mommy," and not contradict. Then you would have strength of the spirit too. So you can have play, you can have a good time, and you can still be of the spirit. I am going to tell your mommy and your daddy, "Don't always tell her, 'Don't do this. Don't do that.'" Because I know you will be responsible.

Acacia and John, if you try to limit her, she won't be happy. First think of Crystal, that she should be happy. And she would like that, that her parents don't always tell her what to do.

> JOHN: Could you talk about what kind of discrimination a parent has to have to see when it is appropriate to offer correction and when it is an interference?

I think love would bring that about. You would know right away. Now the parents only know 'don't.' But if you love the child, it's all right. Why should the child behave like an adult? I want Crystal to be Crystal. Crystal is seven years old; I don't want her to act like a ten year old.

CRYSTAL: But if they say do something —
like put your nightgown on — you should do it?

If your mommy says, ''Sweetie, please put on your nightgown, it is time for bed.'' You should trust your mommy because she loves you.

One begins to trust someone when you know that person loves you. You know your parents love you. You know I love you. Then there is no trouble because there is trust.

I also want you to grow up, Crystal, so that you always have something to give. Always. Do you know I have never said no to anybody in my life. And do you know there were times when I didn't have money for months and months. I used to eat one or two apples a day, or only a chocolate bar all day, but I would never go and work for anybody. Nobody knew I was hungry. So, I am not afraid anymore and I always have something to give.

Baby, when you are born whatever you need is already given, it is already there. Just like your teeth came when you needed them and your mommy and daddy didn't give you your fingernails — they were already there. Everything is always there in the world. But very few people today have trust in God.

CRYSTAL: Why do some people think that to
be someone special and talk to God that they
have to go on a fast and not eat?

That is a nice question.

In the olden days, in the Bible, they used to say that one must fast. And sometimes people fasted one day a week. Fasting sometimes is necessary because it cleans the system and it also gives the liver a time of rest. It is good for the health but there is no need to make it a big mystery. You can fast and fast and fast but that doesn't mean you are spiritual. When I was poor I wasn't thinking about God, I was hungry all the time.

CRYSTAL: Yes. Some people punish themselves and make themselves do things like that.

Why do you think Jesus loves everybody? Because He is always happy. He thinks about you first, about mommy first, not Himself first. That is love. Anybody who is going to talk about Jesus must love the other person more than himself.

CRYSTAL: Probably a pretty hard thing for some people to do.

Yes, that's true. It can be a very hard thing. But it can also be easy too, dear.

CRYSTAL: How can you make it easy?

The fewer ''wants'' you have, the easier it is.

CRYSTAL: What if you have none?

Ah, then you are in heaven. Then you are blessed.

Once upon a time, Crystal, there was a great king. He was a very good man with a large and prosperous kingdom. This king never took one single penny from his kingdom. Do you know what he did? For his work the king would copy books like the Course or the Bible — in those days, there were no printed books — and then he would sell the books he made and he would live on whatever money he received. All his kingdom had righteousness because the king had no ''wants.''

I wanted to do that one time. I wanted to do something very simple so that I would only have enough money for food, clothing, and a house — basic necessities. I used to live on $25 a week. That is very little money. I ate simple food which I like and I sat quiet and went swimming and walking. I was very happy. For three years I never spoke with anybody. Three years in silence. That is almost half your life, Crystal. My mind was always quiet. The brain is not the mind. The brain is to take care of the body. When the brain is silent, then there is the light of heaven in it. It is so happy and content. I was so full of energy and I could really see things of the spirit. Never was I so happy. My house was very clean. That was when some contact got made with Jesus. That was when I found out what I am to do.

CRYSTAL: Can someone know everything from the time he is born?

Yes, Jesus was that way. There were others too. Most of the people whose pictures we have in the Prayer Room* were born that way. They knew from the very beginning.

We have to protect you, Crystal, from stimulation. That is why I was saying that when your mommy and daddy say something, please don't contradict them. Then all your life you could be like those great beings. But if you get too stimulated, the body is going to interfere with the spirit. Just try to contain stimulation. I don't mean all the time. When you play, you get stimulated and that is normal. But not to let stimulation control you. Stimulation is necessary, but don't let it control you.

Look at this picture. This is a sculpture of Lord Buddha. He is very still. When I look at this picture, I come to stillness right away.

CRYSTAL: It is like he is giving you stillness.

Isn't that beautiful? That is what we would like you to know. But if stimulation controls you, it will be difficult as you grow up because you have lots of energy. Do you know what brings Him to stillness? He uses His energy for stillness. He gets the body out of the way and then the spirit is totally still — and it

---

*The Prayer Room at the Foundation for Life Action contains pictures of great beings: Jesus, Mr. J. Krishnamurti, Bhagavan Ramana Maharshi, Sri Ramakrishna, Lord Buddha, Lord Rama, Lord Shiva, Guru Nanak, Lao Tzu, Mother Teresa, the Scribe of *A Course In Miracles,* and others. (Editor)

always has the stillness to give. And do you know what these long ears mean?

> CRYSTAL: That he is wise.

He is wise and he listens. And Jesus said that only those who have "the ears to hear" the Word of God can listen. You would hear it inside of you if your brain becomes absolutely still.

> CRYSTAL: If my brain becomes absolutely still, would I know if it is His voice?

Yes. No mistaking it. It would be so precious and you may tell somebody and they may not believe you. You probably will see that too. You will want to give it with all your love and you will find that most everyone is busy all the time, stimulated.

So we have to start taking control of stimulation from now on. But play and be stimulated now and learn to end it.

> CRYSTAL: Just learn how to end it right then.

You will do it. You have the strength inside of you. God has given you that. You have extra strength when you also know what stillness is. And when you can contain it, then you could help other children.

> ACACIA: Could I ask something? In situations where we ask Crystal to do something and she does contradict, is there some way without causing any upset in either of us that we could bring it to a cooperation?

I am sure she would cooperate now because she has understood it. She has energy. Either she is in control of the energy and then she can come to quiet — and then she will know Jesus — or she gets stimulated. But now she knows that it is harmful. She doesn't want to be controlled by the body. She wants to know what is of God. It may take a little time but you can help her and I'm sure Crystal will cooperate.

> CRYSTAL: I think I can cooperate. I will.

*   *   *

> ACACIA: Taraji, we were shocked to see how jealous Crystal was of the other child, the younger Crystal, when she came this weekend. She was miserable and we didn't know how to deal with the jealousy. Our talking didn't seem to do any good.

Sometimes the older child does get jealous because she is not getting the attention. You have to give the older child attention. That's all. You can't just take her for granted. You know that she has a need. The more attention you give the less aware of jealousy she will be. But it is important not to make her self-conscious. What a gift not to make the child self-conscious!

How little we know of the protection a child needs. Every seven years the cells completely change. Therefore, you have to be present with the child to continually bring him to newness. The child must evolve a totally different set of cells so that by the time he is fourteen he can be responsible, aware, and able to handle puberty and all the issues that will face him then.

Crystal is born out of her parent's flesh and cells. But within seven years we must help her to undo jealousy and everything else that limits her. By the time she's fourteen she will be more herself because we've helped her to come to new cells that are non-prejudiced and responsible. Awareness has come in.

No one knows that. And so the kind of education we're giving is not education at all; it is strictly how to fit into society. Today we take it for granted that divorce, disharmony, living in apartments, and having a job are a natural way of life. The one thing we have learned is how to be irresponsible, and these are the consequences.

It's very interesting that Crystal would say, "I don't like this feeling of jealousy. Why am I suffering?" What can you say to her? Can you tell her that you become jealous also? What does that mean? She is saying, "*I'm* suffering," and we don't know what to do so we give her some cliche. It never shocks us — why don't we know what to do?

What would it take to create the right environment for the child?

*   *   *

Parents have to be very careful about not making the child too dependent. It's very nice the way your child has love for you, Acacia, and you have for her. And now also with John. But if it becomes an indulgence, then to that degree she's going to be weakened. Don't make her attached and don't you become attached. Both of you have to impart order in her life. And if by bringing order she's going to nag and whine and want to evade it, I will hold you both responsible for teaching her evasion. Order is a law. Be very loving to her, but insist upon order.

You must find out what order is. It's not discipline, but something very different. Crystal is swift but we have to introduce her to something she can't manipulate — a law. Because it is of love, it would be her strength. Otherwise cleverness would develop.

All three of you can sit down together and you can tell her, "I love you more than anything else and I don't have to always prove to you that I love you." Ask her, "Are you sure of this — that when I tell you not to do something, that my love is still there?" Ask her to repeat to you how she has understood it. Talk with her leisurely, objectively, apart from an incident. And then when that is understood, if it repeats again, say, "I will spend time with you, but not now.'' Until she gets used to the fact that she cannot manipulate you. Bring her to the point where she can stand on her own feet and not be dependent so that if you discipline her, she's not going to cry or think you don't love her. Then you are also free to do what you have to do. When she comes from school, spend a few minutes with her. Ask her what she wants to do and cooperate to help her find her own feet, her own space and freedom.

To know thyself remains the most difficult of all challenges. It requires no effort. But we are lazy and don't have the time. We can always do it tomorrow; there is constant evasion.

How are we going to teach or awaken Crystal? How did Mary teach Jesus to be content with exactly the way things are so that He would never be touched by conflict or duality? If we felt that we needed to know, then probably we could relate with Mary and she would teach us also.

*   *   *

ACACIA: Crystal has been having a difficult time with her teacher at school lately. She is repeatedly doing things which are not permitted in the class, such as talking or getting up from her seat and walking around. The teacher puts Crystal's name on the board and for each offense, puts a check beside her name. After receiving three checks, she is deprived of playing at recess or at lunchtime. We have tried everything and don't quite know what to do.

Acacia, I went with John to pick Crystal up from school today. She was upset that the same thing happened today — she got three checks again. But she has no second thoughts about it. She is not hesitant. We have to protect her from the second thought, so that she can be with ''what is'' without letting the second thought intrude and start the duality.

Are we not always putting that second thought in the other, whether child or adult? We say things to please or because we want something, and we don't even know it. It becomes second nature. We have brought this second thought, this duality, into our lives for so many reasons, and by that we live. How did Mary prevent that from happening in Jesus' life? He never had a second thought. He was never in conflict. How did she do that?

We are going to try to please Crystal, or become so self-conscious that we won't tell her anything. Or we impose a *don't* which has an *or else* behind it. *Or else* means: "If you don't do it, I'm going to punish you, put you in the closet, put your name on the blackboard, stand you this way or that way." And the child will do it because she is afraid of punishment. Can you have a relationship with a child without *or else*? *Or else* makes the child have second thoughts; it's an easy way of making the child conform. The child is vulnerable and innocent, but you are not. You have chosen to make the child change rather than to change yourself.

What is it that Mary had that we don't have? Mary was content the way things were. She had no opposites, no options, no fear. She could say, "BE IT UNTO ME ACCORDING TO THY WORD."[3] Mary was at peace with *as is*. I wonder if anyone would discover that that's the kind of mother the Son of God would need. She had no unfulfillment, never felt inadequate, had no sense of inferiority, no desire, no wanting. A simple, virtuous woman ever in harmony with herself.

A Course In Miracles states:

> *I am content to be wherever He wishes* . . . [4]

What freedom and space — no second thought. That's what Mary taught Jesus.

Do you want to know *I am content to be wherever He wishes*?

You will soon find out how much power your desires have, that you are a slave to illusions. You will have to come to an honesty like the child has.

I said to Crystal, ''You are going to school to learn one thing — to control your impulses and urges and not to be affected by anything external. When the teacher tells you to do this or that, please do it because in doing it you become a master of yourself, master of your impulses and urges.''

The teacher is teaching you one thing, but you are learning something else. Once you've learned that you will be a unique child in the world. That is why you should go to school — so that you can learn to be the master of yourself. Then no one can make you conform. If the teacher says, ''Don't do this.'' You say, ''Very well.''

I told her how I met my music teacher when I was nineteen years old and what he taught me — that he knew the reality of music and always had something to give; and although I never liked school, I discovered that I was a student; and because I was student, I didn't have to go to school. I said to Crystal, ''You don't want to go to school but you're not yet a student. So, you need to go to school. When you have become a student then the teacher will appear. You will have some connection with him and you will value his wisdom.''

I said I was nineteen when I found my music teacher and I was twenty-six when I found my next teacher, Gianiji, in a train. She said, ''In a train? Teacher in a train?'' I said yes and that he was a very famous man, a very great person. I was so shy and afraid. I wanted to talk to him but I didn't know what to say. I went to him and asked if I could speak with him. But he was busy with the newspaper. I said, ''I am already so scared and when you are reading the newspaper I can't talk to you.'' He folded up the newspaper and turned around to me and was very gentle. He asked me, ''What is your name? Where do you come from?'' We talked a little bit and then the station came and we got off the train. He hugged me. I couldn't believe it. This great man. He said he would come to visit me in my village. I ran home to tell my family and no one would believe me. But three days later he came.

He came and stayed for two or three days. And he loved me. He taught me everything. He asked me, ''What would you like to do? Would you want to be a governor? Do you want to be very rich?'' I thought about it but there was nothing I really wanted. I told Crystal that I never knew that I was capable of not wanting anything. But then I told him that I had one wish: ''I wish I had a brother.'' He was startled and said, ''But that only God could give.''

He went away but two weeks later at midnight a knock came at the door. I rushed downstairs and there was Gianiji. He said, ''I will be your brother.''

Since then I learned so much. And Crystal said, ''You are almost like him with me.'' I told her, ''I will teach you everything. But when you go to school and they put you on the bench for a whole week, you must learn how other children feel who go to school. Then if you don't dislike your teacher but you learn and change, then tomorrow, because you will know how other children feel, you could teach them like Gianiji taught me.''

I asked her, ''Why does the teacher have to put you on the bench? Do you react? As long as you react there are impurities in you which we need to deal with so that you could even be with a bad teacher and never react.''

We have undertaken to be free of ''wantings,'' to live a life in which we are not subject just to the body. This is a very different way of life — one of being a student. A student never defends himself. He need not. He wants to learn all of the limitations the brain puts on him. The brain is the brain. There is no reason for guilt or blame. It is just a discovery of something that somehow gets the better of one, not good or bad. We are just looking at how it operates, how it controls; how when one has a bias, it limits one. Bias is something that has either promotion or defense in it. But when you say, "I want to be in a space where I don't have to defend myself," then you will need a friend or a teacher.

*   *   *

(Crystal had been asked not to come to the Foundation because she was beginning to lose her reverence for the atmosphere. She was losing contact with what the Prayer Room and the altar are for. — Editor)

I felt very strongly this morning to go and see Crystal and spend some time with her. So I went to have lunch with her and then after lunch we talked.

How does one get certain things across to a child? They are just beliefs to her. How would one start to tell her not to intrude upon other people? She wants attention and therefore she goes and intrudes. Of course the child wants attention. If you took that away from the child, you would kill the child. It is like taking sunshine away from plants and flowers.

Nevertheless, the child has this wonderful time to play and the adult has the responsibility. There must be some way of communicating. Everything poses a challenge. We dip into the past and come out with a solution. Because the child is younger, and therefore more vulnerable, we can tell her what to do. So, in the end it always comes down to that — authority.

But I don't know what the answer is. Have you ever come to a place where you can say that you don't know what the answer is? Most of us have a past to give us the answers. But if you go back to memory and the past, your answers are fake. What effect will they have on the child? They will make the child conform until the child begins to behave just the way you want him to. Then there is no more child. The child will start saluting the flag and believing your fears and insecurities, and he will not know who he is.

These are the challenges and questions before us and we have found ways to superficially answer them while, in actuality, we have never really dealt with them. I can see that now, because I am faced with the same challenge.

Something had come to me this morning in a quiet moment, so I went to see Crystal and I said, "Baby, did you know one time, a long time ago, when you used to be lonely, we had prayed that you have another child to play with you? I remember sitting before the altar and praying. The very next day, Libby came to be your friend. Our prayer was answered. That is what the Prayer Room is." Because she observed that it happened in her life, she can have respect and reverence — that when we pray it is real.

And then I teased her that when the other child came, the younger Crystal, she became jealous and was acting like an adult. When I had gone to pick her up at school she said, "Is that girl still there?" So then I showed her that this happens. "When someone else gets the attention you want and are accustomed to, you don't like it." We laughed. It is amazing how much she understands. Her responses silence you.

She said she liked Libby. But I told her that with Libby there was no competition. Now that Libby has gone back to Guatemala, Crystal should be happy with whatever happens. I said, "Crystal, if you want to be my student, then you will never be affected. You will see that everything that happens is good." I said, "If everybody left, I'm happy; and if everybody is there, I'm happy." She said, "If everybody leaves I will still be there as your student." Can you imagine a child saying that? That is some conviction.

So then we started to talk about Jesus, about how He said, ''MY WORDS SHALL NOT PASS AWAY.''[5] I said to her, ''I say with that same word, 'I will always love you no matter what you do. If I get angry, I would still love you; if I spank you, I would still love you. My love would not get affected.'' She understood that if love becomes affected it is not love. But love is also honest; it is not an indulgence. I do not agree with her all the time nor does she agree with me all the time.

Now the right relationship with the altar gets established. Her need is to have a child to play with and maybe we can pray. As far as she is concerned whoever God sends is all right. It could even be little Crystal because there are things little Crystal needs to learn from her, and there are certain things Crystal can learn from her. They both have something unique and are both exceptional. I said, ''When little Crystal first came to visit I didn't give you attention because I had love for you. I never expected that you would feel that because I was affectionate with her, all my love had gone away. Never. If I *tried* to give you attention it would be false. I don't want to do that. I want you to know that my love is there whether I look at you or not. If that is strong then I don't have to be false or pleasing.''

When the parents start to be pleasing, things go wrong. The question is: is it the parents' need or is it her need? You find out by being confronted with the same issue. The adult also wants attention and therefore is pleasing. How can we expect that the child will not also be like that when it is inherent in all of us?

I had said to Crystal that in the world there is no love. She was outraged. ''Why is there no love?'' I said, ''Because everybody wants and no one is giving. Love is something you give. But we all want. That is why there are miles and miles of shops everywhere.''

When I arrived at Crystal's home, she told me she had written two letters for me. Being told that she couldn't come to the Foundation really hit her.

ACACIA: Yesterday, when we went home, it took a little while for the impact of what had happened to dawn on her. We started cleaning and organizing and she went into our Prayer Room to write a letter to you about what had happened and why we were sent home. She cried and didn't quite know how to assimilate what had happened, but she went on her own and wrote this letter:

"Dear Taraji,

"I know the things that I have to change — they are not to leave things around the Foundation, not to use the Foundation as a playground and not to waste. I feel happy to work in the kitchen. I like to give to people. Why I did those things is because I did not listen to my parents. I think I should change because I would be happier of myself.

"A temple is a place where you sit quiet and think about Jesus and pray for everybody. Taraji teaches me to be with Jesus.

Crystal"

ACACIA: The other letter, the letter regarding the ending of this four year phase of the School,* Crystal has been working on for the past several days.

---

*On Easter, 1983, Tara Singh began the One Year Non-Commercialized Retreat: A Serious Study of *A Course In Miracles* under the sponsorship of the Foundation for Life Action. Following the One Year Retreat, twenty students remained with the Foundation to study the Course with him on a one-to-one, full time basis. This study continued for an additional three years. On Easter, 1987, the four year phase of study came to an end. (Editor)

"Dear Taraji,

"I feel grateful for you because you can teach me things. I want to learn from you. I like it when you told me how to hold the glass. I like it when you told me not to be afraid of the dark. I learned that. I like to learn from you. You are the best teacher I have met. I want to give my life to Jesus. There would not be anything more important.

"I would not feel good about not to have a school for children at the Foundation. I am looking forward to having a school because I would like you to teach them to always be happy and grateful. And to teach me how to always be happy and grateful. I would not feel good about the people going to other places because I would not have as many people to play with and I would not have Taraji as a teacher. That is very important to me and it would seem strange to me without it.

"You told me that sitting quiet is important to me. I know that it is important to me but I might not show it. It is not easy to do these things. I am going to do these things anyway.

From Crystal"

It melts one's heart. We are all blessed that she is here. We need her too. What a joy to work with a child, to have a child for a friend.

> ACACIA: I was sharing with Taraji about a difficulty we have with Crystal. When we ask her to do things, sometimes she balks and we lose patience. It reaches an intolerable peak. Taraji explained love to me in a way that I had never seen before — that the parent doesn't need

to be a dictator to get things done. Crystal is a child and it is good to let her be a child. As a parent, aware of the responsibility, I tend to get too serious. But Taraji showed me that if there is love and friendship in the family, she will have respect and love as well and the spirit of coop-eration will come naturally.

She must have the space and the freedom, but once the parent says something, she should heed. But don't make her so obedient. She must have the space. Everything is a challenge. If you predetermine your or her behavior, you are going to destroy something. You can't lay down laws. Relationship is alive; laws are dead. I don't want her to be obedient and I don't want her to be deprived of her own nature — she must play and do things. The thing we need is trust and friendship so that she knows her parents love her, and the parents know she understands. Then we can give space to each other. And it can be done happily.

If she is in the middle of some little paper project and you come along and say, "Let's go, Crystal," she may feel she has to finish what she has started. Include her suggestions. Or if you cannot wait, tell her the circumstances and make arrangements to finish it later. There should always be a reasonable exchange so that it never becomes authority. Even if certain things are not understood, it could be talked about at a later time when there is more space. But make sure that the child's space is not taken over, that she is not intruded upon and walked over. Practical things can still be dealt with. We want it all cut and dried but it is not cut and dried — it is alive.

Crystal, do you see that where there is freedom there has to be responsibility? You cannot only think about yourself; you must think about the other person too. Then you will be like Jesus and always have it to give. Instead of wanting, we are going to have time to give, love to give, affection to give. And all the time you would be receiving — from your mommy and your daddy and from all of us.

JOHN: It is a great responsibility not to fall back on how we have been raised and taught how parents are to be — the expedient way, the tendency. It is not easy. We always want a solution.

That is so true, John.

Let's hold hands and pray that a child be sent for Crystal to play with.

"Lord Jesus, I feel very safe and deeply happy inside when I turn to You and ask. I never feel so happy when I ask anybody else, but when I ask You, Lord, I learn to overcome all doubts. I have complete trust. It makes me feel so good to be so whole. When I ask You I know that You are going to do the right thing, the best that is for me, because I know that You love me. Even if I don't get what I ask for it doesn't make any difference to me. I know that what You do is best. Right now, Jesus, I wish I had someone to play with, someone I can learn from, someone I can teach, someone that You want me to have as a friend. And I thank You for giving me that gift. Amen."

Doesn't it feel good to ask Him, Crystal? Then, if He doesn't send a child, you would have to find the resources to play by yourself. And if He sends a child, then that would be good also. But you are never going to want something different than what He does. You will never find your own strength if you always need a child to play with. In that way, He is teaching you. I can show you squirrels playing alone.

*   *   *

Acacia, since Crystal has so many adults around her at the Foundation — which is abnormal from the point of view that very few children have that — she doesn't value you as much. Have you noticed that? Because she has everyone here, it has become an abnormal situation. There is no longer just mommy and daddy.

Then, when we tell her to have reverence, she can manage without. It shows us that one cannot interfere in nature. Her relationship with you, Acacia, is not the one she used to have. Now she doesn't listen. One never knew that this would happen. But it is amazing what awareness can discover. It can realize things that the thinking process never can.

There is a bonding period between parent and child. That bonding period has been cut short in this case because now Crystal has so many adults. I was thinking that after school Crystal can help in the kitchen and then she can do her homework and laugh and play and meet everyone here. But she should not stay for too long. She should make the contact but go home early so that the home becomes her base. Otherwise, if she grows up this way, she is not going to listen to you or to John. How are we going to get her to a point where she has reverence for your words when she can afford not to listen to them? There are too many distractions. This is what has happened to children. They don't have reverence because they can tell the parents to go to hell.

It seems that she needs more bonding with both of you. This is somewhat of an artificial environment. She becomes attached to the attention and then becomes jealous when the other Crystal comes. We must learn from the fact that the jealousy showed up. To the degree she is jealous, to that degree she is dependent on this and less related with the parents. Are you seeing this Crystal?

CRYSTAL: Yes.

Like if your daddy told you something, you would agree, but if you don't feel like doing it, you just wouldn't do it. I don't believe in wrongs and rights. But I do believe that you won't find the strength inside of you if you always learn to escape.

But if there is only daddy, then you can't escape. You will have to find the strength. For me there is no right or wrong, no good or bad. I want you to be happy and content, but you will only be happy and content if you find more strength inside of you. Otherwise, you could say that you would be my student no matter if everybody left, but it would only be an idea. The strength would not be there. The strength, Crystal, comes when you can say no to everything else because you have found something inside of you. Do you see this?

CRYSTAL: Yes.

Crystal, the only thing that you have to master is stimulation, not to get too stimulated. And we have to provide the proper atmosphere for you. If you become stimulated, there is no Crystal anymore; stimulation is in control of you. You won't listen to your daddy or your mommy. And one day you won't even listen to me. So, if I know that one day you will not listen to me, then I have to help you now to overcome stimulation.

I don't care if you go to school or you don't go to school. But if you go to school and you are still overcome by stimulation, then you will end up being a fool. If you don't go to school and you are stimulated, you will also be nothing. So the main problem is stimulation. And you can only overcome it with the God-given strength inside of you.

We have so much work to do, Crystal. Your daddy works very hard here but I told him, "Your family should be together. You should go home early and you should all go for walks together because Crystal is important." Do you remember when I suggested that you massage your mommy's feet and your mommy massage your feet? That was to help free you from stimulation. Stimulation blinds you to the beauty, the purity, and the goodness that is there in you. Do you know, even when you were jealous of the little Crystal, you were still helping her. I saw how beautiful you are. Sometimes jealousy got the better of you; sometimes goodness got the better of you.

What do you think would help you not to become so stimulated?

> CRYSTAL: I think that if I only did one thing and I never could do anything else until that thing was done, I might not be stimulated after that.

That is so nice. You are wise, Crystal. I cannot think of anything better. I call that seeing a thing through to the end. When you stay with something and see it to the end, then you are no longer stimulated. See what wisdom you have when you are not stimulated? When you are stimulated it is like spilled ketchup.

*   *   *

> ACACIA: I have had a question in my mind for the past few days — it is not succinct but if I could bother you with the extra words.

Bother is the extra word. How can there be bother when there is love?

> ACACIA: I have watched you and felt the difference when we have come to you with anything with Crystal. Your first approach is to talk with her with love. It is overwhelming — to see the effect that that has. I feel the tremendous responsibility in raising Crystal and yet I find, Taraji, that I have to repeat everything with her. I know that a child is a child — that she will continue to run and continue to be stimulated — but what I am wrestling with is the frustration inside of me. I get angry with myself.I think that is part of my headaches. I don't want to hit her and I don't want to hit me. I want some way to help her change. But I am not helping her. There

is something I am doing that is aggravating the situation. When John and I talked with her last night we saw that my words do not mean anything to her.

Neither do John's. That is what is happening now and it will happen more as she grows up. She won't listen to anybody. I saw that yesterday and I was horrified. I used to say that some time ago, that pretty soon she will outgrow the parents and not listen. But you had not really heard it then.

Your question is two-fold. One is that you cannot affect her — neither you or John or anybody else — unless first you change. We want to change *her.* That is conformity, authority, exploitation — which she is not going to stand for. And the world has found conformity and authority as the means for settling everything from international situations to local affairs. That is all we know: the law of might, the law of the jungle.

So, unless the parent changes, the parent has no right to expect the child to change. And if they use authority and fear — ''do this or else'' — then they are promoting consequences. *You* have to change.

Two, you have chosen getting angry with yourself. That is a way of evasion. Does it make you feel very pious when you don't like yourself? Why should you be angry with yourself? It intensifies sorrow doesn't it? That is a good thing to know. So don't get angry with yourself. See the fact as it is.

ACACIA: I want my words to mean something so that I don't keep having this effect on her.

I know that it is very good for your words to be real. But I also see that children learn from very early on how to manipulate. They can be cruel. One of the cruelest beasts on the earth can be a child. Don't ''holify'' them; they can be monsters.

They are of our seed. We glorify the child's innocence, but that is only for a very short time.

Do you know how much that little girl wastes? If she were living with me I would find ways for her not to waste paper. I would give her one pencil and say, "This is going to last you for six months." Some of the finest calligraphers in the world are Arabic and they use only one pen.

How are you going to teach her what simplicity is? She has got so many things all around the house. And then you say you don't want them around, but why do you make them available to her?

So, if you don't come to simplicity in yourself you cannot do anything about the child. If you value change, then the child will value change.

Life has made children impressionable. They imitate. If there is love between the parents, that communicates. If you have reverence for something, that communicates. If you have reverence for your husband, speak tenderly to him and he speaks tenderly to you, then the child will not be insulting nor will she speak casually to either of you. Let her try that with me, I can't say what I would do — it would be unpredictable because it would be an expression of the moment. You might call it anger; I would call it correction.

The longer our words don't mean anything to her, the worse it is going to get. See the difference. If I tell her something, she is going to listen to me differently than to you or John. I don't let her bring this relationship to a common level. It is becoming harder for parents today to bring their relationship with their children to that kind of dignity and reverence. In India, we were taught reverence for the parents, for the elders.

There is a story about a child who used to eat lots of sweets. In India, the only sweet we have is brown sugar. We grow our own sugar cane. Sometimes they put almonds into it; it is natural and delicious. So one day, the child runs in and takes a hand full of sweets out of the terra cotta pot in which they are kept. But the adult scolds him and says, "Don't eat so many candies. They are not good for you." The child could not believe that something so good could be bad for you, so then he went to ask his grandfather. "Grandfather, is eating gur (candy) good for me?" The grandfather said, "You must come back and ask me tomorrow." The next day, no sooner had the child woken up, than he ran to the grandfather. "Grandfather, is it good to eat gur?" The grandfather said, "No." The child said, "But why didn't you tell me yesterday?" He said, "Because yesterday, I had eaten it and my words would not have been true."

You don't have to get angry; you have to come to this integrity. As long as your words are partial, don't expect her to obey you. The child has come to correct both of you. She has brought the two of you together and now you must make the correction in yourselves.

Once you have made the correction, you can teach her. If you are not corrected, you've violated yourself and you've violated her. Children must have reverence for their parents so they heed their words the first time.

You don't have to argue with the child or let the child argue with you. The word is the power. We don't know that power so we want to force the child; we think in terms of punishment. But punishment has not worked. So now you parents are really on the spot. But you can give thanks to the Lord that it is brought to your attention that you must change.

CHAPTER NINE

9

THE CHILD
AND THE SOURCE OF CREATION—
THE NEED FOR REVERENCE

Both the parent and the child are part of creation. If we were aware of this we would be interested in knowing the Source of creation. To know the Source we must have the space to observe all that is part of creation — the plants, the light through which we see, the water we drink. It would introduce us to an awareness of something far greater than anything we have ever known. And with it one would expand beyond all duality, as if awakened by the Reality of the Source Itself. The little activity we experience seems insignificant compared to the vast innocence of the Nameless.

The looking that separates ceases, and we witness the blessing on all manifestation. One comes to a tremendous reverence for the unmanifest reality behind objects. Creation begins to unfold in our awareness as we observe that the plant is related to everything in existence. Nothing could grow on this planet without sunlight. A rock is dormant and hard and vibrates at a different pace, but it is still part of creation. It is in movement, but not as much as water is. Air has more vitality than water and is more subtle. The subtler something becomes, the more essential it is in creation. The Source is not something tangible; it is beyond the physical and therefore beyond the senses.

As you become aware of subtler levels, you begin to see that the five senses can only go so far. But a still mind can move past the physical world. The Source is a state. When man comes to that state he is free of his physicality. This is the only freedom.

According to *A Course In Miracles,*

All things are echoes of the Voice for God. [1]

True reverence is a state in which isolation in time ends. It is a movement towards unity. The Lord's Prayer says:

"THY WILL BE DONE IN EARTH,
AS IT IS IN HEAVEN." [2]

We are given the senses because we live in a physical world and have a body which the earth sustains and nourishes. The water, air, and fire keep it alive. Spirit comes to the world of senses and brings the Light of Heaven to the physical world. Only man is capable of doing this. Of itself, the manifest world remains physical even though it is sustained by Eternal Laws, timeless and changeless.

It is the responsibility of every parent to bring the child to this awareness. Without this awakening the child becomes absorbed in the physical phenomena of change — the activity of his own senses — and he becomes limited to them.

One cannot overemphasize the need for reverence. But reverence cannot be cultivated mentally. You will know it only when you directly perceive the glory of creation in its total relationship. Reverence reaches out towards the One that is. But society as a whole is moving farther away from reverence and relationship. In times past no one on this planet knew the disease of nationalism. There were no passports or even boundaries. But the fragmentation increases daily. Parents must value and realize the harmony of unity and have reverence for the miraculous Source of creation in order to prevent the child from becoming an extension of fragmentation.

Daily we need to make contact with God, the Source of our being, to renew ourselves. Order in life is essential. Meditation is a necessity, for in moments of stillness we discover that after each breath there is a pause. Between the thoughts, too, there is a gap. Time and timelessness coexist in life and nature. It is important for the parent to make contact with this timeless pause, for the very awareness of silence extends itself and affects our lives. These gaps between the thoughts are shortened by stimulation and are often crowded out of existence. We need relaxation to widen them; nature demands it. If we violate this law we become self-destructive.

Whatever we are we extend to our children. What kind of life do you want your child to lead? Obviously, if you relinquish responsibility and allow him to be shaped by society, his insecurity would compel him to join the ranks of employees promoting the status quo. Your love is needed to protect the child and relate him to the *new*, to Eternal Laws.

Before we do anything with the child, however, we have to drop our own opinions and come to newness, untouched by reaction. Come to the peace of God, and the imperceptible action of Grace will enter your life. Then you will invite the participation of the Creator in your relationship with the child.

The real purpose of seeing the false as the false is to make correction internally. Transformation is at the cause level, not at the level of effect. If that awareness, and its inherent correction, does not take place, one becomes subject to the *effect* as a source and is isolated from the true Source. When I am separated from God, I am automatically separated from you. And from then on there is only the extension of separation. Life becomes more fragmented and lonely, and the inevitable by-products of loneliness — fear, suspicion, poor quality of sleep — affect every life. Because you cannot cope you are drawn to television, liquor, drugs, food. The forms may differ but the cause is always separation.

If you and I know we are of the same Source, there is respect and reverence for one another. Without love, there is no peace; where there is reverence, there is no attachment. Now we can understand the deeper meaning of: "AND IF ANY MAN. . . TAKE AWAY THY COAT, LET HIM HAVE THY CLOAK ALSO."[3] The man who can give the cloak must be at peace. Because he has a relationship with the Source, he knows that we are all part of God. The minute you realize that, everyone becomes the same and there is no judgment regardless of what another person does.

As the Course makes clear:

Christ's vision has one law. It does not look upon a body,
and mistake it for the Son whom God created.[4]

Only a person who is in a body, cut off from the Source, would react to what another body does and judge him accordingly. If it is favorable to him, that person is good; if not, he is bad. To the degree we are preoccupied with personality we try to adjust ourselves and be comfortable in separation. When isolated we are always suspicious of the other. Such an existence becomes a seemingly losing battle against our fear and projections. But the truth is, psychological insecurity is manmade; we keep it alive by giving it energy. We have become so obsessed with problems that violence has become the only solution.

It is only when one realizes:

I am not a body. I am free.
For I am still as God created me.[5]

that one can awaken to a state where the world of body attachments vanishes. Such a person has no problems, either of the body or of the world. Thus, he affects the world with his very being.

Give your child reverence and you have given him the power to dissolve problems. But without reverence in your own life you have little of lasting value to give him. The system will harness him to serve it. At the root of this superficial existence is lack of reverence for Life.

The parent has the task of safeguarding his offspring from the strain and struggle of the manmade world. Through reverence we help the child get past the body and the sense of separation. It is true that the body is the means of communication, but what are we communicating through it? Is it love or fear? What would you have your child extend?

Without holiness and reverence there is no relationship. Society has degenerated to the point where there are very few people who can even relate with one another. They can relate with their own needs, their own "wantings," but in essence there is no relationship. Thus children grow up with an attitude of, "I do as I please." They think that it is freedom to live by sensation and gratification. The lure of sex and violence are instilled from an early age. They are the staple of the media — news, advertisements, and films.

Seldom do we find value for what is of the spirit, even though in reality each person is an extension of heaven. We need to see the other person as God created him, not as the manmade world has conditioned him. We need to look upon him with compassion, without judgment. Recognize that all you think of as good, bad, right, or wrong, is of duality and therefore part of unreality, for what God created is the only Law. It is eternal.

How compassionate the law is! Just the love that sustains

creation leaves one speechless. Inspiration widens the gaps between the thoughts and silences our words. How futile is life without this direct experience of our own holiness. As *A Course In Miracles* tells us:

> *Your holiness reverses all the laws of the world. It is beyond every restriction of time, space, distance and limits of any kind. Your holiness is totally unlimited in its power because it establishes you as a Son of God, at one with the Mind of his Creator.*
>
> *Through your holiness the power of God is made manifest. Through your holiness the power of God is made available. And there is nothing the power of God cannot do. Your holiness, then, can remove all pain, can end all sorrow, and can solve all problems.[6]*

We are well provided for — the rivers flow, the birds sing, and flowers grow. All our needs are met by creation. We can therefore have trust in its perfection. Fear is not necessary. The man or woman who has no needs has something of heaven to give to the world. Your love becomes part of existence and you become a co-creator with God because you are bringing Reality to awareness.

Without gratefulness, life is limited.
Gratefulness outgrows needs, ambitions, unfulfillment.
Gratefulness is the holy instant shared with your Creator.
It is direct contact with God.

*   *   *

MEETING THE CHALLENGE
OF THE GROWING CHILD

When I woke up this morning, I was wondering: ''How am I going to explain to Crystal something that is not tangible? How am I going to explain to her that which is of the spirit? She is going to say, 'I don't like to sit quiet.' Children are honest. I know if I use authority to impose it upon her she will hate it. We are very good at that. How am I going to really explain it to her so that she discovers it?'' That would be intrinsic — her discovery.

If she sits quiet and makes contact with the spirit, that will be her strength. That will make her different. But she would say, ''I don't like it.'' So it is a challenge. But it is not a challenge if I go and bully her, persuade her and so on. That is the only way we know — educate them with our prejudice, not awaken something within them that sees. Very few people teach that way, sharing that which is of that instant, that moment. I will not give her anything I know. Imposing our ''knowings'' is all the world has ever done to children. Therefore they become subject to the limitation of the known. Intrinsic is something independent of time and knowing. It is part of wholeness.

Only sitting quiet would transform her life. All our teaching will not do a thing. Just as today she would say, ''I don't want to sit quiet,'' tomorrow when she is drawn to a boyfriend, she would say, ''I love him.'' She will think about him all the time and they will play together. What a joy that is, when you have met someone with whom the relationship is right! It energizes one. But at some level the need is so great in a personal way that one gets deceived. Therefore we want to impart to her that stimulation is external. ''The real would come if you can contain this, and you would know with whom it is a life relationship.'' Then her whole life would be different. That's honest. It's independent, your own direct knowing. That is what she needs to know.

Can you imagine how many centuries man has lived and he hasn't learned to cope with those body urges? The child needs to learn certain things in order to contain them. That would be right education. There are some things you can do only within certain periods of growth. And that is where we feel pressured because we can't keep pace with it. Pressure is something you bring into being but in life there is no pressure.

*   *   *

We need to share with children about growing things, about animals. There is a part of us that melts when we see anything that is innocent. Animals give affection back. What would a little colt do to her? It would awaken so many other things. All these dead toys — they don't give back anything. Children do not even develop responsibility, only attachment.

It is interesting that when my children were young I had gotten them rabbits. They were always concerned. "I think he'd like this kind of grass. I think he'd like this one." And then they'd go out in the field and bring flowers and grass. There was a relationship and they would never want to kill it.

Children are interested in natural things. We are just too busy. It is *our* interest that has died down; they are interested in everything. Being interested brings them more to the present. Homework does not. When children live in the country they want to jump, climb the tree. You can't stop them. When they grow up in the city there is very little natural adventure. Children don't learn to climb trees, jump ditches, or throw stones. They are given dead toys to play with and violence and friction ensue. Games become very competitive. They are no longer just for fun. Look at what has happened with the adults — nobody participates. We have all become spectators.

See how detrimental things have become. Even the food is contaminated with hormones. Look at the bodies of the people, how bloated they are, so victimized and heavy, even young girls and boys. Everything the world is doing now is destructive. Even your own child is no longer safe in the world of insanity. The ethical age of character, strength, and rightness is gone.

It is an artificial society in which almost everything is geared to buying and selling — clothes, food, gadgets. Everything has become mental and further stimulates. We have no contact with the earth, with the seasons, with birds or worms. It is inevitable that a child is going to be affected and get hurt by growing up in this artificiality.

In other cultures, where the family is still intact, even if people are poor they are rich in goodness and consideration for one another. If there are five children in the family and one has special talents, the whole family supports that gifted child. Thus, no one is poor. When he or she becomes successful, the child never wants to separate from the family, but brings whatever he has received financially and shares it with everyone. He is not given any special privileges nor does he look down on the family because he is more cultured. Instead, he reveres them because they made it possible.

Out of the harmony of even the poorest family, things are made possible and genius does not suffer. It is a different way of giving which we do not know in this culture. It is still possible amidst the affluence of the West for genius to go unrecognized and unsupported.

In classical India, when the family saw aptitude in the child for anything of pure Indian culture, they sought out the best teacher. The teacher never charged a fixed fee to be paid. The student would take as an offering the thing he most dearly loved in reverence for the teacher. He would feel he owed his teacher his very life because the teacher awakened him. "You pay this much" did not even occur to the teacher. He could see the sincerity of the student. How interested the student was in coming to self-honesty determined his future. And his gain was a gain for all humanity.

I was wondering what one would do with the sensitive, gifted children that are being born now? They are so far ahead and so direct they are not going to listen to silly parents. What do you do?

The children of today have enormous energy and the young girls will get interested in boys whether you like it or not. But they certainly won't stay with anyone. Just like they will see through the parents, they will see through the boyfriends. The child will discover that this thing called "love" is not really love. She will see through one person, and then another, and then another. She will become hard, disillusioned — very bright, but cynical. She may even become talented at something, but because value for what is of quality doesn't exist in society, nor in the parents, nor in the school, she would have no opportunity of making real contact. And that is the only thing that one can provide. But if you do not have it you cannot impart it to the child.

What would I do with a child? I would impart my stillness to the child and help him to unwind everyday. This is not like a mother fixated on the child; this is having something to give. Only a person who has something to give could prevent certain things from happening. This means that the child would always have a friend.

In the olden days there was an aunt or a grandmother or an uncle, or somebody else in the family, who could be totally with the child, who had something to give. And the children went to such a being who offered a place of solace. One begins to see that what the child needs, these times cannot afford; it cannot afford the wisdom or the quiet, something that could normalize the child everyday.

Sensitive, bright children, have a tendency to get depressed. I saw when the others were playing and Crystal was ignored, she started to crumble. Her whole structure got smaller. So I asked her to come and sit with me.

You can start introducing the child to rightness. Slowly. She could become interested in rightness and see that it doesn't have dependence in it but is something inside. That's what a relationship with Jesus could impart. Do it slowly; don't make it a mission.

Because you have a child, *you* are waking up. Something new has come into your life. You have become interested in having words that are true. By giving honesty to your words you can bring honesty to her. In this way you are changing and growing along with her.The child has brought you to God and to rightness. It is a very different action. That is relationship.

If you impose upon your child, ''Why don't you do what I want you to do?'' you are passing your limitations on to her. Then the child becomes a duplicate. Most parents have made their child a duplicate of themselves. Especially single parents. It is very difficult when a parent raises the child alone. But now, when you try to share with Crystal about rightness, you are not sharing your prejudices; you are attempting to share some insight, something that inspires, something that is new, of the moment. These are the responsibilities of being a parent.

*   *   *

A TALK WITH CRYSTAL

Crystal, to be with Jesus requires overcoming certain things one likes and dislikes. Everyone has time for everything but sitting quiet. There will be something in you that will have a resistance to sitting quiet. It would seem too long and that would be somewhat natural. It is not a bad thing to feel that way. But nevertheless, one would have to cope with that resistance.

CRYSTAL: What is cope?

Cope means to deal with it. You have to deal with it. Because you and I and everyone are a body and a spirit. The spirit does not have a body, the spirit does not live by time. It is of Jesus. It is of God. But the body has resistance to doing certain things like sitting quiet. But if the spirit is strong then it can deal with the resistances of the body. If the body gets

206 / HOW TO RAISE A CHILD OF GOD

stronger, then pretty soon Jesus would be pushed out of your life.

CRYSTAL: I know.

So you should know inside that you can cope with the resistances of the body. When it wants to be sleepy, when it wants not to sit quiet, don't listen to it. And when you don't listen to it, then Jesus' strength is with you to cope with the resistance.

CRYSTAL: Yes.

So then you have become like a friend to Jesus and He would help you to overcome the resistance. You see, we did not start when we were children like you. We started much later and our bodies are full of resistances. So we find all kinds of things to do. We keep ourselves busy like insects and we don't have time to sit quiet. You are so blessed that you want to sit quiet even when you are this age. That is so nice. If you keep that quality, you would be a strength to other children. The love of silence will be a strength for your life. Can you understand that?

CRYSTAL: Yes.

Do you think you would keep it up?

CRYSTAL: Yes.

I can see that you won't feel helpless. You will like sitting quiet more and more if the resistance doesn't get the better of you. You make a decision, "I'm not going to have resistance." You can tell your body and your thoughts: "Be still. I want to be quiet." This determination is necessary. Sometimes, I feel a lot of resistance too, Crystal, but I don't listen to it. And then in no time a strength comes and resistance goes away and then I love the silence.

CHAPTER TEN

10

MARY AND HER CHILD JESUS
THE DIVINE HAND AT WORK

To observe the life of Mary, the mother of Jesus, is to see the Divine Hand at work. Mary refused to be helpless and irresponsible. She grew up in the holy atmosphere of the Essenes* with a mind untouched by fear, insecurity, or doubt. She was not educated in the ways of the world but introduced to her own sacredness. Thus, when the Archangel Gabriel appeared to her, she had a voice of her own which did not heed the second thoughts of duality.

"HAIL, THOU THAT ART HIGHLY FAVOURED, THE LORD IS WITH THEE: BLESSED ART THOU AMONG WOMEN. . . . AND, BEHOLD, THOU SHALT CONCEIVE IN THY WOMB, AND BRING FORTH A SON, AND SHALT CALL HIS NAME JESUS. HE SHALL BE GREAT, AND SHALL BE CALLED THE SON OF THE HIGHEST: AND THE LORD GOD SHALL GIVE UNTO HIM THE THRONE OF HIS FATHER DAVID: AND HE SHALL REIGN OVER THE HOUSE OF JACOB FOR EVER; AND OF HIS KINGDOM THERE SHALL BE NO END."[1]

---

*The Essenes were a religious sect of ascetics and mystics that existed from approximately the second century B.C. to the second century A.D.

Mary had no hesitation. She was innocent of the world of consequences. When she responded, her voice was as direct and conflict-free as the Archangel's:

"BEHOLD THE HANDMAID OF THE LORD; BE IT UNTO ME ACCORDING TO THY WORD."[2]

Here is the divine purpose of the parent. Here is the holiness of self-giving. Here stands the love of virtue that protects one from the illusions of the future. Helplessness never touched Mary, nor her Child. Helplessness comes only with personal goals. Creation is not helpless and neither are we, for we are part of its love and perfection.

What is the root of the insecurity that weakens us? Simply seen, it is the lack of consistency in our lives. We all have goals and ideals, and we believe that the means of attaining them are difficult. Is this not an assumption? The means and the end are inseparable. In awareness they are one and the same. The separation is manmade. Mary was consistent with the Will of God; she did not divert into choices. Therefore, she never deviated from the already perfect "end," to the so-called "means." For her there were no "means" to it. It was not in the future. Her perspective was divine, free of the concepts of time and the projections of personality.

Consistency with the Will of God, then, knows no deviation into the limitations of personality. We find the means difficult because the end is illusory and self-projected. Mary was ever in harmony, knowing the perfection of the present.

What each mother must realize is that with the birth of the child the means are provided; there is no reason to assume projections of lack. Perfection is never absent. The issue is our inconsistency with the Will of God. From the very outset we deviate into self-centeredness and in our isolation we burden ourselves with effort and ambition. This is what we teach our children.

To truly appreciate Mary, to know her stature and incomparable dignity, one can turn to Archangel Gabriel's visit to the high priest, Zacharias, and learn the difference in the quality of response. The Archangel came to bestow the boon for which Zacharias had so ardently prayed.

> "FEAR NOT, ZACHARIAS: FOR THY PRAYER IS HEARD; AND THY WIFE ELISABETH SHALL BEAR THEE A SON, AND THOU SHALT CALL HIS NAME JOHN. AND THOU SHALT HAVE JOY AND GLADNESS; AND MANY SHALL REJOICE AT HIS BIRTH."[3]

But the first response of Zacharias' mind, like that of all mortal minds lacking faith, was fear and doubt. He proceeded to "educate" the Archangel:

> "WHEREBY SHALL I KNOW THIS? FOR I AM AN OLD MAN, AND MY WIFE WELL STRICKEN IN YEARS."[4]

His defiance and obstinacy aroused the Archangel:

> "I AM GABRIEL, THAT STAND IN THE PRESENCE OF GOD; AND AM SENT TO SPEAK UNTO THEE, AND TO SHEW THEE THESE GLAD TIDINGS. AND, BEHOLD, THOU SHALT BE DUMB, AND NOT ABLE TO SPEAK, UNTIL THE DAY THAT THESE THINGS SHALL BE PERFORMED, BECAUSE THOU BELIEVEST NOT MY WORDS, WHICH SHALL BE FULFILLED IN THEIR SEASON."[5]

Compare this with the purity of Mary's spirit and her unquestionable faith in the Will of God. She knew only love that has no interpretations. Mary must have imparted her own peace and confidence — the purity of her innocence — and awakened heaven in the physical body of her Child. He, in turn, taught us, *Each of us is the light of the world . . .* [6]

We should look to what Jesus says about the reality of a

child, whose destiny it is to bring God's Kingdom to earth. In so doing, we may learn directly the joy of raising a child of God.

Parents have to discover for themselves the Law of Rightness. Rightness is forever free of consequences. It is only when the parents themselves realize that they are children of God that they can be free from the fearsome burden of unreality.

> "AT THE SAME TIME CAME THE DISCIPLES UNTO JESUS, SAYING, WHO IS THE GREATEST IN THE KINGDOM OF HEAVEN? AND JESUS CALLED A LITTLE CHILD UNTO HIM, AND SET HIM IN THE MIDST OF THEM, AND SAID, VERILY I SAY UNTO YOU, EXCEPT YE BE CONVERTED, AND BECOME AS LITTLE CHILDREN, YE SHALL NOT ENTER INTO THE KINGDOM OF HEAVEN. WHOSOEVER THEREFORE SHALL HUMBLE HIMSELF AS THIS LITTLE CHILD, THE SAME IS THE GREATEST IN THE KINGDOM OF HEAVEN. AND WHOSO SHALL RECEIVE ONE SUCH LITTLE CHILD IN MY NAME RECEIVETH ME. BUT WHOSO SHALL OFFEND ONE OF THESE LITTLE ONES WHICH BELIEVE IN ME, IT WERE BETTER FOR HIM THAT A MILLSTONE WERE HANGED ABOUT HIS NECK, AND THAT HE WERE DROWNED IN THE DEPTH OF THE SEA."[7]

As you read the words of Christ, give them space. Come to peace, so that the Given is made accessible to you. With the coming of the child, a new awareness is given to parents who are ready to receive.

The serenity of the Sermon on the Mount awakens you to the highest levels of your being. Relaxed and cleansed of haste, you begin to expand in awareness. This new perspective gives us a glimpse of what we would be without the body, not subject to the physical senses.

When one has the "ears to hear,"[8] the Beatitudes lift one

above physicality into another state. Through the Beatitudes parents can introduce the child to his God-consciousness.

"BLESSED ARE THE POOR IN SPIRIT:
FOR THEIRS IS THE KINGDOM OF HEAVEN."[9]

Here Jesus is speaking not of the physical poverty we dread, but of a law that sets one free from insecurity. This poverty is not an imposed denial but a voluntary release from attachments. The action of peace within the self-sufficiency of life lets old attitudes fall away effortlessly, until there is no need to possess things or people. The waste of sacred energy is the issue of our day.

"BLESSED ARE THE PURE IN HEART:
FOR THEY SHALL SEE GOD."[10]

Do you want your child to see God, above all else?

An Eternal Being comes to this planet, makes peace with its laws, and affects time with His Eternity. In the Sermon on the Mount Jesus relates us to eternal life, to our own purity, and to an independent action that ends the cycle of misperception. Thus we discover courage and conviction as if we are reborn and the light of reality dawns upon the planet. This is what children need to know about themselves — their Reality. It brings the so-called learning to an end.

Rightness and reverence are qualities the parents have to live in order to give the world a strong and independent child. Their goodness cannot only neutralize hostility, but can often change the very outcome of a situation. Listen to the eternal words of Jesus:

"BUT I SAY UNTO YOU, LOVE YOUR ENEMIES, BLESS THEM THAT CURSE YOU, DO GOOD TO THEM THAT HATE YOU, AND PRAY FOR THEM WHICH DESPITE-FULLY USE YOU, AND PERSECUTE YOU; THAT YE MAY BE THE CHILDREN OF YOUR FATHER WHICH IS

IN HEAVEN: FOR HE MAKETH HIS SUN TO RISE ON
THE EVIL AND ON THE GOOD, AND SENDETH RAIN
ON THE JUST AND ON THE UNJUST.''[11]

In unity there is not the other. One Life knows only the
creation of Love. What the child needs to know is that there is
safety. The parents' fulfillment provides him with it. When the
parents act with rightness, reverence is inspired in the child.
Reverence brings peace and harmony into relationship. The
child begins to see that life is not limited to physical sensation.

As Jesus prepared His disciples for their ministry, so we
must lead the child to his rightful function for the fulfillment of
his purpose on earth. ''NOT MY WILL, BUT THINE, BE DONE''[12]
is of first importance for clear direction and right relationship
with the Father.

We live in a world of relativity, of loss and gain. The competitive world may make the child feel small and inadequate;
it is the parent's job to help him transcend such comparisons.
Do not treat him as if he were an unfinished adult. He is ever
perfect in his growth. What is of God is ever complete.

Teach your child that all things in life are of equal value. A
tiny flower is as great in its perfection as a snow-capped
mountain peak. The physical eye sees only separation; but
wholeness is of the Spirit. Unless the child is introduced to unity
within himself, he remains subject to the laws of conflict, no
matter how well-educated he is.

> *Conflict must be resolved. It cannot be evaded, set aside,*
> *denied, disguised, seen somewhere else, called by another*
> *name, or hidden by deceit of any kind, if it would be escaped.*
> *It must be seen exactly as it is, where it is thought to be,*
> *in the reality which has been given it, and with the purpose*
> *that the mind accorded it. For only then are its defenses*
> *lifted, and the truth can shine upon it as it disappears.*[13]

What will it take to awaken the child to his Reality? Obviously your own silent mind will be more effective than words. It is your own gratefulness that frees the child and you from the limitations the world is apt to impose.

> *Our gratitude will pave the way to Him, and shorten our learning time by more than you could ever dream of. Gratitude goes hand in hand with love, and where one is the other must be found. For gratitude is but an aspect of the Love which is the Source of all creation. God gives thanks to you, His Son, for being what you are; His Own completion and the Source of love, along with Him. Your gratitude to Him is one with His to you. For love can walk no road except the way of gratitude, and thus we go who walk the way to God.*[14]

Acquaint your child with the ways of a holy life. What greater gift could you give to humanity than that of a God-child, wholly at peace, created in the image of God? Blessed are the parents of a child who is one with the Will of God. Let us not betray our children to indifference and to a superficial life of activity.

Know that what you need to give to the child of God will be given to you. For as you give, you learn to receive. This Truth is what you most need to know: the heavenly Father is ever with you. The love between parent and child reaches Heaven and seeks guidance. The child awakens the parent to co-creatorship as their very life together becomes a prayer. *A Course In Miracles* assures us of Divine assistance:

> *If it helps you,*
> *think of me holding your hand*
> *and leading you.*
> *And I assure you*
> *this will be no idle fantasy.*[15]

Conviction is a matter of decision within oneself: to live by the Will of God and not by the dictates of society. Only then can we truly listen to the words of *A Course In Miracles*.

CHAPTER ELEVEN

11

RELATIONSHIP
AND THE DIVINE MOTHER

In today's world very few people have a real relationship with anyone. As long as the going is good and both parties agree, within that agreement what we call "relationship" continues. But few people know something that is independent of time; few have the conviction to say: "I have formed a relationship with you, a bond, and no opinion, no judgment, or disagreement would interfere with that. Whatever happens, this relationship will not be affected at its core."

For us, what our thought tells us is going to take over; at some point we will be ruled by our likes and dislikes. Can we see that in order to have a real relationship with someone we have to transcend thought? We don't even know that that is possible. Since we are all thought-bound, our relationships are not relationships at all.

All thought is reaction. In fact, almost everything we know is reaction. When we get married we may say, "Until death do us part." But then over differences, the relationship ends. Or we conform one another and think we are compatible. We are always meeting at the changeable level — at the level of thought — where we only have images of one another. And we are totally regulated by these images of each other although images are not true. A human being is beyond images. Instead of confronting the deceptions in our perception, we would rather think that another is wrong. When there is a situation which shows us that *we* are wrong, we want to run away.

We have become slaves of our "knowings." We have a name for everything. "It's a picture. It's a flower." Seldom have we seen or felt anything new. A whole decade could go by without one contact with a second of newness — the unknown. Would you know there is a difference between a carrot and bell pepper — that they vibrate differently? Would you have the space for newness in your life?

Rarely do we touch those we love with newness. If you really loved someone, just by touching their cheek or holding their hand you would be silenced. When that happens, it is new. The new only has it to give. It has no desire. Through you it extends joy, love, kindness, tenderness. When there is that newness you would have a relationship that nothing of thought could interfere with.

Each one of us exists in relationship. Without relationship nothing exists in the world. That is a law, not an opinion. Of relationship, however, we know hardly anything. Nor do we know our function on this earth. There is nothing more meaningful than to know your function because it brings you into right relationship with everything and everyone.

There is a prayer in *A Course In Miracles* which begins:

> *Forgive us our illusions, Father,*
> *and help us to accept our true relationship with You* . . .[1]

We can't accept our true relationship because we are crowded with all sort of projections, illusions, and things we want to do.

This earth plane is a level of two forces — cause and effect. And we must understand the action of cause and effect, which is the action of our motivations, in order to bring our mind to a state where it is willing to empty itself and accept true relationship with God. As long as there is chaos at the level of motives, at the level of cause and effect, our relationship can never be right with anything.

We need to bring about a transformation in our relationships with one another. Families today are falling apart. Something is terribly wrong. Everyone wants to do as he likes, follow his inclinations. But we are utterly irresponsible. What are the lessons to learn in relationship?

A Course in Miracles says that in each encounter there is the potential to learn; that there are some relationships that are just brief encounters, other relationships that are present for life, and some relationships that go on beyond this life. Everything has significance. No one is where he is by accident . . .[2] We must pay heed to everything that happens because life is a tremendous responsibility. But we would rather live at a sublevel, absent from awareness and oblivious to what is going on.

Relationships in the family are long range relationships. They are not casual. And in each one of these relationships, whether it be with mother, father, children, aunts, or uncles, correction is needed. Healing is needed. Compassion and understanding are needed. Thank the Lord it is so, because now we can grow to being responsible and learn to harmonize relationships which have gone on for lifetimes. We will never know the peace of God until all relationships come to love. And if we don't have the peace of God there will be wars. The world is becoming very dangerous but it is still possible for the individual to change.

In relationship how do we become free from entanglements, involvements? The family is subject to cause and effect just as the earth is. One person's debt to another becomes the factor which brings them together. And then they have more encounters within the family from childhood — strong opinions develop about sisters, brothers, mothers, fathers. There is very little reverence left.

Birth, death, and marriage are subject to the Will of God. It is not an accident that you have the parents you do. It is not by accident that you married the man or woman you did. But there is a responsibility to come to peace and harmony with everyone in your family. Start undoing. Start removing judgments. Find out why it is difficult for you to come to forgiveness, why you have such strong opinions.

We are not entitled to opinions because opinions have brought about this chaos. Opinions block the vision of who the other person is. If we limit life to opinion there will be no forgiveness in it. What other freedom is there but freedom from our own opinions? If our forgiveness is genuine, we will see how effortlessly our opinions change. And as we change we become energized because we have put away our resentment and all the "knowings" of yesterday. You may see beauty in another which you've never seen before. Why should you want to rubber stamp each day of your life? Make it new. Make it different. We have to bring harmony with everyone with whom we are related.

In right relationship no one dominates the other. Transformation is transformation *in* relationship; it is not closing your eyes and *becoming* transformed. In bringing harmony you would grow in wisdom. It is no longer abstract. The wise starts with himself because if you start with another, you start with blame. Start with yourself and give the other person the space. If they don't want to change, let it be. That is their relationship with God. In the end we are related only to the Source but we can still love another regardless of what they do.

If you want a harmonious marriage, a harmonious family, *you* have to be in harmony. And the more you change, the more you will make contact with something that goes beyond the physical — thoughtfulness, consideration, and love. In love there is no cause and effect and all relationships must end in love. Once you are in harmony, you are out of it.

So, keep growing that way. Start with your own family — not with trying to deny or get rid of your family. Are you going to be defeated by the little family you are in? Your responsibility is first of all to yourself. If you have forgiven the past, you are with the new and at least one person is not reacting anymore. That is wonderful. In this lifetime, you could end all blocks in relationship!

A Course In Miracles suggests that we are given three times to bring each relationship to harmony. Our only responsibility is not to wish things to be different from the way they are and to meet each encounter with real love. In this way one is no longer part of effect. If the first time you meet you react, the second time you could be wiser, more tolerant because you have grown in goodness. That would be the natural thing if you are growing at all.

Before you go to bed, sit quiet, undo the known. That is the way to grow if you want to come to love. Undo all the events of the day. The brain will automatically bring unfinished issues to your attention because the brain is part of creation and one of its functions is to bring order. We have abused it and have not understood its function. And now it is confused, unfulfilled, hateful, crowded with memories. But the brain is sensitive and alive. It tries to bring to your attention what needs to be dealt with. When you go to bed, sit for one hour of meditation. First everything will rush in, but don't evade it, just see how much you have suppressed, how dull you have been in ignoring it. You have a relationship inside too. Observe.

Slowly awareness would come and the brain won't disturb it. This light, this awareness, this sensitivity and attention would grow. Then you would only observe. You won't have an opinion about *opinions* anymore. You won't interpret things anymore. You'll just see all that is there without interfering with it. And you will see that it has less power because something in you can no longer be affected by it. Your first function is to bring order in your brain and in your relationship with those who are close to you. You are becoming mature. And you would see how the passion and joy in you to end the involvements would grow. You would be at peace.

"Know thyself" is the beginning of wisdom. And when you're liberated from reactions, the intensity of your stillness and innocence would affect mankind upon the earth. Your words would have power for they would not be born of time and personality. Eternal words are like the light of the world. Let us leave behind some eternal words upon this planet.

*   *   *

Edgar Cayce[3] had predicted that in the modern countries, where society has become so scientific, man's brain will become dull with routine. He would not see much of the sky and the sun; he would be in the house, the car, the office, the restaurant, the theatre. He would be limited only to routine which takes attention away. Mr. J. Krishnamurti talked about this routine existence with disgust. "Twenty years in an office, same thing, day and night, day and night." The same train, same car, same house, same food, same Saturday. Everything routine.

In this way a species of man is evolving that is very limited. He only needs outlets and to be told what to do. Everything classic is being eliminated from man's experience because we don't have the necessary span of attention. A very small part of the brain is active. All it knows is what it wants. It doesn't know what to give.

Who is going to know his Reality or a life free of consequences? Who will know what it means to be productive or what it takes to be self-reliant? To have conviction? To go past reaction? What place does such a man have in this society or in the present world, anywhere? A man who doesn't accept any belief, any system of thought, any nationality, any dogma?

What a horror it is that we have become such specimens, almost computerized, that we can't seem to step out and come to an awakening or to integrity.

When we do, we will be grateful. Gratefulness is everlasting. It is not for a thing. It is for having discovered who you are — your own unlimitedness, your own holiness. Just by being present there is the ending of the past and future. Man is eternal; he is not of time. Past and future become real only when we have made ourselves children of routine and bias, and live a life directed by external forces.

> *You are the work of God, and His work is wholly lovable and wholly loving. This is how a man must think of himself in his heart, because this is what he is.*[4]

*   *   *

There is an affirmation in one of the lessons of *A Course In Miracles* which, if realized in truth, would bring us to fulfillment. It is possible to know, beyond the words, beyond the concepts, the truth of:

> *By grace I live. By grace I am released.*
> *By grace I give. By grace I will release.*[5]

You could say, "I don't know what grace is. I don't even know what life is. I only know my constant need for something — a perpetual state of unfulfillment, of ever wanting something 'other.' I want something and move towards that but once I get it, I move towards something else."

We cannot seem to put an end to our constant "wanting." We have a sense of insecurity, inadequacy, unfulfillment, and then we need pleasure, outlets, evasion. Something very active in us is constantly seeking all the time.

If you have understood this, you would see that it is the *seeking* that deprives you. Seeking perpetually keeps its isolation going; it doesn't know one moment of contentment. Contentment is where the seeking has ceased. There is a prayer in *A Course In Miracles* which says: *I am content to be wherever He wishes . . .*[6] When that is so, there is no seeking in you. There is no such thing as a place for the content person. You have come to the right place — the place of your own contentment. That is our real nature.

The supreme thing is to know who you are and to learn that *By grace I live* frees you from everything external. You will have no worry, no anxiety. This is a chance to be a human being. This is an opportunity to come to an awakening of sanity. *By grace I live* purifies one from all fear, all concern, all "knowing" — everything is gone. Grace would fill your mind and heart when you are cleansed of all your "knowing." Then you extend grace.

The first thing is to see that you are a victim of the world — a victim of "wanting," experiences, sensations — and that you have nothing to give because you want; therefore, there is enormous waste of life. When you discover that you need to be released, then grace has meaning for you. "*By grace I am released* from my unfulfillment, from my sense of lack, from wanting direction. I am at peace with myself. *By grace I give. By grace I will release.*" In a world where everybody wants, there is one person, one human being who has something to give. And because it has released you, you release those with whom life brings you into contact because you do not want anything.

Just being who you are brings the Kingdom of God to earth. Each person is born for this. That is our function. The only thing that matters is your knowing that you live by grace, are released by grace, and by grace you give. Can you imagine always having something to give, rather than to want? Because you are always receiving. Then you will be lost in the purity and the inspiration of your own unlimitedness. Grace makes it possible to realize this truth. Nothing external can rule you and make you react. Grace is an action and your life is an extension of that grace.

*   *   *

Being from India, I had heard from childhood about the Goddesses Durga, Parvati, Saraswati, Lakshmi, and Mother Kali, all representing the Divine Mother. There are many pictures and sculptures of these Goddesses in India. In the Christian world, we are limited primarily to Mary as the representative of the Mother.

Recently there arose in me an interest to know the Divine Mother. I had actually been repulsed by the morbid images of Mother Kali with her tongue dripping blood, wearing a necklace of skulls. I had avoided it, satisfied with my conclusions. I could live without knowing.

Aren't we all quite satisfied with our conclusions — our "knowings" — although they may have nothing to do with reality? Our liking, disliking, understanding, or not understanding all fall into the realm of opinion. Don't we all live without knowing the truth, without knowing anything real? We can even destroy each other over opinions and yet they aren't true at all. If someone disagrees with us, we could disown them — our children, our mother, our father, our friends. Every single person could disown another person over some issue, some opinion.

The Holy Mother has many names. In Hinduism, a name signifies the attributes of the person. For example, Lord Shiva has one name as a householder, one as a dancer, one as a musician — these are different aspects of him. Lord Krishna has twenty names. It is the same glory, just different aspects of it. Goddess Durga is one aspect of the Holy Mother, the Divine Mother. Mother Kali is the feminine force — another aspect of the same Mother. Sarada Devi, Sri Ramakrishna's wife,[7] was also the same Mother, just a different aspect.

When I attempted to find out about the Holy Mother, I wanted to know it with newness and not with someone else's thought. It started with a prompting inside, an interest within me. I wanted to know it directly. When we want to know something we usually go to the "known," begin to do research, go to a bookstore or a library. But I would not go to the "known," therefore I had to be content to remain in the realm of uncertainty. Knowing is the bondage. If you really understood this you would have brought an end to a pattern that has ruled your life. You would have brought an end to unfulfillment with its urges, boredom, loneliness, and curiosity.

So this inner impulse, something startling, took place within: "Who is this Divine Mother?"

In order to know what is whole you have to come to wholeness. You must never accept what your brain tells you for it knows only the partial, never the whole. Start undoing. A miracle may happen and you will know who the Mother is. And it won't be from thought. Interest has vitality, alertness. When you become attentive everything external ceases. An awakening begins to take place and starts to unfold. It isn't anything outside. You are in a different world, a world that has no duality in it. You begin to discover *yourself.*

The concept of a Mother God is something new to the West. It is not something one gives oneself easily to. We see God as a father, all-powerful, all-knowing. In the West particularly, God as a mother is unheard of.

I began to see that when there was stillness in the whole, that was God — the Unknown, the Formless, the Nameless. And then it extended and expressed itself. This expression became energy, the energy of Love that created everything. This energy is feminine. This energy that extends itself is the Mother. She is the Source behind appearances that multiplies into a million shapes, names, forms. Love extends and becomes creative.

The Mother is called *maya,* or illusion. She has the function of helping the person to be caught in illusions, and she also has the function of helping the person undo illusions. Without illusions there would not be the external creation. The manifestation which we see only exists at the level of illusions. As *A Course In Miracles* puts it:

> *Nothing real can be threatened.*
> *Nothing unreal exists.*[8]

So the Mother dissolves illusions and she promotes illusions. She promotes illusions to keep creation going because she created it. What she created, she promotes. Illusion is the knowledge of ignorance or separation. It will come to an end because it has the capacity to destroy itself. One can see in the world today how bound man is to belief, sensation, pleasure. The Mother is the master of the ending and the end is guaranteed. You can go to the end through suffering and demoralization — you just degenerate more and more until you cannot even use your brain. Or you can end by becoming enlightened. What is your relationship with her? When I discovered this, I shivered.

If you want to go on producing illusions, she says: "I am the Mother. I cannot keep my creation going without them. In the end, there is only God, nothing else exists. Only in illusion does this world exist." Nothing that is external, that is limited to the human brain is real. That which is real has no name or shape or form; it is not subject to time or to appearances.

And then it came to me directly: If you would recall that you have a Mother, you have nothing to worry about. I know for a fact that I have a Mother and therefore I have no problems. I have what she embodies as a part of me. There is no opposite to it; I am not separated. She creates even the prophets, the sages, and the Incarnations. She is the energy. She knows to love what she created. The real nature of the woman is to protect what she has created.

So the Divine Mother, the Mother of the Universe, is the nearest way to come to knowing God. When we see Mother Kali with the skulls hanging around her neck, her hand with a sword dripping blood, her tongue hanging out, it is to bring us to awe that there are other forces to correct the illusions we are caught in; we had better step out of consequences and live a life that is virtuous.

When the direct contact with the Mother was made, the words were: "Say to yourself: 'You have a Mother.' And everything will disappear." It takes away the concepts and brings you to contentment, to the action of grace. No matter what situation it is, the Divine Mother is accessible to you.

CHAPTER TWELVE

12

THE GOD-CHILD AND THE WORLD TODAY

Seeing the external world as it is means seeing without condemnation. In the purity of true seeing there is no reaction. Just to witness the drama of humanity is enough.

In this spirit of observation, let us look over the span of several centuries since the time of the discovery of the New World by Columbus and see what similarity they bear to the twentieth century. This may reveal that all the changes, progress and prosperity, freedom and literacy, are no changes at all in reality. Greed is greed. Fear is fear. Wanting and wishing are what they have always been.

For centuries, religious authorities ruled the day. They proclaimed their sovereignty and required absolute obedience. No one was allowed to question or disobey the orders issued from above. And eventually obedience was regarded as a great virtue.

In looking at politics we see how kings and feudal lords took control of the people, and their authority remained unquestioned for generations. Slowly, however, unrest began to grow until revolutions erupted — French, Russian, Turkish — as servile man began to challenge the burden of authority. History has recorded it all — the bloodshed and tremendous suffering. It took centuries for consciousness to explode out of the mold shaped by the authoritarian religious leaders and monarchs of Europe.

Today people's energies are being drained by corporations and profiteering organizations. The privileged classes have worked everything in their favor to maintain the advantages of the status quo. And nobody has questioned the inadequacies of politicians, even though they have failed to bring peace to the world. As it has for ages, the propaganda to protect these vested interests still controls the mass mind. Men are mobilized, drafted, and sent to kill the "enemy" — human beings they have never seen before. Although there has been a shift from religion to politics, it is the same belief system based on individual helplessness and dependence.

Today the industrial economy with its machines, artificiality, and need for outlets is playing havoc with man and nature. Attached to success and profit, it is utterly indifferent to what it manufactures. Human energy is being used for the unbridled production of armaments. The laws that govern the system's economy are not based on the natural principles of wisdom, simplicity and "LOVE YE ONE ANOTHER." They are based on status and authority. The spirit of man continues to be crushed for the sake of the advantages of those at the top and our so-called freedom of religion and politics has not freed man from hunger and poverty. Every nation, every city, has its slums.

Affluence today thrives on the frustration of man by offering him indulgences to compensate for his routine life. It is another system of exploitation that lives off human existence. Inherent in this misnamed prosperity are the seeds of its own destruction.

We are bringing up children in an economic system that controls almost every facet of life. It has in its power all the advantages of science, the communications media, and education, to prepare us to acquire the skills it needs to run its enterprises and agencies. It owns the oceans, the airways, the minerals, and the manpower. Everywhere man is compelled to support the build-up of armaments for the destruction of mankind.

Prosperity has its consequences which may prove the worst of poverties. Mankind has survived poverty but one wonders if we will survive the consequences of the next twenty years.

Only a few men of Divine Perspective are aware of the fallacy of it all and the illusion of helplessness that is imposed upon man by manmade power structures. Everything man has ever done, is doing, or will do at the time level, results in consequences. As consequences multiply, the intensity of loneliness increases. The efficiency of fear and insecurity enters and lays the foundation for self-destruction.

*　　*　　*

I wonder if it is possible to share something and, just in the sharing, bring about a total change of value in a person?

Each one of us has to face the fact that we are irresponsible people. If we saw the fact of this and if we didn't condemn ourselves, we would begin to discover some of the traits of irresponsibility. Only when we see that we are irresponsible — when we come to "what is" — does some other action take place. The discovery and awareness of Truth is all we need because then we would change.

If you *interpret*, however, then it doesn't go any further. All of our education is based on interpretation, explaining *about* Truth because it doesn't *know* Truth itself.

What is irresponsibility? How did it come into being? How

did we become its victims? When a person is irresponsible he lacks wisdom; and without wisdom he is not going to be able to love. Irresponsibility is a kind of selfishness. ''I do as I please.'' Irresponsible people are produced by the present culture and the present educational system.

When we are irresponsible we become children of the world of illusion, the world of unreality, the world that is separated from the Will of God. No matter how erudite you are, if you are not related to the Will of God, you are caught in the illusion of unreality. Within the illusion of unreality there is only irresponsibility and interpretations.

With modern society, more education came into being: justifying the interpretations, or rather, saying that within the illusion, we can have peace; within the illusion, we can glorify the flesh.

In his book of discussions with children, parents, and teachers, *Think On These Things*, Mr. J. Krishnamurti pointed out:

> ''Life is really very beautiful, it is not this ugly thing that we have made of it; and you can appreciate its richness, its depth, its extraordinary loveliness only when you revolt against everything — against organized religion, against tradition, against the present rotten society — so that you as a human being find out for yourself what is true. Not to imitate but to discover — *that* is education, is it not? It is very easy to conform to what your society or your parents and teachers tell you. That is a safe and easy way of existing; but that is not living, because in it there is fear, decay, death. To live is to find out for yourself what is true, and you can do this only when there is freedom, when there is continuous revolution inwardly, within yourself.

> ''But you are not encouraged to do this; no one

tells you to question, to find out for yourself what God is, because if you were to rebel you would become a danger to all that is false. Your parents and society want you to live safely, and you also want to live safely. Living safely generally means living in imitation and therefore in fear. Surely, the function of education is to help each one of us to live freely and without fear, is it not? And to create an atmosphere in which there is no fear requires a great deal of thinking on your part as well as on the part of the teacher, the educator.

''Do you know what this means — what an extraordinary thing it would be to create an atmosphere in which there is no fear? And we *must* create it, because we see that the world is caught up in endless wars; it is guided by politicians who are always seeking power; it is a world of lawyers, policemen and soldiers, of ambitious men and women all wanting position and all fighting each other to get it. Then there are the so-called saints, the religious *gurus* with their followers; they also want power, position, here or in the next life. It is a mad world, completely confused, in which the communist is fighting the capitalist, the socialist is resisting both, and everybody is against somebody, struggling to arrive at a safe place, a position of power or comfort. The world is torn by conflicting beliefs, by caste and class distinctions, by separative nationalities, by every form of stupidity and cruelty — and this is the world you are being educated to fit into. You are encouraged to fit into the framework of this disastrous society; your parents want you to do that, and you also want to fit in.

''Now, is it the function of education merely to help you to conform to the pattern of this rotten social order, or is it to give you freedom — complete freedom to grow and create a different society, a new world? We want to have this freedom, not in the future, but now, otherwise we may all be destroyed. We must create immediately an atmosphere of freedom so that you can live and find out for yourselves what is true, so that you become intelligent, so that you are able to face the world and understand it, not just conform to it, so that inwardly, deeply, psychologically you are in constant revolt; because it is only those who are in constant revolt that discover what is true, not the man who conforms, who follows some tradition. It is only when you are constantly inquiring, constantly observing, constantly learning, that you find truth, God, or love; and you cannot inquire, observe, learn, you cannot be deeply aware, if you are afraid. So the function of education, surely, is to eradicate, inwardly as well as outwardly, this fear that destroys human thought, human relationship and love."[1]

Fear, an aspect of ignorance, limits life to body existence. For the most part, in this overly externalized life, irresponsibility is mistaken for freedom and the need for outlets, for pleasure.

In the same chapter, Mr. Krishnamurti explains the function of education:

"I wonder if we have ever asked ourselves what education means. Why do we go to school, why do we learn various subjects, why do we pass examinations and compete with each other for better grades? What does this so-called education mean, and what is it all about? This is really a very important question, not only for the students, but also for the parents, for the teachers, and for everyone who loves this earth. Why do we go through the struggle to be educated? Is it merely in order to pass some examinations and get a job? Or is it the function of education to prepare us while we are young to understand the whole process of life? Having a job and earning one's livelihood is necessary — but is that all? Are we being educated only for that? Surely, life is not merely a job, an occupation; life is something extraordinarily wide and profound, it is a great mystery, a vast realm in which we function as human beings. If we merely prepare ourselves to earn a livelihood, we shall miss the whole point of life; and to understand life is much more important than merely to prepare for examinations and become very proficient in mathematics, physics, or what you will.

''So, whether we are teachers or students, is it not important to ask ourselves why we are educating or being educated? And what does life mean? Is not life an extraordinary thing? The birds, the flowers, the flourishing trees, the heavens, the stars, the rivers and the fish therein — all this is life. Life is the poor and the rich; life is the constant battle between groups, races and nations; life is meditation; life is what we call religion, and it is also the subtle, hidden things of the mind — the envies, the ambitions, the passions, the fears, fulfilments and anxieties. All this and much more is life. But we generally prepare ourselves to understand only one small corner of it. We pass certain examinations, find a job, get married, have children, and then become more and more like machines. We remain fearful, anxious, frightened of life. So, is it the function of education to help us understand the whole process of life, or is it merely to prepare us for a vocation, for the best job we can get?

''What is going to happen to all of us when we grow to be men and women? Have you ever asked yourselves what you are going to do when you grow up? In all likelihood you will get married, and before you know where you are you will be mothers and fathers; and you will then be tied to a job, or to the kitchen, in which you will gradually wither away. Is that all that *your* life is going to be? Have you ever asked yourself this question? Should you not ask it? If your family is wealthy you may have a fairly good position already assured, your father may give you a comfortable job, or you may get richly married; but there also you will decay, deteriorate. Do you see?

"Surely, education has no meaning unless it helps you to understand the vast expanse of life with all its subtleties, with its extraordinary beauty, its sorrows and joys. You may earn degrees, you may have a series of letters after your name and land a very good job; but then what? What is the point of it all if in the process your mind becomes dull, weary, stupid? So, while you are young, must you not seek to find out what life is all about? And is it not the true function of education to cultivate in you the intelligence which will try to find the answer to all these problems? Do you know what intelligence is? It is the capacity, surely, to think freely, without fear, without a formula, so that you begin to discover for yourself what is real, what is true; but if you are frightened you will never be intelligent. Any form of ambition, spiritual or mundane, breeds anxiety, fear; therefore ambition does not help to bring about a mind that is clear, simple, direct, and hence intelligent."[2]

Mr. Krishnamurti had placed a great deal of emphasis on education and started numerous schools in India, as well as one in England and one in California.*

Human life is boundless. It represents all of eternity. All of the universe is focused in the human being. We have reduced ourselves to such limited existence that, out of frustration,

*For further information regarding Mr. Krishnamurti's work, contact the Krishnamurti Foundation of America, P.O. Box 216, Ojai, California 93023.

mankind is heading toward worse and worse disasters. But there are Eternal Laws that remain unaffected by the mortal fuss of artificial superiority or inferiority. The circumstances that surround our helplessness are not real. There is another approach to life, independent of it all, regarding man's relationship with God, man's relationship with man, man's relationship with nature. The individual who has a voice of his own, having freed himself from conditioning and prejudice, lives according to Eternal Laws.

How vitally important it is for both parents to assume the responsibility of bringing up the child without a sense of inadequacy, without a sense of being a victim of the manmade world.

The father represents justice and strength. Where there is strength, there is no judgment. It has the vitality never to get into duality. It is not brutal, physical strength, but strength of character and integrity. The mother represents the gentleness of compassion that forgives and does not acknowledge the illusions of the world as truth. The parents, who themselves were not raised consciously, now have the opportunity to raise their child according to Divine perspective.

Be grateful to know that each soul, having its Divine purpose to fulfill on this physical plane, provides all that the body needs for its function. Raising the child of God is a *shared purpose*. The parents, as co-creators, are not inadequate to the challenge of bringing up the God-Child. You have within you the power to change the destiny of stars.

New consciousness dawns upon the age through those who have outgrown the illusion and the deception of "littleness" imposed upon them externally by society. The action begins with the parents when they provide the environment in which the child flowers in virtue and in love. Let us begin now.

*   *   *

When I was coming out of my room this morning, two of the children at the Foundation came up to me and we hugged and hugged. Most of us don't know what a hug is. A hug is when you are present. If you still have thought going on in your head, then it is not a hug, it's a formality. In a hug, you get so close that you don't even know you're you and the other is the other.

I noticed that to be with a child brings you to stillness and calmness. It slows down everything. Your hand moves more slowly. Everything becomes more gracious as you become gentle — all of you. Your whole rhythm changes. When you meet an adult, that doesn't take place. Meeting a child you both meet instantly. Meeting an adult you meet a problem; you have to get the problem out of the way before you can make any kind of a contact. Children have no problems; you can communicate something that is not of words.

The child doesn't know dual things or cleverness. He is factual without even being aware of it. We can't be factual even when we try. We're going to be polite, we're going to be sentimental, we're going to be all kind of things. With a child there is no "going to be." He just is. How much one can learn from how precise and exact a child already is!

It is almost impossible for children today not to get influenced. The externals intrude upon every cell of their bodies — through sounds, desires, fear, insecurity, violence, greed. But the children born today are far more powerful in the spirit; they are unique, exceptional. Parents should prepare themselves and not limit the spirit. Because *A Course In Miracles* is here, it is possible to raise a child of God. The Word has come with its power of the Absolute, the Thoughts of God, that would make things work. The child's spirit is indomitable and cannot be undermined. One should not underestimate the child nor limit or judge the power of the spirit.

QUESTION: When do they lose the spirit?

When the parents impose their frustrations on them, when the schools computerize them, when they've got to live in this world and get a job, then the conflict begins. But it starts with the parents. When they are lonely they need a child and the child becomes the toy. Then when they are busy, that becomes more important and the child becomes a nuisance. How many times during the day is the child a nuisance and how many times is he a toy? Very little time is left for the child and the parent to be just child and parent.

> *QUESTION:* Will this book that you are writing enable the parents to help the child keep his pure spirit?

To the degree the parents are capable of receiving what the book says. It all depends on how much space the parents have to understand it. How much the parent has awakened his own potentials will determine his relationship with the child.

If the parent lives in a fragmented world, he's going to transmit those limitations. Where is the parent who has no limitations, who lives in the external world but is not of it? Can the parent remain a parent in order to protect the child from the externals that try to invade upon his life? The parent has to awaken the child to his own awareness, his own discrimination. To educate the child is to harm him, but to awaken the child to awareness is to be responsible.

The minute the child is sent to school, the school will shape him to fit into a skyscraper. The parents knowing this have a responsibility. But since the parents have no direct relationship with the source of creation, they say, "What can we do? We have to send our child to school." The parents' helplessness is going to limit the child. But if the parents see that they are betraying their own child by being helpless, they would come to a rebirth merely because they want to bring the child up right.

This rebirth rarely takes place in the parents because they

have great faith in their helplessness. But when they want to protect the child from conditioning, from being programmed, the parents can act and change their lifestyle because their child is their extension. If they can't be true to their own child, they will not be true to anything else either.

Which one of us is going to bring about that change? Mr. Krishnamurti had said to me, "People seldom ever change." They can always justify. "What am I to do? I'm all alone. I have two children, I have to work." But I say that other potentials come with the child. The child brings the potential to be free and to free even the parent. But this requires trust. And that's one thing we don't know. Everything we know is an extension of ignorance and therefore an extension of doubt, fear, and limitation. If we could really know the truth of *Nothing real can be threatened*[3] we would know the child is protected and the parent is protected. When you know:

> *Nothing real can be threatened.*
> *Nothing unreal exists.*[4]

you have revolutionized your life. Who is going to do that? Does this society allow it?

The only thing we need to realize is the truth of:

> *By grace I live. By grace I am released.*
> *By grace I give. By grace I will release.*[5]

The world is going to influence the child; other children are going to affect him. But can you awaken the child and bring him to awareness so that constantly you are releasing him, releasing yourself, releasing your neighbor with the grace that has become real to you? You may even come to a point where you have no more "wantings" because you have discovered that all is perfect, accomplished, and provided. But it is very difficult to bring this into application. Somewhere we are all defeated and we just accept ideas.

There may be better possibilities for the child because he is in the present. For me, it is like meditation to be with a child because there is nothing to be undone in him. One can come to a total calm which the child feels. In fact, they are very drawn to it. Without mentally knowing why, they just sense and feel that this is different. That kind of contact is what we need to make with each other and the child. It's easier with the child because he still has innocence.

*   *   *

If you are in a large city and feel trapped in an artificial environment and wish your child had the space of the country-side and open sky, or, if you are in a small town filled with gossip and small talk, and its earthiness gives you a sense of isolation from the sensitive vitality of creative people, know that at the relative level there is no such thing as a perfect place. Wherever you are, transformation is possible. The wise does not seek another place; he only leaves the place where he is when doors open and the other is offered. All will be provided. Your right action has tremendous potentials.

There were times when I was a stranger abroad and had no money, nor did I have the skills to get a job or the willingness to work for another. Oftentimes I did not have money for a meal. And yet my children went to the most exclusive and expensive schools. Whenever the time came to send money for their tuition and expenses, it was always there. I was surprised how many different ways the need was met and I asked Mr. J. Krishnamurti, "Does Life take care?" He said, "Yes, if you completely let go." It took all the anxiety away and, for years, one way or another the money would be there. I would never borrow nor accept charity. I know this is a law — rightness is provided.

There were many other needs I had and I wished the money would be there, but it was not the same. Heaven provided for the children. It requires the highest of discrimination to know what a need is and to give honesty to everything one does. Your own virtuous life awakens the potentials and an all-embracing awareness that has its own direction and ethics.

Such a man stands always in the eternal present. He knows no lack. Being free of lack is the most powerful action known to man. Its simplicity contains the light of heaven for it is the rare individual who has overcome ambition and insecurity. It requires an internal transformation. Once this is realized by one individual, society is transformed also. The action of sanity starts with the one person who recognizes his identity with God and lives by forgiveness and eternal gratefulness. Not being ruled by opinions, he does not judge his brother.

Parents may say that they cannot find a good school, cannot find Gianiji in a train, cannot go to Shankaracharya.* What can they do? One would want to give up. But if you look at it calmly it may not be difficult at all. What seems difficult is the undoing, the unlearning; what seems difficult is to cope with one's irresponsibility. It shows how far we have deviated from being responsible human beings, as parents, families, and neighbors. If parents do not have an alternative, then *they* can become a Gianiji, a Shankaracharya. The child could go to the best schools, but if the parent is not a Gianiji, it will not matter. First of all, parents have to change.

*   *   *

IRRESPONSIBILITY WILL DESTROY MAN

The world is in such a state that only weakness seems to work. Everything is based on thought and reaction, not on space, giving, or freedom. What kind of affluence is it when you do not own your own home, when you don't have your own space, when your life is not productive in the true sense?

---

*See Introduction.

The external situation is always impossible. We can elaborate upon it, but the result would be that one would come to the realization it is too vast, too complicated. What can "little me" do? Granted. But it is possible to make internal corrections, for that is where the misperception is. Anyone reading this book who feels helpless against the external world of society and its demands has not yet understood that man is never helpless, that for him to master himself is always possible. When that correction is made, it has its effect on all of mankind.

One Mother Teresa makes the correction within herself and finds her own boundlessness. She corrects the misperceptions of mankind for now she has something of her own to give. Gandhi made the correction within himself and was able to affect the externals.

When you are overwhelmed as a parent by the world, it is because you have not corrected the misperception within yourself. That is man's first responsibility. Deal with yourself. Once you have come to wholeness you will have a different relationship with the world and you will have something to give to your child. Always remember, the world is abstract, but you are real. Nothing of time has power over you unless you allow it.

Yes, in this highly externalized, violent, and materialistic society, it is possible to be at peace within yourself and have the space and the sanity to live a life of rightness. It is possible to discover that the power of rightness is subordinate to nothing. It is possible to communicate with a child and awaken a sense of awareness in him so that he can protect himself from the invasion of the externals.

The child has the potential to revolutionize the family. The birth of a child is a great event in creation. Its significance goes beyond the frontier of time and body.

*   *   *

WHO KNOWS THE RESOURCES
OF BEING EVER CONSISTENT WITH THE WILL OF GOD?

The child is born with his own resources
to know freedom from need
and to realize his own God-given Identity.
The purpose of birth is Rebirth.

The parents are blessed by the love they feel
for the child God entrusted to them.
The child brings the parents to a shared interest
which has great vitality.
Two people putting their minds together
can do anything under the sky.
Once the polarities are in unison,
the action becomes creative.
It knows no limitation.

Be independent and learn to act from freedom.

It is compassion that awakens the parents
to the harmony of a higher purpose
that instantly overcomes the issues
and limitations of personality.

> *Be not content with littleness. But be sure you under-*
> *stand what littleness is, and why you could never be content*
> *with it. Littleness is the offering you give yourself. You offer*
> *this in place of magnitude, and you accept it. Everything*
> *in this world is little because it is a world made out of*
> *littleness, in the strange belief that littleness can content*
> *you. When you strive for anything in this world in the belief*
> *that it will bring you peace, you are belittling yourself and*
> *blinding yourself to glory. Littleness and glory are the*
> *choices open to your striving and your vigilance. You will*
> *always choose one at the expense of the other.*

> *Yet what you do not realize, each time you choose, is that*

your choice is your evaluation of yourself. Choose littleness and you will not have peace, for you will have judged yourself unworthy of it. And whatever you offer as a substitute is much too poor a gift to satisfy you. It is essential that you accept the fact, and accept it gladly, that there is no form of littleness that can ever content you. You are free to try as many as you wish, but all you will be doing is to delay your homecoming. For you will be content only in magnitude, which is your home . . . .

You who have sought and found littleness, remember this: Every decision you make stems from what you think you are, and represents the value that you put upon yourself. Believe the little can content you, and by limiting yourself you will not be satisfied. For your function is not little, and it is only by finding your function and fulfilling it that you can escape from littleness.[6]

Everything in creation exists to bring man
to perfection.

You have to change.

Because you can change.

Heaven is with you.

There is nothing my holiness cannot do.[7]

To trust the Word of God
you have to question the conventional ways
of a borrowed lifestyle.
Know that you are renewed
by the energy of the newborn child.
You need not conform to the externals anymore,
but bring a new order
and new values into your life.

Such an action has a small beginning
but it has the power to uproot empires.
Start where you are,
confident of your own potentials.
Rightness will endow you
with the strength and conviction
necessary to set yourself free from bondage.
The child's need is for you to be transformed.
This is your need also.

The child is fully provided,
as Love is protected.
Gratefulness inspires the strength.

Resurrection is the message of Christianity.
The child is born to bring the parents
to Resurrection and, like Jesus,
humanity to rebirth.
We must live by:

"IN GOD WE TRUST."

A Course In Miracles is an absolute necessity
for the parent to come to new values
and a different thought system
from the one he knows.

Bring the child to attention
so that neither you nor he
dip into past memories.
When something is shared,
if you can come to attention
and not bring in the past,
the fact can be seen.
The past brings defensiveness.

The child's spirit is incorruptible.
Beware you do not mislead him

with a lifestyle limited to your own experience —
insecurity, prejudices, jealousies.

Beware of the tendency of struggle and effort
on which one relies to solve projected problems.
Struggle and effort
are born out of reaction to a situation.
Action that is independent of personality
dissolves misperceptions.
Thus, first there must be internal correction.
If we ignore the Holy Instant,
keeping past experiences and memories alive,
the "me and mine" remains intact.
This is the challenge that we evade —
the undoing of the "me and mine."

Parents must come to a life of virtue.
If you are serious
and want your child to grow up
in an atmosphere of sanity and quietude
you have to give him the space
of your own peace of mind.

The simplicity of self-honesty
is the wisdom that corrects the illusions
of thought-deluded brains.
First and foremost,
the parents must bring the mind to silence.
There are a thousand artificial barriers
to the sanity of peace of mind.
Know that integration within yourself
is your primary responsibility.

The day, awakened by the dawn, enters
and the light, with its energy,
is upon the earth.
With the night comes the peace
for man to renew himself.

The child needs sleep
so that he can grow inwardly
and awaken the light within him,
so that he, with his own Divine Intelligence,
can be the light to the world.

Humanity needs children
who are free from the educated ignorance
of man's malevolent mind
destroying the world
with its fear, violence, and commerce.

How would you protect your child?

CHAPTER THIRTEEN

13

THE PATH OF VIRTUE

Inner awakening should be the most important thing in one's life. Our first responsibility is to know who we are, not who God is or anything else. We must realize that we are thoroughly programmed, inside and out. Just by becoming aware of this we would start to undo. You might say, "I was always afraid to look within because I thought I would see how ugly I am." That is all right. It is just your opinion that it is ugly. Slowly you would begin to discover that you continually underestimate yourself. Why is it we are always moving away from what we are? Unless a man learns who he is and what he is here for, there can be no knowing of truth. How can he know his real function without knowing who he is?

Almost everything depends on our capacity to receive that which is ever present. What determines how wise or how sane a person is, is his capacity to receive. Through *A Course In Miracles* you can come to a real gratefulness of the heart, a greater capacity to receive than you ever had before. Gratefulness is the strength that increases the capacity to receive.

Somehow we have the capacity for wrong thinking and wrong values but not for truth. The result is that our lives go wasted. Without the Course, I don't think any one of us would know which way to turn.

One must start by bringing order into one's life so that the values of the earth have less sway. Making space within and emptying the mind is the beginning of a religious life. To empty the mind you need order. That is the issue. But we want to help our children without taking care of our own unwillingness to change. This will never work. If inner awakening is not of first importance, you can do all that you want and it will have little effect; your child will become just like you.

When the parents and the child come into the atmosphere of the Course, and have right relationship with it, you would see how harmoniously things would work. Do not accept *littleness* as real and I can assure you of one thing: once you have determined this is what you need to do, it is already accomplished.

*   *   *

All men have urges born of thought. These are self-centered, and constantly motivate and manipulate us. We have become so engrossed in urges that they have taken over. But there are also natural impulses, miracles born of love — a different pulse beat of Life within us.

The child is born to the mother to awaken her to the impulse of miracles. Miracles relate one with Life; urges limit one to the body. If the mother stays with these impulses, she will impart universality to the child. If she falls back on urges, she will condition and isolate him. And there will be no relationship, only dependence. Thus, without strength or truth, life becomes a search for expediences. There is no strength in the absence of simplicity.

Simplicity is not poverty; it is a flower of wisdom not burdened with "wishes and wantings." There is a Chinese proverb which says:

"We never buy more than we need.
We never need more than we use.
We never use more than it takes to get by,
until we learn to need less."

Lead your child to an intrinsic way of life, one that is neither commercialized nor ruled by ambition. It is the happiness within that will sustain the child, and what he does will give expression to his spirit.

Teach your child not skills, but love to share.

Teach him to have more space in his life,
the richness of stillness.

Teach him to widen the gaps of silence between
the thoughts with relaxation.

Teach him that all things in their origin
are of the One Source.

Teach him to pray for his adversary
to regain his own peace and harmony.

Teach him to take prayer beyond words,
and you will be teaching him the way to heaven.

Teach him not to be controlled by another,
and he will be able to dissolve conflict within himself.

Teach him to bless all things with his peace.

Teach him non-waste and the love of conservation,
to be a friend of trees, dawn, and twilight.

Teach him simplicity and gratefulness,
to love virtue and to have no alternatives.

Teach him to be a friend unto himself.

A child is the son of man and the Son of God. The son you perceive outside yourself is yours; the other rests with his heavenly Father. The parents have the choice which they would let him be. But the purpose of parenthood is to return the child to God. To raise a child of God is to allow God to participate.

*   *   *

Excerpt from
Lesson 182
(from *A Course In Miracles*)

"I will be still an instant and go home."

This world you seem to live in is not home to you. And somewhere in your mind you know that this is true. A memory of home keeps haunting you, as if there were a place that called you to return, although you do not recognize the voice, nor what it is the voice reminds you of. Yet still you feel an alien here, from somewhere all unknown. Nothing so definite that you could say with certainty you are an exile here. Just a persistent feeling, sometimes not more than a tiny throb, at other times hardly remembered, actively dismissed, but surely to return to mind again . . . .

We speak today for everyone who walks this world, for he is not at home. He goes uncertainly about in endless search, seeking in darkness what he cannot find; not recognizing what it is he seeks. A thousand homes he makes, yet none contents his restless mind. He does not understand he builds in vain. The home he seeks cannot be made by him. There is no substitute for Heaven. All he ever made was hell.

Perhaps you think it is your childhood home that you would find again. The childhood of your body, and its place of shelter, are a memory now so distorted that you merely hold a picture of a past that never happened. Yet there is a Child in you Who seeks His Father's house, and knows that He is alien here. This childhood is eternal, with an innocence that will endure forever. Where this Child shall go is holy ground. It is His holiness that lights up Heaven, and that brings to earth the pure reflection of the light above, wherein are earth and Heaven joined as one.

It is this Child in you your Father knows as His Own Son. It is this Child Who knows His Father. He desires to go home so deeply, so unceasingly, His voice cries unto you to let Him rest a while. He does not ask for more than just a few instants of respite; just an interval in which He can return to breathe again the holy air that fills His Father's house. You are His home as well. He will return. But give Him just a little time to be Himself, within the peace that is His home, resting in silence and in peace and love.

This Child needs your protection. He is far from home. He is so little that He seems so easily shut out, His tiny voice so readily obscured, His call for help almost unheard amid the grating sounds and harsh and rasping noises of the world. Yet does He know that in you still abides His sure protection. You will fail Him not. He will go home, and you along with Him.

This Child is your defenselessness; your strength. He trusts in you. He came because He knew you would not fail. He whispers of His home unceasingly to you. For He would bring you back with Him, that He Himself might stay, and not return again where He does not belong, and where He lives an outcast in a world of alien thoughts. His patience has no limits. He will wait until you hear His gentle voice within you, calling you to let Him go in peace, along with you, to where He is at home and you with Him.[1]

CHAPTER FOURTEEN

14

TALKS WITH PARENTS
Part I

FAMILY RELATIONSHIPS
ARE BREAKING UP

PARENT: In today's society one of every two marriages fails. Family relationships are in a rapid state of deterioration. I, and others that I've known, have tried various avenues to bring about some harmony in our relationships. Some of us turned to psychology and self-help programs, some to religion. Others have sought another relationship. But the fact remains that things are getting worse, not better.

What is the real function of the family? And how can proper relationships be formed within the family unit?

I don't think that I can give you an answer. That is the function of specialists who fragment life and pretend to know. For that, high fees are charged. We have to see the fact of this. We think that we cannot solve our own problems; therefore, we turn to specialists. Because we feel inadequate we become dependent. Anyone who encourages inadequacy and dependence pretends he has solutions, makes a living from other people's problems, and is a party to bringing about the present state of affairs in society.

What do you think a wise person would do? He would introduce you to potentials within yourself and would not take the position of being superior. What kind of society do you think he would foster?

There is no longer wholeness in our way of thinking and this very lack of wholeness is what is bringing about the fragmentation in the family. But where would you find a person who extends wholeness and has a total view?

We have to make corrections at a totally different level. The questions that you are asking are at a level which cannot be answered. But they can be explored and together we can discover. This is friendship. This is humanism. It cannot be commercialized or bought and sold. Without compassion society would fall apart. But now we feel we must pay for it.

With the advent of modern society, the serenity of the human mind is being invaded upon. It no longer has the capacity to learn, for learning requires the space to give and to receive. Affluent society is so inwardly poor that it uses the space to earn more, and to produce more and more illusions, distractions, dependence and artificiality. Everything is geared toward harnessing your energy to make the system work. And you leave your children behind. Then when they grow up you complain that they are not respectful, that they are drawn towards drugs. Do you think that families are breaking up because somebody put a spell on us? *You* are breaking up the family. What is your lifestyle? What are your values?

Are you willing to face the facts of your life? You would plead helplessness and need an expert. Why should you feel helpless? To do the right thing you need not feel helpless at all.

Why are divorces taking place? Because you don't have anything to give. You *want* from your wife; you want her to conform to you and she wants you to conform to her. Each believes in self-centeredness, competition, watching out for himself. Where is love in this? Where is giving in this? Where is the affection of sharing — not just what is yours and hers, but something that is born of goodness?

Have you ever shared affection with someone? It will free you from all desires. Just to be affectionate. When affection holds the hand of a sister, she is uplifted. When affection looks at a younger brother, he is forever protected. Where there is affection there can be no insecurity. Where there is goodness there is no self-assertion.

As life becomes more self-centered, there is a per capita decrease in affection. There is more isolation, which ultimately leads to divorce. Not that being divorced is any happier than being married. It is shifting from one to the other. Trust is gone. You have lost trust in yourself and you have lost trust in the other person. The lack of relationship is painful, and the human brain becomes preoccupied with that hurt. It is inevitable that hurt feelings will occur, but affection could correct it. When there is no affection, you need a lawyer. He sets everything aflame. Where there is one lawyer, he hardly makes a living; where there are two, they both prosper. Where there is one saint, the whole village is tranquil. There is the tranquility of dawn and twilight; he doesn't take sides.

You need friends today to vent your frustration. But that is not friendship. Friendship is where you can share your innermost feelings, where you can talk about how difficult it is to be truly honest and about your lack of contact with that which is eternal — that you feel isolated from everything and want to bridge the gap and come to peace and stillness. Does anyone have a friend today?

Have you ever tried not to allow falseness to touch you? Have you ever felt that your life has made you dependent? Does it pain you that you are not yourself anymore? Do you want to correct it so you can live a life that has rightness in it — where you are not bought and sold?

The wise person never makes survival his first concern. Making a living is the least important aspect of life. Every rat, dog, and monkey survives. We should be inspired by the perfection of creation. The tree has never known a problem. The birds do not have courthouses.

One has to change one's values. Learn about wisdom, its simplicity and self-reliance. You would have something to give that is born out of gratefulness. What you give would be wholesome. Now you give your energy to get a paycheck. And you spend most of it on non-essential things because your life is artificial. You sell yourself because you don't have anything of your own to give. Everyone is compelled to do so and we call it a high standard of living. Our high standard of living has brought in a high standard of violence, high standard of tension, high standard of drugs, high standard of neurotic people. It is time for us to question our high standards.

Thank God that in the middle of this insanity, here and there, are a few people who have integrity. But for the most part, integrity is non-existent. We are being destroyed by the work that we do; it is the enemy of man. There is no reason we have to work so much. To produce what? Missiles, torpedoes, computers? We needed leisure with our children, cities with trees, parks, gardens, and flowers. What has affluence produced? The ugliest cities the world has ever known.

For the sake of our children, it is our responsibility to outgrow the society and to know what is essential and real and what is false. Otherwise, the teenagers will get worse. They haven't received the affection or the love and the whole world is luring them with sensation, pleasure, outlets, and stimulation.

It is unlikely that they will ever express who they really are. They will be drafted and compelled to contribute to the civilization of mercenaries in the offices and factories. The corporation is not concerned with your life. It is only concerned that you are there at nine o'clock, that your clothes are clean, and that you have the skills to produce. It doesn't care where you live or what you do.

What can we expect of teenagers? We have externalized their lives and now there is no reverence, no real sense of beauty. Our clothes are not even real; they are not cotton, silk, or wool. No. They are fashionable.

Do you know what it is like to have a mind that is untouched by the pressure of time and haste? Look at the wonder and the beauty of a carrot. So orange. Just the color of it could stop your mind from chattering. And when you eat it, you have a different relationship with it.

Can you introduce your children to something that is real, something eternal, something that God created? The pit in the fruit, so solid, has the potential to produce a thousand more fruits. The potential of one seed introduces us to the abundance of nature. The richness of life would take man out of his thoughts of poverty and inner littleness.

Only when man knows his own strength and inherent wisdom is civilization on the right path. Then it introduces the individual to his own dignity and he wouldn't fit into an office any longer. He would have his own work, his own expression; he would make whatever he is doing holy; he would not produce a thing that is unessential but something that meets needs. Man cannot live without wisdom. Where there is wisdom there is harmony, tolerance, and "the ears to hear"[1] another's cries. And then you meet your brother with love and goodness in your heart. Wherever that takes place, it is blessed. We can bless every relationship with the goodness within us.

*   *   *

DISCIPLINE

> *PARENT:* It seems very important today for parents to instill a certain amount of discipline in their children so that they can be more responsible in life.

Yes, but are the parents responsible? What do you mean by discipline?

> *PARENT:* It could mean anything from . . .

But how did you mean it, how do most people mean it?

> *PARENT:* Well, it is used in several ways. One is in terms of a habit or good behavior that the child learns which endures throughout his life. Another would be something that is done to the child, as a form of control, in order to shape and correct his behavior.

So our concept of discipline is something that you do — you impose — to correct behavior, seemingly for the child's own good. Can we then see that discipline that we impose in one country is what makes people nationalistic, that makes them want to give their energy to being soldiers or clerks? This discipline herds people into certain patterns of thinking. Do you, the parent, want to protect the child from that discipline or conform him to it? What do you want to do with the discipline?

> *PARENT:* I think most people want to make the child fit into set values which the child himself doesn't know.

Would you call that discipline? Is not your telling the child what to do and not do a form of conformity? Is discipline conformity?

That is how the world knows it, isn't it? It is quite simple. The child is helpless and you mold him. You are conveying your belief system, your prejudices, to the child. That is the discipline of imposing external values.

But what if the parent were aware of that and said, "I don't want to create a duplicate of myself, a carbon copy of my frustrations." What then? The action must always start with the parent because the child is vulnerable. That is the one good thing that the child has that you don't have. He is vulnerable.

What we commonly call discipline isn't discipline at all. Generation after generation we have clipped the very wings of the child, taking away his vulnerability, taking away his spontaneity by putting on him a mold that is made of time and not space.

That is the discipline that we know. It is very important that we get to know it thoroughly. Could you come to a place in you that is not prejudiced and conditioned? By doing so you would make more space within yourself just by seeing how wrong it is and how it has damaged, molded, and confined *you*.

That would be the first step. And then you would realize how difficult it is to cope with those tendencies with which you were conditioned at an impressionable age. You would probably have to struggle for years to get to a point where you are not helpless against those tendencies, those hurt feelings and confusions that have taken the space away from you. You have to come to the horror of seeing it and then move from a space that is not conditioned — not disciplined. See how the conditioning has limited you, made you a citizen rather than a human being. You would begin to touch upon a space within you that is incorruptible. And that is what you would want to impart to your child rather than external conformity. Then your disciplining of the child would awaken him not to be false. If you don't have the space, then you impose. If you have the space, you awaken. The real meaning of the word discipline is to awaken.

If you can bring the child to that awareness, it is probably wiser than any kind of education, any kind of external discipline that you would ever impose upon him. The discipline that is externally imposed is based upon insecurity. But the discipline of that incorruptible place within you, that you are trying to awaken in the child, is based on an awareness of that which is not real, of that which is external to its own nature.

Which discipline would you give your child? The discipline of freedom or the discipline of conformity? Only love is free; only awareness is free. Conformity binds, molds, conditions, and subjects.

We are all trying to educate the child — the schools, parents, and the state. But what is that education?

> PARENT: It is a preparation. The child is
> being prepared to ...

To serve the state, to serve the vested interests of society? By and large, that is it, isn't it? Can we be honest about it?

> PARENT: But then the question comes, if
> they don't have a skill or an ability or training,
> they will be unable to survive in society.

You ask, ''If the child didn't have skills how would he survive?'' All of the animal kingdom survives. The earth actually exists to serve man, and you are talking about survival! ''Without this education, this conditioning, how would my child survive?'' Wake up from your insanity.

Isn't man only endangered by man today? We have to wake up from this illusion. I am saying that either you impose the past upon the child and continue what you call history, or you could come to a moment of sanity and see this for what it is and possibly open the child's eyes to see it for what it is also. Then you have disciplined the child never to be deceived. Because you have disciplined him never to be deceived, you have probably freed him from being dependent. The wise parent would introduce the child to his own awareness, rather than to the outside world.

If you ever touch upon wisdom, then you would no longer be a citizen but a human being. And whether your child is in Hungary or he is in Russia or he is in America, it doesn't matter; that is external. You would introduce the child to the potentials inherent within himself. When that child is introduced to those potentials he would have the capacity to relate with eternal forces, with laws that are eternal.

You want him merely to adhere to the laws that are manmade. But that is conformity, and certainly not education. It is living in the dead of yesterday. It has no morality, no virtue, no goodness, no ethics whatsoever. And you think that unless your child conforms he cannot survive. But you have killed him already. Without discovering his own potentials and knowing that he is part of that which is eternal, he is as if dead. When you have related him with Eternal Laws, however, he won't fit into anything. Such a child brings something of the Kingdom of God to the earth, the light that sustains creation — not the physical light, but the light that he *is*.

We don't want to go that far. Everybody is helpless because we are drained and dissipated. There is no knowing of truth and our lives are a lie. We are all ready to be trained.

And then we talk about wanting to correct the disorder outside. Disorder outside is only caused by the disorder within. A person with order within is part of the universe. He is never isolated from life. Life is compassionate, creative, and independent of personality. But the energy of thought and its friction is what you want to discipline and train the child with, to give him direction, plans, ambition, and status. It is another form of self-destruction.

No wonder when the child grows to be a teenager he has no respect for his parents. They say one thing and they do another. There is no reverence because the parents are hollow, shallow, and superficial. They pass the dull day of their life with the same routine — meaningless jobs, newspapers, TV, petty talk, and quarrels. They are without a voice and laughter. And the children go out searching because they think that they might find it somewhere else. And what do they find? They find some kind of intimacy with their own age group because they can share their prejudice against the adults. And the adults have their own prejudice against the teenagers. But the adults are the ones who started it. When the teenagers meet they have something in common and can laugh about things they don't like in their parents; a bond is formed. But it doesn't last because it is based on reaction.

At its root, everything that is external and manmade is reaction because it is not part of the action of Life itself. There is only one Life of which we are all a part. That one Life is sustained by a Love that is indivisible. It has no nationalities, no conformity, it is ever giving. Its resources are boundless.

The responsibility of the parents is to introduce the child to the spirit within the body. Then the child would make right use of the faculties and abilities of the body; he would develop the means of expressing the particular gifts and abilities he brought with him to this earth. If a particular child's gift is for growing things, he would grow things and find peace. And you would not train him to be an engineer. If the gift of the child is to play music, you won't train him to be a doctor because if you do he would be false.

I once observed an incident at a progressive, private school in New York which illustrates how even well-meaning parents can impose a false direction on a child. The headmaster had the parents of a six year old girl in his office for a routine parents' conference. In the course of the conversation these parents mentioned that their little girl loved to paint and draw.

"No, she does not," said the headmaster.

The parents protested, saying they had stacks and stacks of her paintings at home. Again the headmaster said, "No, she does not."

They were becoming annoyed and tried to convince him, "Do you think we are lying?"

The headmaster, whose school allowed the children to freely choose their activities during the course of the day, was not persuaded. "If your daughter loved to draw," he said, "she would be doing it here, too. She does it at home because that is apparently the only way she can get your attention and approval."

If the parents had their way, one day their daughter would be convinced she wanted to be an artist and she would be sent to the best art school money could buy. She would probably die without ever knowing what she really wanted to do. That is how misdirected most of us are.

God entrusted the parents with the function of awakening the child to his own identity, the holiness of which encompasses the whole universe. Each child has the inherent potential to be God-like, for he is an extension of God, unlimited and absolute. Your responsibility is not to limit your child. That is what we do when we encourage him to identify with the body and the physical faculties of the brain.

First find out what are the abilities your child brought. When you do not have the love, you send your children away. Baby sitters, cribs, schools. The child could be without imposed schooling until he was seven or eight. Now they are sent at three and even younger. All those years of affection are taken away and they feel lonely but don't have the words to tell anyone. And then when they are teenagers and can express themselves a little more, you want to confine them. But you didn't give them the love and the affection that they needed.

The home is not a home so the children leave. Women work today; they don't want to be mothers. They want to be wives and are as interested in variety as the man is. The woman of today is not necessarily satisfied with one husband. And there is not even one husband for most of them. It is just flesh and stimulation. We are ruled by sensation because we don't have anything of our own, eternal self to give.

> PARENT: In what way could we change the quality of our lifestyle so that it would move away from the direction of stimulation to which we are all prone?

The first thing that you would have to move away from is the pressure of time. Can one meet the child with leisure? Could you give that quality of purity and space to the child?

Then you are responsible for being a parent. Then you are responsible for being a teacher. And certainly you have something to impart that the child needs to learn. But let your learning be an awakening of the child's own potential; don't try to fit him into society.

I think parents need to read certain books. There is one that Mr. J. Krishnamurti wrote entitled *Think On These Things,* (Harper & Row, 1964) which addresses fundamental issues of education. Krishnamurti's writings are the best ones to start with and to end with, for he doesn't teach, he awakens. In this book he shares with students, teachers, and parents who participate and pose questions.

There is no such thing as teaching, only sharing. And what is shared is always eternal. It makes space and lifts the pressure of time. It gives one the gift of Divine Leisure and you become your own self, expressing your own beauty, your own goodness.

FEAR

> *PARENT:* We have a difficulty with our child. She wakes up every night with fear. The fear takes different forms, but fear seems to be the issue. How can we end a child's fear that seems to be innate?

The first question is what is the source of fear? Unless we get to the source of it, we will associate it with a certain incident or a certain occurrence. Fear itself is the basic issue, not how it expresses itself.

> *PARENT:* Our tendency is to look for some incident the fear might be related to — that she is afraid of the dark, or afraid of noises, or having nightmares.

Look at the incident, but only in order to get to the root of it — the fear in mankind as we know it.

I wonder if anything else in creation knows fear? There might be fear in the jungle, the fear related to survival. There is a natural response — sharp reflexes, speed, heightened sensitivity. Faculties develop to respond adequately to danger. There is alertness. But that is not the case with psychological fear. We have to understand what fear really is in order to respond and deal with it in the child.

Sometimes the child wants attention. The mother takes her and pampers her and gives her what she wants. From then on it could be the need for affection and you call it fear. So there is a great deal we have to look into before we say fear is the issue.

One must question. "Is it lack of affection? Or is it fear?" That places a challenge before the parent. But we want to make the child's issue the problem, we want to make the child the patient — correct it in her. Could it be corrected in the child without the correction in the parent? To correct fear in the child, we must first correct it in ourselves.

But we rarely want to deal with the source. It is an opportunity for the parent to find out how fear comes about. It may have nothing to do with what is external.

The person who has freed himself from fear, who has given the attention and discovered how fear works — where it originates, how it can be dissolved, how it can be dealt with — has a gift to give to all mankind. One person who becomes attentive to that. One child has raised a question about being afraid and one, rare parent has the space, the intelligence, the love, the goodness, to find out what that is. That parent has given all children in the world a present.

Why is it that we want to find ways of expedience and evade the discovery of what fear is? That parent would have to discover that fear and thought are connected, that where there is no thought, there is no fear.

Maybe at one time, the child got frightened. Now that memory produces fear when something similar happens, and every time the fear gets stronger. How are you going to free the child from the thought that produces fear in the mind? Can you free the child from his own mechanism of producing the fear?

In actuality, in life, there is no fear. Fear is manmade. All wars are born out of fear and insecurity. It is a very rare person who has solved that problem. Then he has the love to give to the world.

If you want your child to be free of fear, you have to change your lifestyle. Then you will give the world a different child. It is not something another can analyze, diagnose, and prescribe a solution for. The parent must take the responsibility of finding out how fear originates and how thought maintains it. The parent has to come to an intensity of awareness that precedes thought. In that state there is no fear. Are you willing to live that kind of lifestyle? Are you willing to pay that price? The price is not money, it is just being interested. If you loved your child, you would, wouldn't you?

Then you could make her aware that fear exists in her memory. She tells herself she is afraid and then the body, or the brain becomes afraid. You say, "Well, she will keep on believing she is afraid." Of course she will because you have not brought her to a state that precedes thought. Can you free her from that deception without bringing her to another wholeness, to another energy, another vitality that is untouched by thought?

We want to play a role with the child. We still have fear, but we say: "Don't be afraid. It's only your thought." But have you ever noticed how children listen to children because they are not playing roles, one is not correcting the other?

It is the primary responsibility of the parents to see that the child is never conditioned and that as he grows he cannot be deceived by his own thought, or by anyone else's.

Where is the man who will not blame himself, nor his wife, nor his children, nor his job? Today, everyone blames the teenagers. They are disobedient, overly stimulated, drawn to sex, drugs, and violence. We think we are all right and the teenagers are bad. What kind of thought is that? A thought that has no love in it, no forgiveness in it, no goodness in it. Who do you blame? If you blame society, you invariably blame yourself also. But there are no problems where there is no blaming.

I don't accept problems as real. It's not that problems do not present themselves. It's just that they can be met adequately and dissolved right then and there. Is there a problem when you are clear? Come to clarity and from there you can make a decision. Rarely do we make decisions. We make choices based on preferences, advantages, and loss and gain. But clarity does not have self-centered considerations.

The problem comes and we want to get away from it. But see how nice it is to meet it headlong. We all have that capacity — to undo, dissolve, and come to clarity — so that we need not ever carry the burden of problems in our mind. The time to solve it is the minute it appears. But we want to solve it in our own favor. That is really the problem.

We have to play with our children. We don't play anymore; we don't even laugh anymore. That is really the American way of life. We are reduced to spectators.

Instead of making children responsible we give them bouquets of fear — over simple things like crossing the street, cutting with a knife. We need not ever tell children what to do if we would share with them, out of mutual interest, in order to make them responsible. That is how friendship is born, laughters are born. And that relationship keeps the parents alive. But we think we are doing the child a favor taking them out to the park. Then self-consciousness comes in between parents and children because they are playing a role.

Communication is important and bonds need to be established. It requires stillness. When two people meet within that stillness, there is a bond and you want to hug one another. Mischief and laughters are the gifts of God to both the parents and the child. Children love to be caressed. In fact, everyone does. Somehow we have taken the affection out of life — between husband and wife, brother and sister, friends. We don't have the leisure to be affectionate.

We have become very pleasure-oriented. And pleasure is regulated by sensation; the sensation of food, sex, and loud music is all we know. Slowing down has become the problem. Eighty percent of all problems are born out of lack of relaxation. We don't even relax in friendship. Affection demands relaxation.

It is not duty-bound, nor does it have the pressure of time in it. When you are spontaneous you are not regulated by thought. Something of your real nature comes in and that real nature has something of life in it, not just the way you are conditioned.

When there is thought, you have habits and you are conditioned. Play is an opportunity to step out of that. Within the realm of self-consciousness there is no play, there is caution and calculation.

If you could get interested in doing something with the child, then you've got a friend. Interest takes you out of self-consciousness and introduces you to the energy of the present. It can give to any situation, rather than assert and demand. But we don't want to take interest in the child's interests. We don't want to interrupt our routine.

Any person who wants to know what relaxation is, in the final sense, would discover that he can't have any goals in life, no direction, nor plans. As a good citizen you'd say that's worse than not having arms and legs. But it never occurs to us that *then* you may be an extension of the Will of God. It does not need any direction because it is always with the stillness of the present. That is the action of Creation extending what is eternal. Peace, love, light, and joy would be present. Why would you want to have a direction?

The Will of God is the ever-present. It doesn't have a past, doesn't have a future — so it doesn't have a goal. The tree is the tree and it grows because it is part of the same extension. True life has no direction, no plan, because it doesn't have insecurity. It is part of the indivisible energy of love called the Will of God. To be one with the Will of God is to be a light for all times, for all men that would come after you.

PARENT: How did we come to this very alienated, isolated state?

What we are seeing now began not too long ago in this country. World War II brought prosperity and the mentality of "get rich quick." Salesmen were rampant and ladies without much depth and character betrayed themselves by wanting to be something other than what they were. They began to wear a mask. Everything became artificial and fashion came into being. In one glance, can we see all of that as a background?

Where did it start? It started from conception. There are certain vibrations when the creative moment of conception takes place. Although the action takes place within the body it is an action of life, not an action of the body. What kind of vibration does the body have that is going to produce a child? Is it preoccupied with lack? With desire? Constantly looking for something outside itself? Or is there contentment in that womb, in that person? That will determine a lot about the way the child is brought up. He is forever affected by the atmosphere of nine months in the womb.

And then with boy babies, they are circumcised very soon after they are born. Have you ever thought what that does? To introduce the child, as soon as he is born, to pain? It is one of the first things that is registered on his sensitive brain. Will he ever forget that first touch? He doesn't know the name, but for the rest of his life that memory will be with him.

How many mothers have felt, "I want my child to be different?" Can they afford it? Can they afford to come to something natural? We don't even have natural thoughts. The schooling we receive distorts our brains and makes us controlled by a sense of lack.

What is the lot of a woman today? Deprived of true affection, she can only be desired. That is not love. Could you love someone without desire? Really love him or her? How would you touch that person without the desire? There would be compassion. But we don't know that. We can't even give that to our sisters. We are so stimulated.

Life meets needs. In India, it is the householder's responsibility to feed the man who is in search of God. Observe what the efficiency of war produces and how it affects the economy. Today, there are so many surplus goods in the world, but the business mind doesn't want to meet a need. We sell things but we don't meet needs. We would rather throw away butter, wheat, milk than meet the need of poor and starving people in the world.

> "The twelve-nation European Community spends $63,000 an hour to store 1.4 million tons of unsold butter in refrigerated warehouses. Its mountain of skimmed-milk powder rose this summer to 988,000 tons."[2]

What kind of parents produce the kind of child who will not meet a human need? Are these children expressions of our helplessness?

Children who have not received love or human kindness cannot be contained. We are totally identified with the body and the body is producing degenerate children. But you are not only a body. That is what must be discovered. We have to shift our identity.

PARENT: How do you keep a child's innocence intact?

The child is born innocent. His innocence is not impressed by status. He responds to a totally different sensitivity. The child hates no one. He doesn't know duality. This is God's gift. Your responsibility is not to impose your conditioning on his innocent mind.

How do you protect innocence? You protect the child by awakening awareness in him. But you can't awaken the awareness in him if you don't even know what it is yourself. We don't know what the holy action of creation is. The divine action of Life takes place in it. If we abuse it, and it becomes a pleasure, then we love each other for awhile before our minds and opinions change. It has nothing lasting to it. Nowadays, children are growing up without fathers. And you know the rest.

You may say, "God's gift? I gave him birth!" Oh no you didn't. The action of creation takes place when a man and woman come together. That action is involuntary, for it is an action of Life. It is entrusted to you when you come to a certain age.

Begin to wonder! We are never struck by the wisdom and perfection of creation. Inspiration doesn't seem to hit us anymore; nothing seems to affect us. The very birth of the child! That the conception is involuntary and the child is entrusted to the woman who is giving and passive!

If we could only observe the innocence and holiness of the child, then we would learn what to do. We learned something about Crystal today. The teacher accused her of something. I said, "Listen, baby, don't get into rights and wrongs. Jesus said, 'RESIST NOT EVIL.' Can you still love your teacher? Are you going to get affected?" She said, "No, I am not affected."

But I see why the teacher would get upset with her. She can't sit for five minutes. The parents must discover what the child needs and resolve to provide that. What can we do to bring the child to stillness? She has so much energy, so much vitality in her, and she wants to do things; that is beautiful. What can we do to bring the child to stillness? We had suggested that she massage her mother's feet, and her daddy's feet, because when you are massaging someone's feet you come to stillness if you are really present. The same with washing clothes by hand or cutting vegetables — anything like that has the capacity to bring the mind to silence.

If you want to know a child, or anyone, you have to come to self-giving. It is a principle. You can massage the child's feet to calm her, and come to silence together. Then you can teach her to massage your feet.

We have been taken away from what is natural. There is no direct contact with the mud and the feet, or the eyes and the tree. Some of us do not even know what love is. If we knew it, we would give it. Love is something you must give. In the giving you know that it is love. When that isn't there you make demands out of your unfulfillment. And there are thousands of miles of shops everywhere to cater to that unfulfillment. The offices keep the shops open. There is nothing left but money.

Also, we must have order in our lives. There is order in the universe. This order is mathematical. Nothing could function without order. You have a pen; the pen has order. If all the ink came out at one time you couldn't write. A door has order; the hinges give it order. Everything in the heavens has an order. What is the order in your life? Confusion, fear, and insecurity are of disorder. Every time you look at a tree, if you could see it faster than thought, that tree would introduce you to order. Silence is order; activity disorder. We are not related with nature. If we were related with nature its mystery would move us. Everything in nature exists to take us out of our confusion and disorder.

CHAPTER FIFTEEN

15

TALKS WITH PARENTS
Part II

RESPONSIBILITY

Bringing up a child demands responsibility. But we are irresponsible people. Mercenaries. We just have jobs. We are trained; we work; we are told what to do. That's all we know. And this is respected. Nobody realizes that people conditioned in this way from childhood are incapable of responsibility.

At the irresponsible level divorce is all right, selling somebody wrong things is all right, doing unessential work in an office is all right, war is all right. People with authority and power use employees for their own ends. The employee is the pawn. That is what life is reduced to. Parents don't even have time to be with their children.

Most of us have been irresponsible all through our lives. How are we now going to be responsible? What are we going to give our children who are growing up in an atmosphere of ir- responsible people? It seems overwhelming. How can one cope with it? There are so many factors. The child grows up and meets other children — irresponsible children — coming from irresponsible homes where there are no ethics, no standard, no conviction, no integrity. They know nothing about what it is to be a human being.

See how things have degenerated! There is no wisdom in society and none in us. How few parents have the integrity to say, "I won't do meaningless work. I live a simple life and am somewhat self-reliant. I cannot afford to be nationalistic because I have seen that it leads to war. *I am as God created me.* [1] I am a responsible human being."

Today, mankind in general is body-bound, regulated by the gluttony for food, the vanity of clothes and makeup, and the sensation of sexuality. What else is our economy based on? Schools fill the function of training you to go and work. No longer do you receive an education. Education would mean finding out who you are and awakening you to your own potentials. Instead, specialization is emphasized. You are not a human being — you are an engineer, a computer programmer, a teacher. But what are you going to teach? What you learned from another? One would think a teacher would teach everything in creation because he has insight and has ended his separation from God. These are high standards, but they are accessible to a man or a woman who would not compromise.

One should question: "Why does a child need two parents?" Little bit of a thing, why two parents? Nature could have devised a way in which only one parent was needed, that a woman on her own could have a child. Why is it that there are two? Because that's the kind of energy needed to responsibly bring a child up in a balanced way and to awaken other potentials in the child. It would require two parents because the child has two polarities.

If there is only one parent, the child can get the better of him, no matter how good that parent might be. It is imbalanced to begin with because the child is born of two polarities, and he needs both. Therefore, wisdom demands that if they have brought a child into being, whether they like each other or not, they have to be responsible for the child and find other potentials within to cope with the situation.

A function of the child is to bring the parents together. That is in his own interest and in the natural order of things. One must heed Life as Life is. To the degree the single parent can come to transformation and a different way of thinking, to that degree he will bring about a wholeness for his child in one way or another. If the parents are separated and harmony or reconciliation is not possible, it may be possible for the grandparents to help raise the child. Could you, the mother or father who has the child, yearn to come to harmony with your parents if they are alive?

We have to reverse the process of separation and abandonment and become closer with one another. Something else will take place if you are willing to consider this. There are other potentials in harmony. Divorce is born out of isolation but you need not isolate yourself. If one parent could make this change you would see something else happening that cannot be predicted. But correction must be made for its own sake, not with the condition that things will happen in a certain way. That is wisdom.

Parents, especially single parents, have to be aware that very early on the child begins to manipulate. They must be watchful not to harm the child by agreeing with him all the time, thus depriving him of strength. If the child can manipulate you, you are encouraging a dependence, a weakness, and a trait in the child. First the child has heredity, now he takes on the parents' weaknesses. And parents let him get away with manipulation in the name of love. But that is not love; it is just sentiment — *your* need for affection. And it weakens the child.

One must give the child the space and the freedom. Don't try to make the child an adult. Let him play, be carefree. In modern society, children have to learn so much so fast that they don't have time to play. That's criminal. I don't see why a child has to go to school at such an early age. But since they need office workers, the child goes to school so they can have the mother come to work.

We don't have extended families anymore. It has become rare to have grandparents, aunts, uncles, nephews, and cousins living nearby — so that the child is part of a larger family. The truth is that the child is everyone's child. But when one is isolated, there are only limited ways of coping. That one parent suffers and so does the child. And there is degeneration with each coming generation. More irresponsibility. There is little the mother or father can do.

Where is the love? Love would require some responsibility. Can you say, "As long as my child is this age, I will not work?" In this society nobody is going to listen to you. It is not a society that welcomes a child, or tries to produce a child that is God-like. While, in truth, humanity may even *exist* just for that purpose.

So the parents have to take the responsibility to bring the child to a different perspective — one of wholeness. They have to live an ethical life. The parents should both decide which way to raise the child. "We'll give her the space she needs but certain things she must not do." Start with a few small things. "On these we are uncompromising. And when she comes to you and says, 'Daddy's telling me this.' You say, 'What daddy is telling you is what is right. I want you to know what reverence is. He loves you.' And when she comes to me, I'll say, 'No, I'm sure of one thing, that your mother loves you and she knows; we owe her that respect. Listen to her.' "

Then, even if the parents disagree with one another, as far as the child is concerned, they are united. Both must become *one voice* so the child doesn't think, "This one I can get to."

And the child is going to pester you like nobody's business. But soon she will find out that you are not the same mother, not the same father. You have to change. It's going to be a little harder for the mother because the child is going to melt her heart. But the child requires for you to impart this strength to her.

When she's being difficult, you could say: "If you keep dragging this thing on, you'd better go to your room." Once you've said something, that's final. Once you have said it there is no conflict in the child. What is said is *so.* Do everything possible, but when you see a pattern you have to put to an end, then act.

There are terribly undisciplined children in this country. Why? Because there's lack of love. Everybody is busy and the children's characters are neglected. Respect is a very important thing. The parents have to free the child from the mania of wanting and feeling, and introduce him to another strength within. The parents must bring him to an awareness of rightness.

Awaken a sense of responsibility in the child without punishment, without blaming, without making the child feel guilty. Do it with a great deal of love and intelligence. Thus, while you are awakening the child, you are also being awakened to what love, intelligence, and responsibility are. We have to learn as much as the child.

* * *

THE SOLAR PLEXUS

Each parent has a bond with the child. If you were a sensitive mother and your child was in China and had an accident, you would know it. There were animal experiments made in Russia in which mother rabbits were wired electronically and then their babies were taken in a submarine to the bottom of the ocean and slaughtered. When the baby rabbits were killed, they found that their mothers registered a reaction.[2]

Life is one. This is not a theory; it is a fact. It is most prominent between parents and children. The child always feels the mother and the mother feels the child.

This bond between parent and child is related to the solar plexus. So little is known about it by science. It functions with invisible silver cords which extend regardless of distance. When the solar plexus is seen by another eye, we see that the cords come out like strings, or wires. When your heart wells up, the solar plexus energy then goes to your child. Or the child runs to the mother because the child is connected in this way also. When I am loving a child all her little wires are around me. And when she wants something, I see her solar plexus activated, and it activates mine.

When there is such a strong bond we can see that no situation is hopeless. If we're going to be responsible, ethical, loving, we have to go beyond bodies, beyond physicality. We have limited children to physicality and thus they can be made into good employees, better soldiers, avid customers. As long as you bring people to a lower level, society flourishes. But if you aspire to other values, you discover what a curse and a disease affluence is without wisdom and without simplicity.

Children are beautiful all over the world. But the environment in which we bring them up has its effect. What is our environment in the West? Television, movies, and videos are shaping the environment. Where are the wise people of this country? Individually, I know there are parents who are conscientious, but it hasn't become a larger issue in which it is everyone's concern and responsibility to protect the child's space from being intruded upon by artificiality. It almost seems too late. Nobody listens.

But because the bond is there, the parent can communicate something that God would like to be communicated to the child, that a real parent would like to communicate to the child. It's not impossible; it's merely that the other way of life has become so much of a habit.

It is not necessary to feel limited and defeated. Rejoice in the fact that you are entrusted with a child to be brought up responsibly. If that is the value you hold dearest to your heart, then it's done. It doesn't take time. This very day you can come to a new perspective.

* * *

THE RIGHT PERSPECTIVE

We have to live a life that would be approved of by the Christ. It cannot be *belief;* it has to be *lived.* Your values have to be much larger than self-interest. The child needs to be exposed to that which is eternal, that which is virtuous. This is very rare in the world today. How would you raise a sensitive child? You would be blessed to know that with the sensitivity of the child comes the atmosphere to raise him.

The parents have to change when the child is born. Their superficial life must go. Now they have to be a couple that personifies responsibility. If they have any options, when difficulties arise they would justify and compromise. But the child needs their harmony because he is a creation of the two. Disharmony weakens the child and promotes conflict. Thus he will never know conviction or the strength and faith that come from harmonious parents.

The birth of a child should make divorce impossible.

If we can come to the right perspective — that we are going to live by different values — then eighty percent of the agreement is there. Both parents certainly want to do everything to have harmony between themselves and with the child. The little issues can get corrected if the larger perspective becomes clear. We have to take it out of the realm of problems. First see this is how you want to live.

> *PARENT:* My husband is not affectionate and I don't know what to do. Could you help me to approach this problem?

There is a beautiful story of King Louis of France and Antoinette. Antoinette was a princess from Austria; her mother was the queen of Austria. The marriage between Louis and Antoinette was an arranged marriage. Antoinette was very attractive, fiery, and well cultured, but her husband would not have anything to do with her. She must have had a great nobleness about her, a sense of dignity, but he would not even look at her, or touch her. He had no sexual inclinations at all.

Because she was dignified she couldn't even tell anyone. But she never looked at another man.

For over a year, possibly years, it went on that way, day in and day out. Louis and Antoinette would have large parties with ballroom dancing and here is this beautiful, red headed young girl — probably everybody desired her. But she was poised and made no demands. Her mother wrote wonderful letters to her saying the only thing in this life that brings happiness is one's relationship with one's husband. She couldn't tell her mother, ''I don't have a husband.'' She remained who she was, with her own strength; she didn't have alternatives; she didn't have choices.

After years and years, one night Louis reached out and held her hand. It's probably the most poetic action in the history of France. She could not describe the beauty, the joy, the happiness. It was her goodness that brought it about.

What it is that moved Louis is what we have to discover. He didn't want sex, obviously. That was not his need. It was the goodness and the virtue of the other person that would not compromise which flowered and merited something. What kind of inner strength she must have had! Just their holding hands — from there it began. It totally turned the tide.

One must start from strength. Your own goodness would win the other. You need never be weak. Just see what your strength would do. And then you will have that strength to give to your daughter. She is going to have boyfriends right and left and the boyfriends would want her. If you don't have the strength, how are you going to impart it to her? Everything that happens has something divine in it and can bring us to strength. Weakness and gratification exist everywhere, but strength does not exist. We have to surround this child with that kind of strength — that we live for something nobler than body needs. When you are with goodness, you will see that body needs will get met also. If one person is stable the whole family is stable.

Bring a correction in yourself irrespective of your husband. Then you are no longer the same person. And that will make him change too. He will have to find out what constitutes being a husband and a father.

You have to bring this kind of nobleness into your family. Overcome petty-mindedness, reactions, ''wantings.'' Prepare yourself in this way. Learn to love one another. Once you have become strong you will have no problem whatsoever with your husband. Each person must make the correction within himself first.

There is a condition to everything in life. When the Author of *A Course In Miracles* says: *I will teach with you and live with you if you will think with me,*[3] it contains a condition. It is not child's play. It demands application, and then all options fall away.

But in today's world relationship is fast disappearing. There is not the deep sharing of our aspirations in life. We are working people. No one has imparted other values to us.

If you would go to a real Teacher, the first thing he would teach you is *dharma* — the life of virtue. Simple things — wash your hands before you eat; bless your food; bless everything you do. Parents must learn to impart something eternal to their children. That is real education.

> *PARENT:* How does one encourage stillness or silence in a child?

There is a quiet that you can demand of a child by imposing your will on him. And then there is a natural quiet that already exists in the child who has not been crushed, forced, or walked over. This quiet can be nurtured.

With your daughter yesterday, I noticed that she had the quiet — she was in a different state. But then all of sudden she got up and left. What do you think she needs to learn? Let us give this some attention and learn from the situation. We observed that she was quiet in a natural, normal way; she was not made to *be* quiet. So then why did she get up and leave? Anyone else in that state would not want to get up.

Continually we have to be able to learn. If we already ''know,'' then that is a block to learning. What we know doesn't apply to the living moment. If all I know is that she should be quiet, then I will not be her friend.

What I observed when she got up and left is that there are impulses and urges in a child, like there are urges and impulses within us. When the urge comes, the child heeds it. We have to teach her — the parents can teach her by doing it first themselves — that those urges are going to come because that is the function of the brain. ''The brain is not going to let you be quiet. It is going to make sure you get up and go. But this you must master. This is what you are to be in charge of, not let the impulses be in charge of you."

Start from the basis that she is quiet. Then the impulses come. She doesn't know what to do with them; it is natural for her to pursue them. We pursue them all the time and it creates conflict. Can we teach her something very different? That sitting down quiet is one part of it; then, there is another part — when the physical body, the brain, uses the energy of silence to take her away. How are we to bring about this kind of strength and awareness, that unless one is in charge, dignity and poise would not come into being? Only a person who can contain his urges and impulses will have a face that is unique. Silence acts upon urges and impulses and they begin to subside. It is a critical point; otherwise, the urges act upon the silence.

But we can't ask the child to do things we don't do ourselves. That is always the difficulty. We have to assume some responsibility for having the privilege of telling the child what to do.

*   *   *

PARENTS

How difficult it is for us to receive love! We have been harmed, damaged, perverted. We cannot really love anyone — our mothers, our fathers, our wives, our children — not really. We use them.

When the child is born we can't recognize his innocence. If we did, we would protect it, not indoctrinate it. Instead, we put our insecurity and all our prejudices in the child. That is what we are teaching our children. Everything is based on irresponsibility. And finally, when you meet someone who is responsible, you can't understand his language, you can't receive.

It is the parent that has to be educated. Then that parent can transmit something real to the child. Now the mother has to work, prepare meals, and take care of the home. Observe. What is society doing for the child? The child is then left in schools to which he, naturally, doesn't want to go. It is difficult to break loose of the bondage of the system. The die is cast. We have to make a real, heroic effort to free ourselves.

If the child lives in a house where the bed is made, clothes are hung, towels are folded, then that child obviously has order without your trying to tell him anything. The action must begin with the parents.

This is one of the only cultures where the child is regarded as an interference. We give them anything to entertain them. Television has become the third parent. There is not the right relationship. The right relationship is to bring the child to some kind of discipline. She may not like it, but without it the system will shape and condition her.

In other cultures, children are always taught to work and they love it because they love to imitate. It is natural. Crystal has made an agreement to help with the cooking every day after school. We have to teach her that she can't just say one day, "I'm going to play with Libby." She has to learn to be consistent. She can see Libby at other times. That is what I mean by order.

I said to Crystal today, "There are a few things you are not going to like to do. If I were your age I wouldn't like to do them either, so you have a friend. But I have seen, Crystal, that if you only do things you like to do, then you will never know the strength in you. You will always go for the weak things. Since you want to find the strength in yourself, you should welcome things that are difficult."

Because the children who are being born today are so exceptional, you can talk directly to them. They understand so much, so quickly. But we need to be mindful not to be a teacher of ideas to children. We must find meaningful ways to relate.

The lives of great people are wonderful for children to be exposed to — people like Florence Nightingale, Helen Keller, Thoreau, Lincoln, Gandhi, and others. Children love to hear what they were like when they were children. It is also important to expose them to the lives of the great Incarnations — Jesus, J. Krishnamurti, Lord Buddha, Sri Ramakrishna, Ramana Maharshi, Lord Rama, Lord Shiva, Lord Krishna.

> *PARENT:* I find that I am embroiled in problems — my own and other people's. What would help me change this?

The God-lit man gives one simple key. And it is worth lifetimes because it is unlikely we would ever come upon it ourselves. When I first met Mr. J. Krishnamurti, he said to me, "There are no problems apart from the mind." Since hearing that I have never been the same. It silenced me for years.

All problems are self-made. Nobody has ever given any one of us a problem. All problems are self-created. "There is no problem apart from the mind." If you could remember this key you would never be subject to reaction; you could free yourself and stand independent of the mortal fuss. You would be the one person without a problem because you have realized there are no problems in life. There are problems at the level of conditioning but there are no problems in life. It is this truth that will introduce you to your own holiness. And that you need to know.

God is the Light in which I see.[4] Unless we see with this light we will only see a fragmented world. We will be caught in our opinions about that fragmented world and never see reality. That is the tragedy. It is at the cost of seeing reality. To see reality we have to come to awareness. *God is the Light in which I see* all that is holy, all that is real.

There is a beautiful story of a monk in Peking — full of passion, fire, radiance. He wears a saffron robe of renunciation and a shawl and he sits in meditation. The people of the area are affected by his Presence as they realize they have a God-lit man amongst them.

Then a strange thing happened. There was a rich man with a beautiful daughter. One day they discovered that she was pregnant. This was an outrage. She could be stoned. They had a problem. When they asked her who the father was, she was so frightened she said that the father was the shining-faced monk. They were shocked. ''Why that scoundrel!'' Now they really had a cause. Word spread like wildfire. They sent the girl away to have the baby and when the child was born they brought it to the monk. ''This is yours. Take it, you wretch!''

Do you know what the monk said? He said, ''Is that so?'' They put the baby in his arms and walked away. The baby began to cry and the monk went and begged for milk. After a while he walked out of Peking. Nobody missed him. Everybody knew the truth.

Some time later the girl who accused him was bothered; her conscience was disturbed. She went to her parents and told them that the father of the child was not the monk but the fisherman's son. They were horrified. ''Oh God, what have we done?'' They went running all over to find the monk. When they finally discovered him, they apologized and said, ''This is not your baby. We are so sorry we accused you falsely.'' And they took the baby from him.

What do you think he said?

''Is that so?''

If you are free of reaction, you never get caught in the mortal fuss. Now you have the key that can liberate you from your problems — *THERE ARE NO PROBLEMS APART FROM THE MIND.* All problems are self-made. Don't ever believe in your helplessness. You would not be reading this if you were helpless.

> *The ego thinks it is an advantage not to commit itself to anything that is eternal, because the eternal must come from God. . . . The ego compromises with the issue of the eternal, just as it does with all issues touching on the real question in any way. By becoming involved with tangential issues, it hopes to hide the real question and keep it out of mind. The ego's characteristic busy-ness with nonessentials is for precisely that purpose. Preoccupations with problems set up to be incapable of solution are favorite ego devices for impeding learning progress. In all these diversionary tactics, however, the one question that is never asked by those who pursue them is, ''What for?'' This is the question that you must ask in connection with everything. What is the purpose?* [5]

> PARENT: Why do I sometimes feel so helpless and confused? I like what you are saying, but all I know is that I am very restless. I don't know what to do.

If you look around, you will observe how still everything in nature is — absolutely still. Observe the stillness; come to stillness. Stillness is a state in which you are not of the flesh. But to come to it the body must be in good health, not abused. If it is not in good health, then it is the function of the brain to alert you — you need rest, food, order. As long as we keep driving it, we will not know that which is not of the flesh. Man is becoming more and more restless.He knows activity but not stillness. Activity without stillness becomes self-destructive.

Years ago, when I was in silence, at one point I was very

depressed. I couldn't do anything about the depression. I didn't want to read anything. I would go out and walk on the beach, but when I was out I wanted to be in; when I was in I wanted to be out. Do you know why? Because when the brain doesn't like something, it says, "You should be in Yosemite. You need nature to be silent." Or the brain shows you pictures of yourself doing something else. My brain was projecting lovely images. When I didn't give in to those images the depression came. We become victims of the experiences our brain projects when it is bored. That is where experience is born. The brain starts reminding you. That is the core of the issue and we all avoid it. Mine was an extreme form. If someone told me I would die tomorrow, I would have said, "Why not today?"

But one day as I was walking on the beach, I heard direct words within me saying: "Keep the discontent burning. Don't try to escape it. Don't let it defeat you." I said, "That I will." Nothing external can have power over a man if he can stand firm. After that, something within me burst open. All my energies came into play when I sat quiet. Since then nothing external has touched me. Don't accept any escape. Keep the discontent burning. Otherwise you will never know the reality of your own light.

When the Light of heaven dawns upon the brain, it is no longer insecure, it is no longer confused. It begins to extend that Light, that Love, that Oneness. In the absence of it we remain prisoners of our own personality and idiosyncracies. To know yourself is to know your God-nature, not what society conditioned you to be.

CHAPTER SIXTEEN

16

WORKING WITH A CHILD — CRYSTAL
Part II

Crystal, there is a part in the *Text* of *A Course In Miracles* which reads:

> *A wise teacher teaches through approach, not avoidance. He does not emphasize what you must avoid to escape from harm, but what you need to learn to have joy. Consider the fear and confusion a child would experience if he were told, "Do not do this because it will hurt you and make you suffer; but if you do that instead you will escape from harm and be safe, and then you will not be afraid." It is surely better to use only three words: "Do only that!"*[1]

Crystal, these are words of Jesus. If a parent or a teacher tells the child, *"Do only that!"* they should not have to make big speeches. But if the child doesn't listen to the teacher, to the mother or the father, then they have to go on explaining. If we have respect for one another and I say, "Crystal, don't do that," then right away you should stop doing it. You should not be so interested in the reasons because you know that I love you and what I say is true. There should be that kind of trust between us.

"Do only that!" This simple statement is perfectly clear, easily understood and very easily remembered. [2]

This is true for the child and the parents as well as the teacher.

The Holy Spirit never itemizes errors because He does not frighten children, and those who lack wisdom are children. [3]

CRYSTAL: What is itemize?

He doesn't say, "You did this wrong. You did that wrong. And you did the same thing wrong yesterday." The Holy Spirit just says, "Do only this." Not what not to do, but what you should do.

When we don't have the wisdom, then your mommy and daddy and myself are like children too. A wise person is someone who really knows. Whatever he says is how he lives. I can't tell you not to eat ice cream because it is bad for you and then go and eat ice cream. My words would not have any effect. One cannot tell another what to do if he is not doing it himself.

A wise person is someone who knows truth, love, and gratefulness. He is a friend of everything. A friend of a deer, of a rabbit, of a child, of a tree. The one who is wise is always a friend because the wise person always has something to give. The person who is not wise has nothing to give; he always "wants."

Don't you see that if we ask you if you want to help in the kitchen, you are happy because you are giving? There is always happiness when one is giving. When we don't give we resort to "wanting."

The Holy Spirit never itemizes errors because He does not frighten children, and those who lack wisdom are children. Yet He always answers their call, and His dependability makes them more certain. [4]

Anything you would ask of the Holy Spirit or of Jesus, They would give. You don't even have to ask; They just give. If you know that Jesus is taking care of you, you would say, "Thank you, Jesus, for all that You give." We usually think that we have to take care of ourselves.

Crystal, there are a lot of things I don't know. And I'm so glad that I don't. I always like things just the way they are. If I don't know, then I can ask you; but if I know and you are not included in it, then that's not as nice. So, maybe you like me because I say, "Crystal, how can we do this? How would you like this?" And whatever you say I will consider. A real teacher loves the child and is willing to listen to what the child needs and the child listens to what the teacher asks. So, if I say, "Crystal, do this." Then you would say, "All right."

It is all a matter of friendship and whether we love each other. If there is no friendship, you won't be so willing to do something. If there is no friendship, you would stay with the "wanting." But if there is friendship you would listen. To the degree that we love each other, we are helped to outgrow "wanting." We have more and more "wantings" when we are not happy inside. Can you see that?

CRYSTAL: Yes.

And wherever there is "wanting," there is fear. All your life when you get to be ten years old, when you get to be twenty, forty, sixty years old, you will find that where there is "wanting," there is fear. Until you find happiness inside of you, you are going to be "wanting." But when you are full of joy inside, whatever you do would be honest and would express your happiness. Happiness expresses happiness. If I am not happy then I express "wantings." The happiness is in everyone, but very few people know that it is there. The Course says: *I am the light of the world.*[5] Very few people, Crystal, have ever found that light.

To find the happiness inside, you have to relax. If the four of us cooperate — Acacia, John, myself, and you — we can make the space for you to find the happiness inside. Crystal, it took me fifty years to find it. I would like you to find it now while you are a child. I would like your mommy and daddy to find it now also — to find that which God created, not what the shops give.

Crystal, it is easy to say that you would like that now, but what can we do when you are stimulated? What do you think would help?

> CRYSTAL: It would help if I had something to do that takes a long time. Some kind of work or something that takes awhile to finish and I can't do anything else until I am finished with that.

You are so wise. I wish you'd come and sit here. You make me cry you are so beautiful. I feel so blessed to know you. What you said is very true. I would have never thought of that. You are saying that you want to give. In some strange way it is a giving. You really waken me to love inside of me.

Crystal, I wish that you would try to do something for me. I don't want you to promise because I know that it is very difficult, but would you do a favor for me?

> CRYSTAL: Yes.

Would you always listen to your mommy and your daddy?

> CRYSTAL: Yes.

You won't argue?

> CRYSTAL: No.

I want you to always listen to your mommy and daddy

because otherwise you would be lost. They really love you. And they both need you. We all need to change, Crystal. That you are so willing to change gives us the strength that we can change also. And it is so nice that it is possible to bring a child into the world that knows something of love, of truth, of peace; a child that has happiness inside.

How can we help you, Crystal, not to get so stimulated? If you are given a long project that you can be with for awhile, in the doing of it — and you do things so well — you would come to stillness and quietness in yourself. But we don't want to use being busy to come to happiness. I think it is nice that you want to do things, but one must also spend quiet time without working.

I remember when you were younger you used to love sitting quiet. Now you may still like it but it is harder for you. Once you are stimulated you may make yourself sit, but you are not quiet. So how about having a regular time, morning and evening, when you would sit quiet? Maybe it would sustain you through the day.

CRYSTAL: I would like that and I will do that.

That's so nice. Crystal, I don't want to force you to do anything but we have to help you overcome drifting. Otherwise, you will never find the strength inside; you will just work in an office to make money. If you find the strength inside, you will want to do what is meaningful and Christ would accompany you. To be interested in something is the most wonderful thing. Interest overcomes physical laziness and other weaknesses.

*   *   *

John and Acacia, when it becomes the parents' need to be with the child, the child becomes an indulgence for them. Things won't work. Time and time again parents have made that mistake. And the child is exploited. And Crystal is going to understand what is taking place very quickly. She is going to notice whatever is false, especially if she is close to me. That is the only thing I'm going to teach her — not to be false. What a challenge it places before you. How wise creation is to entrust two beautiful parents with a child that is going to weed out the falseness in their lives. Falseness could be over-affection, over-attention. Whatever is false. She won't accept falseness and if you don't get rid of falseness in relationship to her, you will harm her, cripple her.

How responsible we need to be. Never to touch her when it is one's own need. It is for you to decide. Each person has the same challenge. We want to teach the child but if we don't have the ability to learn, we won't have anything to teach her. It's as simple as that.

I can deal with Crystal easily enough, but to deal with adults is more difficult because it is harder for us to change. The issues are psychological. There is an emptiness inside of us. She is to find the happiness within while we need to change our tendencies. If I am always bored and wondering where Crystal is or what she is doing, I have to discover why my mind is wandering, why I am so dependent on her. And if I totally ignore her, I have to find out why I don't know how she is. It's a clear direction. Can one be aware without anxiety or dependence? Everything one does can be false and it can be right also. It requires great discrimination to know the difference.

The basic issue is to overcome and undo one's own tendency of dependence, of indulgence. As you have seen, there is hardly anything that she misses. And when she is stimulated, she may have a need for you and you may have a need for her, and each side can exploit the other. But if that happens now, one day she is going to be like the leaning tower of Pisa. The corrections have to be made within. She is young and needs to learn, but you need to undo your tendencies.

John tells me that she will agree for the moment because that's the right thing to do. But then when she is in the midst of the stimulation in a store, she forgets and she can't hear. Similarly, when we are in the midst of our tendencies, they get the better of us. Inner correction has never been easy. But without inner correction, nothing comes to rightness. Inner correction is the best gift one can give to oneself.

At this age she would be willing to cooperate. But the way she is growing, a time would come when she won't listen to you, especially if your dependence on her continues. She would know there is a weakness and a falseness in you and to that degree she won't listen. We must see that she will never know happiness if we don't awaken the potentials and strength within her to cope. She is free only in God — which has nothing to do with the lures of the earth. The answer for us is inner correction. And the only thing that can correct it is coming to rightness. That means making real changes in one's own nature. If you are never helpless, she won't be helpless. If you are never false, she won't be false.

> *ACACIA:* I don't think I have ever seen my attachment so clearly.

That's what is false — the dependence and the attachment. We even call it love. Most parents become attached when the child is very bright. The child gives the parents status.

> *JOHN:* I see that it is possible to change. It doesn't seem like that much of a challenge.

But attachment may not be aware of attachment. Do you think that people who are attached are aware that they are attached?

> *JOHN:* You might become aware of it if you became defensive when confronted with it. You should become aware at that point that something is going on.

But you have to see, John, that attachment is not fully aware. It would have been corrected long ago if you were aware. Now you have to listen totally differently. See that it is possible for you not to be fully aware. Maybe you can quietly point out to Acacia and she can to you, but don't argue with each other. Listen to each other and try to correct it. Don't argue or give justifications. "Thank you for pointing it out." Attachment is deceptive to begin with, so it will breed other deceptions.

Everybody in the world believes they want to correct themselves, but I have not seen one person who really does.

> *ACACIA:* One area where I feel inadequate is when she blatantly tells me, "No." I don't know how to respond.

The way she was talking shows me that she will outgrow you soon.

When she contradicts you, ask her if Jesus would like her to speak that way? Remember, God would never have entrusted you with this child if the potentials were lacking in you.

*   *   *

What are we going to do with willfulness in Crystal? I noticed today, when Crystal was getting into the car with her mother, that she always wants things "her way." When I asked Acacia how they dealt with it, she said, "We take privileges away." I asked her, "When did I say punishment was the way? If you don't learn to deal with it without punishment, there will be consequences."

Acacia could have noticed, "My goodness, she always wants things her way." And then begin to question, "Is it right to deal with this by taking privileges away? Will that correct this tendency in Crystal?"

Do you know how they deal with willfulness in a child in India? The child is brought up with reverence and parents lead a righteous life. The child is taught never to contradict. I never contradicted my aunt; I would never contradict even those teachers whom I knew were not righteous. It is a self-mastery. Here children are going to be subservient when they grow up — subservient to a system that has no regard for them. And yet they are given the illusion the world revolves around them. It is deceptive and harmful.

*   *   *

Today I was explaining to Crystal that the younger Crystal is coming back to visit. She was happy to hear that. But I said, ''Don't get jealous. I love you and my love would never change. Very few people know what love is. Love does not change.''

She asked, ''Why? Why don't they know it?''

''Because they have 'wantings.' ''

'' 'Wantings?' ''

I said, ''You may want a jacket and then you would want to go to the store to get it.''

''Do you mean I can't go and buy it?''

I said, ''No, that's not what I mean.''

''Do you mean Jesus will get it for me or someone will bring it?''

I said, ''No, He won't give you the jacket. But He will give you an intelligence, a clarity, to understand everything. He will take care that you will never be cold. That is all. Because He gives everything that is needed, He will meet the need of the cold. Not the way we have opened shops.''

Then I went on to say, "You have eyes and they are very sensitive. To protect the eyes, there are the eyelids. Without the eyelids, the eyes could not stand the strain. When the child is a baby, there is milk in the mother's breast because the child cannot go to the shop. The child can't do anything, so it is provided. Then when the child grows up there is no more milk in the mother's breast but there are fruits and vegetables that the earth gives. Every need is met. We think that only by going to the store is it met. You will have enough intelligence to know what to do about the cold — and whatever you needed to keep you warm would be there."

Crystal listened very carefully. I said, "Because God gives eyelids, milk, everything, we have to put our "wantings" away. That is the difficult thing. His love doesn't change. Everybody else's love changes. Today you like this; tomorrow you may not like it. Everything is changeable except Jesus — He never changes."

And then I said, "I love you. And if I cut your hair or teased you or ignored you and you could still say, 'Taraji loves me,' then you have understood what love is. I love you and, if, when the other Crystal comes, you get jealous, then you don't know that my love doesn't change."

Crystal said, "I won't be jealous." I said, "You don't know what jealousy is. When you go to school and you don't get the attention, you feel miserable, don't you? When everybody is giving the other Crystal attention, you need the attention, don't you?" She understood that outcast feeling. "That is what jealousy is. Everybody wants attention. And when everybody gives the other child attention you will see how the change will start taking place in you. Your "wantings" will show up. Your "wantings" will prevent you from love." It really hit her.

In order to have the strength, there has to be one relationship that you do not touch with doubt. Remember my relationship with the Dilawa?* It brought order into my whole life. It becomes your first thought. But if you are going to assess it when the going isn't according to your preferences, then you are not a student. You are still regulated by thought and the personality.

Nobody can be a student unless he gives second place to his personality in relationship with one person, his teacher. Therefore, you must have enormous discrimination before you accept a teacher. It is the strongest relationship in the world. No other relationship compares to it — neither parents, nor wives, nor husbands, nor children. If other things are more important, then coming to transformation and inner correction are not possible. It is as simple as that.

*   *   *

(During a session in which Tara Singh was sharing with the whole group at the Foundation, Crystal started to become restless. — Editor)

Are you tired, Crystal?

CRYSTAL: Not tired, just bored.

You need not be bored, baby. Children need to play. Whenever you feel that way, you ask your mommy or daddy or someone else to come with you. I would say, "Please go and be with Crystal." I don't want you ever to have a bad feeling. I don't want you ever to know depression or sadness. I want you only to know gratefulness, only to know gladness. There is to be no conformity. Whatever you need, we will try to meet.

STUDENT: Crystal will probably never know the kind of acceptance she has found here. The world will want to control her and try to tell her

---

*See Introduction, pages 22-29.

what to do. But you allow her to be herself. What is being given here will always be with her.

We have to do it in another year or she is going to be out of control. She is growing too fast. She is almost eight now. By the time she is ten she will tell us all to go to Timbuktu.

It is very important to keep pace with the way the child is growing. Unless the husband and wife are in harmony, there will be consequences. She is going to grow faster, and they will regret it for the rest of their lives. She needs the atmosphere of shared laughters.

> JOHN: Taraji met with Crystal, Acacia, and myself last night. I saw parts of Crystal that I had never really seen in her. The potentials that started to come to the surface! It was as if I had been introduced to my daughter for the first time.

*   *   *

We usually discipline a child in a way that provokes reaction and defense. It is best not to discipline the child in front of others but help her contain herself. For example, regarding table manners, if I discipline her in front of others, she will learn to defend. It would be better to talk with her later.

Everyone defends against his inability to deal with a situation. If we defend, we do not learn. But when you come to a point where you do not defend, you can be objective. We must help the child to come to that objectivity.

*   *   *

Crystal, if Jesus were eating with you, would you run around? How would you show respect? You would make some demand on yourself, wouldn't you? It is hard to change but if you love someone, you make that demand on yourself. Mr. Krishnamurti was my Teacher. Because I loved him, I learned how to sit, how to talk, how to listen, and live right. If I didn't love him, I would not have learned it.

* * *

(There was to be a surprise celebration for one of the staff members of the Foundation and Taraji shared this secret with Crystal beforehand. Crystal told the person prior to the celebration. When Taraji saw this he confronted her but Crystal tried to evade him by justifying what she had done. Taraji was firm: ''Why did you tell her? That is not friendship.'' Crystal was very affected and cried very hard. — Editor)

Crystal, you must love the truth if you are going to be a student. Everyone justifies, but justifications are never true. Very few people really love the truth; they love answers. Their answers are an evasion — half-truths. Everyone has answers but very few people have the truth. I don't want you to give me or yourself answers. That is not friendship. That is not right relationship.

You have to be honest and never justify or assume, saying, ''I thought this . . .'' When there is fear one does that, but when there is no fear, one can be honest. The main problem of man today, Crystal, is fear. Everyone is afraid to be honest. When you are afraid, you have an answer. But you don't need to be afraid. Mistakes are good; that is how one learns. Without making the mistake you would not have learned to correct it. Now you will never do that again, will you? And now you also know never to justify and never to give answers, but to find the truth within yourself.

CRYSTAL: Yes, Taraji, I will never do that again.

When I asked you why you told Norah the secret, you could have said, "I couldn't resist it." That is honest. I would love that. But cleverness, justifying, saying, "I thought this or that," are ordinary. To be honest is to be religious. If there were one child, Crystal, who was honest, Jesus would walk with that child.

Schools do not teach honesty, Crystal, but if you want to be honest you will get to know yourself as God created you. You will find great happiness inside you — great blessings. And you will not need anything from the outside. Jesus had happiness inside of Him and He was always giving. Your clear, honest voice, Crystal, would be like an eternal note of music.

John and Acacia, we need to raise Crystal so that by the time she is 13 and 14, she is fully in charge, able to handle external activities and distractions and able to reach other levels within herself.

*   *   *

Crystal, last night when you were not well, you hesitated a long time before you said that you were tired and that you wanted to go home. Is it possible that you don't ever have to hesitate again? That you don't have to think twice? If you feel tired, come and tell me right away. I would say, "Yes, you may go home." There should be no second thought that maybe you should not say that. I respect how you feel.

Often, as children grow up, they begin to hesitate before saying how they feel. It becomes a little dishonest when they start thinking too much. I want to have a relationship with you, Crystal, where you can express to me exactly how you feel.

When children want something, they wait until their parents are happy and then ask them. Thinking comes in; scheming comes in. "If I ask mommy, she will say no. But daddy will say yes."

It is very important to have a relationship with one person where you can be who you are, where you don't have to think about it, where you don't have to be nice when you want something and not nice when you don't want something, where you can be spontaneous and express right away how you feel. Supposing a fly sits there. My hand goes this way and brushes it away. I don't have to think: there is a fly, better get it off, and then do it. No. It is immediate and direct.

You are going to see, Crystal, as you grow up, that older people are not spontaneous but children are. It is so nice when children say something spontaneous, like when you came back from seeing your father's friend and said, "He's boring. The most boring person in the world." That was spontaneous. No adult would say that. They will think it is not the right thing to say. The adult would not say what is true and because they cannot say it, something is not right inside.

The minute you feel you are tired and you want to go home, then know you have a friend and a teacher and you can tell me. I will understand that you need your mommy or your daddy to take you home.

But the other thing, Crystal, is that if I said, "No, you cannot leave right now," then you should not contradict me. Just like I will accept whatever you say, you would accept whatever I would say and never ask for explanation. You may contradict other people and say, "No, I'm tired. I want to go." But not your teacher.

Where the teacher is concerned, you should not use thought. One way it is spontaneity; the other way it is trust. It is not subject to right and wrong. I should never have to explain to you why you should go or why you shouldn't go. Maybe your parents could do that, but not the teacher. I never contradicted my Teachers no matter what they said, whether I liked it or didn't like it. Crystal, how do you understand this?

CRYSTAL: That I should say what I feel when
I feel it. Just say it.

Yes. And I will never think it is good or bad; I will think you
are honest and love that. This is one relationship where honesty
is more important. You can tell me anything. No hitches. People
don't like honesty because they always know right and wrong.
All the time they are little judges. And they all have problems.

Honesty is important. But the teacher has the same privilege.
He can say, ''No,'' and you will not question. Not then. Later
on, he could explain it to you and you could say, ''Ah, I never
saw it that way. I was just controlled by feelings. I didn't go far
enough.'' You will learn to go beyond feelings when you love
honesty and have right relationship with a teacher. You will see
how you just get limited to feelings. But you must want to know
honesty first. That is what the teacher can teach.

CRYSTAL: Yes I see that.

There is little spontaneity and little respect for honesty in this
culture. We only have respect for wrong and right. And because
the parents do not necessarily know anything beyond right and
wrong, good and bad, they are fortunate indeed to find a
teacher who can take the child beyond duality, beyond conflict,
so there is no conflict within the child, no good, no bad, no ''I
don't know.''

*   *   *

Crystal, baby, whenever there is something that you want
to do — (many, many times you'll forget, but try to remember)
— see if Jesus would like you to do that? Ask yourself, ''How
would He think about this?'' And then see if you can do without
doing that thing. If you could do without everything, He will
hold your hand and bless you. Nothing external would control
you and you would begin to value stillness more than activity.

Out of that stillness would be born an action that is not activity and He would be with you.

*   *   *

We can observe certain things and get to know ourselves just from the way things are. Before we came into the Prayer Room for the session, Crystal fell asleep there across three chairs. The room is small and we cannot quite fit everyone in with her lying on three chairs. Several of us began to make adjustments because we need the seats, but I said, "No, don't move her. Let her stay there. We will manage."

It is wonderful to have respect for a minority. What is a minority? The child can be told that she must be thoughtful, she must be considerate, she must be this and that, so that you get the two seats from her. All over the world, the minority suffers because the majority has the power. We all follow that trend. Jesus was a minority and the majority crucified Him. This you know as a cliche. When you know the reality of it, then you'll have a different respect for "what is." "What is" is that child is entrusted to all of us. We have never made a demand on ourselves for another kind of intelligence that is of the moment. You might interpret this to mean that we should pamper her. But that is not what I am talking about. If we woke her up and asked her to move, would the child somewhere not know that you do not have the love you boast of, that you cannot give the child the space? She may not get upset, but would you not be showing her your littleness, irrespective of whether the child consciously understands or not? If you have learned to give space to another you are enriched. Have you ever given space to another? If not, then you don't have the space within. But if you have the space within you, then you will give it to another too.

*   *   *

I saw Crystal hanging on to her mother today. Acacia must like it or she would not allow it. She should cope with the issue and find a way to deal with it. I was busy at the time and I didn't point it out. But one does observe. Crystal knows that. Every time she is doing something wrong and I am there, I try not to meet her eyes because I don't want to humiliate her. But sometimes it does take place in a split second and she knows right away. She may not correct it, that's all right; I know that she is aware of it.

So I said to her, "Crystal, it's not right for you to lean on your mother so much. When you grow up you'll find out how parents destroy children and children destroy parents. Always leaning on someone would prevent you from knowing your own strength. This dependence would make you weak and helpless. When you were a very young child you needed to lean, but now that you're growing every day, please try to bring about that balance. For you are not only a child of your parents, you are also a child of God and if you want to know Him you must stop leaning. It is for you to decide."

It was a real communication. This sharing is probably the finest form of teaching. A real teacher teaches Life. He doesn't need books. He always has something to give.

Can you imagine, when one speaks words that are realized, what light they would have, what conviction they would have? The words of a responsible person!

It is so nice to know a child. There is nothing purer than the friendship of a child when it is not sticky. They haven't learned to lie yet. There is less pretention. We should never try to conform the child. It will encourage her to lie.

*   *   *

John and Acacia, I think that there are some changes which have to take place in your relationship with Crystal. She gets stimulated and therefore wants more distractions. The parents, having seen that, discover that it is partly due to them. And they have to change in order to give a different atmosphere — so that it can be healed before the seven years are over. Every seven years the cells change and, during that time, all the limitations that the personality projects must be undone. It's a tremendous responsibility. The child is born of our flesh and blood and therefore she has the same tendencies we have. That is called heredity. If the parents notice a tendency, the parent must first correct it in themselves and therefore provide an atmosphere for the child to outgrow it. Parents have the responsibility to help the child outgrow heredity.

The child brings a blessing to the parents and is blessed by the parents. That is right relationship.

Crystal is going to make you responsible. The child leads man to God. Because you love the child you've got to do something. It takes care of unwillingness. There is nothing like a child in the family. Saints never need them. But worldly people need children.

*　　*　　*

Yesterday Crystal had an accident on the bicycle with John. I telephoned her as soon as I heard and told her that one of the advantages of getting hurt is that she can prolong it, that she would not have to go to school. "Enjoy it. Look at all the good things in it. You are like a queen getting all the attention — that is something to be grateful for! To conform does not take any intelligence; but to take full advantage of privileges does. I learned by learning to outwit the adults. I like children who are mischievous, inventive, and honest."

She said she was going to school tomorrow. I said, "It's not necessary. It won't make any difference. But if you want to learn to be *honest*, that's a different story. Then God will provide you a school. That's not what they're going to teach you at the public school. In most schools, assumptions are all right, projections are all right, justifications are all right. I am going to weed them out of you before they strike root! But I never want you to be afraid to be honest. If you are not honest, schooling will not make any difference.''

When I talked to her about her accident, I told her that accidents are a natural part of life. ''You're going to have more. They're part of the adventure of life. I fell off a camel three times. I take pride in every scar and mark on my body. There are like memories of the mischief!''

I also told her about Alec. (Alec is a fifteen year old boy at the Foundation.) One day he was experimenting with his mother's car, which was parked in the driveway of the Foundation. He thought, ''I'll just pull it out of the driveway for her.'' Instead of putting his foot on the brake he put it on the accelerator and broke down the garage door. Oil was behind the door and it spilled over everything.

When Alec told his mother, he was scared. ''I'll pay for the door. I'll clean up the oil.'' And his mother was upset. When they came to tell me that Alec broke down the garage door of the Foundation, do you know what I said? ''I am so glad, Alec. That is exactly what boys are supposed to do.'' He was shocked and delighted. We all laughed. Since then we have been real friends. Why do we make everything into guilt, fear, and punishment? Children are children. Boys are boys.

*   *   *

Crystal, when you told me yesterday that you wanted to get a kitten, I began to think about it. Do you know why people like pets? Because they are lonely and bored. Animals belong with nature, not locked up because of man's ''wantings.'' If you had a kitten it would have to stay in the house all day. That is not natural for an animal. Animals are meant to be outdoors.

In the beginning, dogs were kept to protect the farm and help with the other animals. Now people have taken them inside and even drive them around in cars. Can you imagine anything more foolish?

*   *   *

Every parent does the best he can. There is hardly a parent that doesn't love their child. But parents have to come to a point where they love the Will of God better than their own ideas. They must do their best and leave the result to whose child it is — God's. But not in a defeatist way. If you are defeated, you won't do anything. So even if God would like you to get him into a better school, if you do not become a co-creator, it is not going to work.

In the end, it is the child's destiny. One should not ever get so fanatic that this is the only way and never mind God. We have to come to the conviction to do our very best — rise to higher purity, to more and more self-reliance, more and more wholeness — and then leave it. There is something you can love more than the child. And that is the Will of God. In the end it is only the Will of God that has no opposite. Only that is right. Isn't it amazing how the child helps to bring about certain corrections in the parent?

*   *   *

Today, I was sitting quiet and then I heard the children in the garden. I couldn't sit quiet any longer — just their voices were irresistible. So I opened the balcony door and motioned to them. They came up so gently sensing the quiet that was with me. When they sat on my lap, they stayed for a long time without moving. We were so affectionate. No words were needed. Something else wells up within — the love for children, the love for life. You experience a happiness that you never knew existed. You could see how Jesus loved children. The Holy Mother, Sri Sarada Devi, said that every child is of God. How can children be what we think they are?

Something within them wells up also when they meet someone who wants absolutely nothing from them. Not wanting anything has become a force of having something to give. Everything is absolutely natural. Very happy and thoughtful, no pressure of any kind, no competition and yet impressionable.

As the little one was putting on her shoes she said, "Taraji, watch. I can tie my shoelaces." And Crystal said, "I couldn't do that at four." One sees that the younger they are, the more capable they are of quick understanding, of grasping something direct.

Most people think that children are important to them, but actually, rarely has the child been important. Giving them geography has been important. Shaping them has been important. Poisoning the child with insecurity, fear and ambition has been important. Our beliefs have been important to us, not children. It is amazing that nature would still allow us to give birth to children. Most of us love children as a duty, but *we* are more important or something else is more important which invariably has its root in status, in something you want to prove, with which you want to justify your existence. I don't have to justify my existence anymore. There is more space and more peace. Children were always important to me, but not in the deep sense in which they are now. Now they are important in that being with them brings one to a state of fulfillment and wholeness.

It is a blessing to be with children and to allow yourself and the children to be. How beautiful when you are not in contradiction. Usually, the only time we are not in contradiction is when we are gratifying ourselves in one form or another. But this is very different. It is so simple and all-encompassing because it doesn't want, and it doesn't *not* want. For the first time, you are true to yourself.

And if you do share something with the children, it is not your own, it is of that moment. And what they share is not something they've learned. It is spontaneous, direct. When you come to that which is of the moment, nothing else that has its roots in tomorrow or yesterday has any meaning. That is the Divine Leisure children provide.

One appreciates that these two children are different kinds of children. I don't think that society can take them over. They have something in them which they will retain. They will always have different values. They are clear about what they want. They are not lost, sloppy, heavy-headed, or dull. And they are very loving. There are probably others like them who are also being raised differently.

Parents at one time used to dominate their children simply because the parents were insecure economically, psychologically, and so forth. But life is training parents now that it is not necessary to pass on worldly insecurity to the child. One need not worry about what they are going to do when they grow up. Nobody will walk over them. They will retain something of their own because they won't as easily be false as other generations were. They are too intelligent, too independent of the world outside. They are connected internally and that is their great strength.

Just giving space and letting them be would be wise. When I say, *let them be,* there is no doing in it at all. You must try to understand this by bringing it into application in your life. Just be yourself and let something else come in. It transcends doing. It is a Presence which can be said to be religious — a state that is not of ideas. When you are not "doing" then your mind is free. The free mind becomes part of something that is not of time and not of "knowing."

When I am still the children sense something in me they never knew before and come to a state where they become interested in a deep way in music or something of the spirit. It brings them to wholeness, a moment outside of time, outside of sentimentality, outside of body senses and manipulation, to another serenity that is an extension of Life.

Then the child begins to express the love in him, that is independent of him. Ideas and opinions are substitutes to love. All our knowing is a substitute for love. Only in love is there no lack. Something else becomes more important as givingness in its natural form expresses itself. It has no names; it is another sensitivity that is not personal. To bring the child to that state the parents must first come to it themselves. They must have it to transmit it.

In ancient times, the parents took the child to the men of Holy Presence to invoke that state in the child, to bring him to rebirth where he knew the actuality of *I am not a body, I am free...* [6] That was the actual beginning of "school." Look where we have come!

*   *   *

LETTERS

September 12, 1986

Dear John and Acacia,

You must have realized by now
that for Crystal to BE what God created her to be,
you, as parents, would not only have to change
superficially and intellectually,
but you would need to live an impeccable life of honesty,
wholly given to God.

Thus the child brings the parents to sanity,
to rightness, and a virtuous life.
We have been brought together.
The Divine Hand is in it.

Much love goes to you,

Tara Singh

*   *   *

December 25, 1985

Dearest Crystal,

Merry Christmas!
This is the day Lord Jesus was born
and we must not tell a lie or be false to ourselves.
If we can do this in remembrance of Him,
then His purity is born within us,
and we become awakened with a new intelligence.

We will never be confused or have problems
because we will think with the pure energy of Jesus' thought
that will free us from world-mindedness.

Dear Crystal, as you grow older,
you are going to have to make decisions in your life,
and many times you will be confused
and feel the need of a friend
whose words value what is eternal and of heaven.

I would be your friend.
You have my promise.
And no matter what you do, this friendship will not be affected.
It is based on love —
the space beyond good and bad, right and wrong.

I offer you the gift of this friendship
on this day of Christmas.
And I pray to Jesus for an angel to accompany you
all through your life.
Know that you are strong enough
to be an extension of God's Will on Earth.

Affectionately,

Taraji

*   *   *

September 16, 1986

Dear Crystal,

We have just returned from our trip to Yosemite. It was so nice to sleep on the ground. Have you ever slept on the ground on your back? There are forces in the earth that energize the body. There have been many wise people who walked barefoot because of the earth currents. One of these was Socrates. He was a God-lit man who lived a life of virtue.

We drove soundlessly through the pine forests of Yosemite. Man can live without trees, but forever in his life there remains a sense of lack. By seeing the waterfalls, cliffs, and mountains in Yosemite Valley, your mind is silenced. I will teach you to see things.

Seeing is a very swift action. It takes place instantly, if you are alert, and brings you to wholeness, to the vitality of the present. But most people look through thought and they have never yet seen anything directly.

I have only met a few people in the world who had the capacity to see without thought interference. To see is to be one with all creation. Seeing is the purest form of meditation. It ends separation. There is no such thing as you and the tree. There is only *attention* and *seeing.*

People look but they do not see. And you are going to be awakened with an energy within you so swift that you would be ahead of thought. You will see directly that the holiness that God created is the same as your own. Then you will never waste and you will have reverence for all that exists.

Recently I had said that I would write about discipline. Discipline, as generally understood, is something that is imposed upon a person — especially children. If you do not do as you are told, you are punished. Foolish men have given this attribute of punishment to God also. They have invented a hell where they think God burns people. Well, they can have that kind of hell for themselves. You and I don't want that. When you grow up, people will try to convince you with the fear of punishment.

So what is discipline? Discipline has no authority in it. It is the understanding that you and I can share that brings Divine Order into one's life. Discipline is born of direct clarity in you. No one can discipline another from the outside. A true teacher does not tell a child what to do. He awakens the interest in the child to come to his own clarity. Without this inner clarity, everyone is blind and boring.

Affectionately,

Taraji

*   *   *

May 15, 1987

Dear Taraji,

My mom has read me the book of Soordas.* I felt very happy after I read it. I felt so happy that I even wanted to sit quiet. It was probably the first time.

I still let my ''wantings'' control me. I would like some help to learn how not to let that happen.

My mom is reading me *Women Saints — East and West, Living Birds,* and the *Ramayana.* Thank you for all the books.

I send you a big hug.

Crystal

---

*Soordas was a renowned, enlightened, blind musician, born in India in 1478 AD, who sang of his love for Lord Krishna. (Editor)

CHAPTER SEVENTEEN

17

A CALL TO WISDOM

Throughout history and evolution, there have been major discoveries which have drastically altered the lives of men. When man discovered fire, the wheel, agriculture, or sailing on the sea, each discovery revolutionized life upon the planet. Observe how far the discovery of the wheel has come. Almost all machinery is based on it. See how far the use of fire has gone. We have tamed the fire and brought it into the home. At one time, it was inconceivable that one could do that. The first ship must have been very primitive. How many centuries did it take to put the sails on, to go longer distances, to carry water, food, and even fire over the sea? There have been basic discoveries out of which everything else grew, refined itself, and evolved. Each new generation added something.

Now the pace is very, very swift. What is the difference between children born today and their parents who were born in the post-war era? In what sense is today's child different from one born fifty years ago? A hundred years ago? To understand the difference, you would need to know something of the evolution of humanity — its history, agriculture, economy, politics, literature, rural and urban life, transportation, communication.

The gap that presently exists between parents and children is wider than has ever been known in history. Parents and children today live in totally different worlds. What has happened between the post-war period and today is so revolutionary it has changed everything that is manmade. Parents have never known a childhood or youth like the one their children are experiencing. Two factors have largely been responsible.

First, the large scale shift of population from rural areas to the cities has affected every aspect of society. When man was in his own environment in a rural setting, he had his own home. Home was already provided like the sky and the earth. When he came to the city he rented his dwelling. The shift from owning to renting made life impersonal. When he was in the rural area he had his own work; when he came to the city he had to get a job. When he was in the rural area the father passed on his work and his home to his children, who in turn took care of their parents. Now this pattern is broken. There is nothing to pass on and it is inconceivable that the children today will take care of their parents. The change that has taken place is drastic and yet we are not totally aware of it. There are no relationships anymore, only expediences.

Second, with the advent of the computer the human brain has become almost outdated. Today the child is born in the electronic computer age with which the parents have no real connection. Just the video machines astound the mind. These changes present entirely different issues than man has ever had to face. We have to see this as a fact.

To read this carefully would create a crisis in your life. If you read it casually it will do nothing.

We are not aware that almost everything has been taken

away from us. It doesn't occur to us that we have nothing to give our children. What would your child have? Influence and opinion that are of someone else? See what has happened in such a short period of time. Which one of our children is going to have a normal life? Which one of them will even have a wife or a husband? You have to get a job — it's the only thing you know. Man used to use horses, donkeys, cows, camels — today he uses human beings.

Before the war, ten dollars was a lot of money. In India you could buy a hundred pounds of wheat for fifty cents. Now the value and place of currency has totally changed. Currency is more in control of man than it has ever been. What will happen from now on we don't know, but a totally new era of economy and the media has dawned in the wake of the computerized age.

When Gandhi asked people in India who ruled them, they answered, "God." They didn't know about the politician. Today currency rules man. What, in actuality, is money? It is of the world, like fear, insecurity, and greed. Without these, would exploitation, corruption, and slavery be possible? Are not our religions, our educational system, and our governments run by money? They are not run by wisdom; they are run by expedience. With money man is bought and sold. What worth do you put on your life? The fear of unemployment today is greater than the fear of war.

On our own we do not have the intelligence to question. Many people say television programming is nonsense, but they don't try to do without it. Most of us live hypocritical lives. At the relative level "this and that" can be both true and false. But they are equally meaningless. We cannot seem to go beyond the meaningless. Where are you? Have you anything of your own to say or are you a mere echo? Everything in our lives has become planned and calculated.

Today the human being functions like a machine, destroying

himself in the conformity and illusion of achieving. He is always working, doing, producing; but in reality, it is *his* own energy that is being exploited. The machine-like routine, in which there is no vulnerability, no spontaneity, no Divine Leisure, no contact with anything real, is destroying man. The dead are born again to kill and to die. There is such strong unwillingness to heed the Voice for God. And there are very few teachers in the world who have something of wisdom to impart. Where is the timeless being who has reverence for One Life and for humanity?

No longer is there real education; there is only the acquiring of skills for survival. The state is very particular about the child going to school and learning a skill. It is not particular about morality. You can have total freedom to do what you like — sexual freedom, indulgences, outlets — but you have to be at the job on the button. You cannot violate the tax laws but you can violate all moral laws and ethical principles.

Now, as children grow up, there is almost no way their parents can help them. If they were living in the same world, yes. But now whatever you would tell your child to do is outdated. He would be laughed at if he listened to you too much. If you try to impose certain morality on him, he won't have a single friend and it would most likely be a hindrance because the children must be able to cope with the present reality.

Children today do not receive enough love, warmth, or laughters. Both parents have to work. And because these very sensitive children have not received what they need, they become depressed. They lack energy because nothing seems to have any meaning. There are no moral values in their lives, nothing virtuous or noble. No contact. They may as well be children of typewriters or copying machines.

Why is this happening? And why is this happening more so in affluent societies? It is a by-product of city life. People have more respect for their cars than for their children. And then the children become "punks" because they have not received the love they needed. Why do you think the "punks" wear black? Because their parents are dead. We need to wake up to what is happening.

Do you know what the "punks" need? They need to be productive. They are sensitive enough, however, to see that whatever society has to offer is part of nothingness. They don't want to be just a number or a name and so they would rather be "punk." Do you think the mercenaries are any better? There are many lonely young people today who are so frustrated they want to degrade themselves. Because they are not connected they become sad and self-destructive.

They need to be productive as you and I need to be productive. Can one be productive without self-honesty? Self-honesty is a great gift to oneself. I may not know the truth, but the gift of self-honesty helps me not to hide or evade anything.

There is an inner harmony that comes from eating food that is grown in the area where you are born, that is conducive to your vibration. As life has become more artificial, this inner harmony has all but disappeared. We grow up without ever having loved a tree because we never owned one. Never having had our own land, we are not connected with the soil that sustains. We think it is the bank that sustains, the paycheck that sustains. We are totally isolated and go to school to be processed like a can of beans, coming out with a skill to do a particular job without ever having had real, direct contact with anybody.

According to Hinduism, all of the ages of man, from the beginning of time, are divided into four yugas or epochs — Satya, Treta, Dwapara, and Kali.[1] Each yuga exists for hundreds of thousands of years. Just like it is difficult for us to count the stars, it is difficult for us to comprehend the span of each yuga.

Each yuga has a different level of energy. Satyayuga was all spirit and no matter; bodies were made of light. In Satyayuga everyone spoke the truth and because their Word was the Word of God, they could do anything.

Gradually the decline began. In Tretayuga there was a little more matter. Although they spoke the truth they also began to think *about* it. They still lived by ethics and virtue but they had the ability to come in and out of physical form. In Dwapara, the separation began as interpretation and identification with the body became more dominant.

In the present age of Kaliyuga there is more matter and less spirit. It is the most dense. The higher realms of the spirit seem not so accessible; nor is there any apparent unifying intelligence, only separative forces. Therefore, we are endangered, insecure, afraid, doubtful. There is no love, only exploitation, corruption, abuse — whether it is between man and man, man and woman, parents and children. It is an age in which the truth becomes the lie and the lie becomes the truth.

Energy is energy. How it is used shows if there is wisdom or selfishness. There is a lot of energy available today but we are more irresponsible than ever before and are deteriorating at a much faster pace. And now the computer has come. What is it going to do?

In his later years, Mr. J. Krishnamurti* was extremely alarmed by the influence of the computer. He talked about how the human brain would degenerate and become more and more dull because man would only know what he is told; he would function by the rhythm of routine since by nature he is a creature of habit. Routine avoids challenge; it avoids being responsible to the spirit that we are. It is a sublevel existence in which one doesn't have to think. The danger is paramount

---

*See, for example, Mr. J. Krishnamurti's Saanen Talk -5, 1983. For a paraphrase of portions of this talk and further discussion of these topics see *The Future Of Mankind — The Branching Of The Road* by Tara Singh (Foundation for Life Action, 1986), pages 5-19. (Editor)

because the computer and the robot can do a better job than man. One computer can contain the brains of six geniuses. Your little brain is incapable of coping with the computer's genius brain thinking on one issue. Mr. Krishnamurti had warned us and I wonder if anyone heard him. Having heard it now, what are you going to do?

The computer has expedient answers but no regard for rightness. It is going to enhance corruption, monopoly, and exploitation because it is born out of them. If a corporation is not successful, it can become successful by manufacturing arms. Ethics do not matter anymore. The computer controls more than one realizes. Its influence has been extensively planned. Man is run by money, so the economy can be controlled. Man is run by the media, so the media can be controlled. It plays with the world.

Every political, economic, and social speech that is written is devised by the computer brain. It knows what the public wants to hear and that is what it delivers. We do not go far enough to find the truth of a situation and we stop short by being appeased or satisfied. If what is said confirms our reaction, we are satisfied; we need not be bothered anymore. We have oversimplified everything and to our oversimplified brain, the computer controlled communication gives the appropriate answer. Truth is no longer valid or needed. Nor has ethics any real meaning or merit. This is Kaliyuga.

But truth is a light and a power. Men who live by it have other energies to bring to this planet. When you live by truth you are not part of Kaliyuga; you are part of something sublime. You are entitled to bring the Kingdom of God to earth. That is your function — to have something of your own to give. It is a contribution that one makes for centuries.

If you do not come to having something of your own to give, the computer is going to get you. Its brain is far superior to yours. Every little impulse and urge, disappointment and satisfaction, is measured and predicted. The experts know what size shoes your brain wears. It will be supplied and you will never know that you died without ever having lived.

One hears people say that they don't want to influence their children, that their children have their own lives to lead. But that is ridiculous. Your children are being influenced elsewhere. We never see the fallacy of our way of thinking. We have to see that they are being influenced and you are being influenced. It is better to find out what influence is than to say you are not going to influence. That is indifference and casualness. What are you going to do about influence itself? What would it be like not to be influenced and not to influence? If you are in a state where you will not be influenced, then possibly you can make the child aware of what influence is. It doesn't matter whether the parent influences or somebody else influences, wisdom is what is needed.

Everywhere someone is trying to influence another. No one realized how capable the media was going to be at influencing the human brain. Every war, every tyranny, every violation can be justified. The trend is frightening. The bliss of ignorance is what the multitude prefers. Indifference. Thus you annihilate yourself in self-centeredness. You have gotten your cookie and everything is all right. There is no moral cause, nothing you live for. Life becomes more fragmented, more separated, more isolated in its delusion. It is quite a crime when man is not related to life, to his brother, to nature, or to God.

Where is the whole man? Are we not more helpless now than ever? Even our brain is no longer our own having become so totally conditioned and dependent. We need vulnerability to have original thought. But that is rapidly disappearing. Vulnerability is when one does not defend oneself; there is innocence, space. But spontaneous action no longer takes place in us. And today's child will never know what vulnerability or spontaneity is. Urges, yes; innocence, no.

This is actually the status quo in the world today. The parent cannot even help the child because there is no morality in the world the child is going to live in. Unless the parent has outgrown dogmas and belief systems, what is he going to give to his child?

You have to turn the child inward. But first see what difficulty *you* have in turning inward. Loneliness comes in and loneliness needs distractions. Outlets flourish — films, television, videos. We think it is progress but the result is that we are more dependent than ever, having become a prisoner of our limitations.

There is nothing you have now to give to the child — not only materially but of wisdom. Rare is the child who comes to know his own wholeness. What are we going to do about the situation as it is now, not as it should be?

It is necessary for the child and the parent to both become interested in that which is of God and to outgrow the things of the world together. Having homes to give didn't work, nor did passing on your profession. The only answer is to come to that which is timeless. Now it is the parents' need. They must come to disillusion; they must come to discrimination; they must come to rightness. That is why *A Course In Miracles* is upon the earth. It is the Divine Hand in our lives.

SALVATION IS THE ONLY PURPOSE OF LIFE.

A Course In Miracles makes having something of one's own to give possible for parents, non-parents, and children alike. It makes it possible to come to self-reliance. Nothing like the Course has ever happened in the New World. Virtue, rightness, ethics are restored. If we have the discrimination, a turning point has come in man's life upon the planet.

The Scribe of *A Course In Miracles* asked why the Course was being given at this time, and was told:

"The world situation is worsening to an alarming degree. People all over the world are being called on to help, and are making their individual contributions as part of an overall prearranged plan. Part of the plan is taking down *A Course In Miracles*, and I am fulfilling my part in the agreement, as you will fulfill yours. You will be using abilities you developed long ago, and which you are not really ready to use again. Because of the acute emergency, however, the usual slow, evolutionary process is being by-passed in what might best be described as a 'celestial speed-up.' "[2]

A Course In Miracles comes at the time of "celestial speed-up" to impart energy to those who are with rightness. The potentials that are available during "celestial speed-up" are enormous. Nothing is impossible. It provides the grace, the vitality, and the resources to awaken man from a routine, demented life. It can change the destiny of stars. Man need not live in misery any longer. You will be able to respond to man's suffering when his economy and his gadgets and his laws based on abstract doubt collapse. Those who have harnessed the energy of "celestial speed-up" will be humanistic. We are part of the "celestial speed-up" and we need to move at its pace, with its resources. The Grace of God is upon the planet.

How many teachers are needed to save the world? "One," says *A Course In Miracles*.[3] That one touches many as his light and peace are transmitted. Those who are willing to receive will be the students.

> *A teacher of God is anyone who chooses to be one. His qualifications consist solely in this; somehow, somewhere he has made a deliberate choice in which he did not see his interests as apart from someone else's. Once he has done that, his road is established and his direction is sure. A light has entered the darkness. It may be a single light, but that is enough. He has entered an agreement with God even if he does not yet believe in Him. He has become a bringer of salvation. He has become a teacher of God . . . .*

There is a course for every teacher of God. The form of the course varies greatly. So do the particular teaching aids involved. But the content of the course never changes. Its central theme is always, ''God's Son is guiltless, and in his innocence is his salvation.'' It can be taught by actions or thoughts; in words or soundlessly; in any language or in no language; in any place or time or manner. It does not matter who the teacher was before he heard the Call. He has become a saviour by his answering. He has seen someone else as himself. He has therefore found his own salvation and the salvation of the world. In his rebirth is the world reborn. [4]

Except for God's teachers there would be little hope of salvation, for the world of sin would seem forever real . . . [The teachers of God] *are not perfect, or they would not be here. Yet it is their mission to become perfect here, and so they teach perfection over and over, in many, many ways, until they have learned it. And then they are seen no more, although their thoughts remain a source of strength and truth forever.* [5]

In this book I have tried to come to a common ground where a communication between parents and children can take place. Can they both grow together? Can they have a spirit of adventure irrespective of the fact that their backgrounds are different? Could they get interested in what is new?

This is a call to wisdom.

CHRIST'S VISION

Let not the past obscure the now to you.
For thus you waken happily, with joy
Upon your heart and eyes, to see a world
Awaiting to be seen aright at last.
How beautiful the newly-born! For they
Reflect their Father's Love, their brother's care,
The happiness of Heaven, and the peace
That is their true inheritance. It is
On them you look. They have no past today.
All darkness vanishes, and Heaven's smile
Presents a world from which the past is gone,
And present happiness ends all despair
In shining silence and simplicity.*

*From *The Gifts Of God,* by Helen Schucman, page 5.

ADDENDA

WILL LEARNING
PROVIDE THE ANSWERS?

QUESTION: Why is it that we continue to pursue our tiresome daily routines? We all seem to be on a merry-go-round that we cannot escape.

Well, there are a number of reasons. We need to know something about the human brain: it has its own images and projections. And whatever we project — whatever the brain projects — we believe, and then pursue. This limits man a great deal. First we project, then we believe, and then we pursue. And by this process of thought we define our whole existence.

We have to see that what we have projected, and thus believe, may not be true. And then the question is, "What is true?" In a very simple way I would say "what is true" is not part of relative knowledge. Only the Absolute is true and it silences the brain.

This discussion has been adapted from a radio interview with Tara Singh conducted by Michael Toms of *New Dimensions Radio*, San Francisco. — Editor

QUESTION: And how does one know the difference?

When the conflict ends one knows the difference. The brain's images end. One does not have to presuppose how it would end. It ends. When this duality within ourselves has ended, we become whole and related to something that is eternal.

QUESTION: In America, it seems there is a momentum and quest for self-improvement and self-development. We continue to pursue more and more. What about the drive in America to accumulate more knowledge? Will knowledge provide the answers?

I would begin by asking, "What is the temperament, the vibration and the purpose of America — the New World — in the whole scheme of Creation?"

The New World gave man the enormous opportunity to free himself from feudalism, monarchies, religious organizations, and so forth. It was a land far across the ocean. Courage was needed to cross that ocean and to leave something behind — to take the next step, so to speak. I think it was Whitman who spoke about how many hundreds of years man must have walked along the shores of Europe asking himself, "What is across this ocean?" They took the step and came. That was extraordinary.

So the people who came *started* with the concept of not wanting to be exploited anymore. And consequently, the human being and human rights became important. Each person had a say in the matter. That was the New World. And the function of the New World, as I see it, was to come to new consciousness.

There were two currents from the beginning. On one side

there was no real respect for nature or for man. There was the annihilation of the Indians, the perpetuation of slavery, and very little care for culture or conservation. The other side was represented by the Forefathers who stood for virtue and nobleness. For example, Jefferson stressed that in a democracy we should be able to vote for a person from our own community — someone we knew — someone who lived by some moral principles and ethics. He cautioned the nation to relate to the land and not become too externalized. Our function was "IN GOD WE TRUST." These were different values altogether. Just look how far astray we have gone.

Then Lincoln spoke of extraordinary things. He said that if this nation stayed with rightness, rightness would be provided with the instruments of safety. Do we care for rightness now or are we motivated by self-interest? Is there the ability to care for the needs of the people?

In the years since World War II, America has become the leader of the world. Because we have become the example, our next step is important not only to the individual American but to the world as a whole. Affluence has opened many doors and the world is excited about it. Other people still long for what we have because they have known only poverty. But there is now a tremendous kind of disillusion in many people here. They have seen that education has not solved the problem of man's peace within or without. Neither has science nor the many other things they thought might give them happiness. They see more mental problems, crime, broken families, loneliness.

America has something to give to the world. It has the energy either to externalize tremendously or to discover something more within.

QUESTION: Does it require us to look at our own lives and notice how little time we seem to have for the process of living, as opposed to the race of pursuing our projections?

One of the things I discovered, Michael, was that when we limit ourselves to our body senses, life becomes very self-centered. The body senses want experience. In fact, they are limited to experience. But this can be one's own discovery — that the body senses crave experience and love pleasure. And when we seek pleasure, we become the victims of our own seeking.

Now, is there something beyond experience? Can I ask that question — not looking for a quick answer which would be a cliche — or am I content to know the body senses have their cravings and they rule me? Do I want to ask the question, ''Is there something else?''

That something else may free me. It may make me aware. And this awareness may have nothing to do with the body senses at all. It is another kind of awakening. And any individual can do it.

There is a great deal of beauty and gladness in life. Gladness and happiness are within man. We have to lead man to himself — to his own resources. And that is becoming harder, isn't it?

QUESTION: Going back to the earlier part of our conversation, you were talking about truth, Absolute Truth. How does one know what is a right course of action? If one looks at two schools of thought, each thinks it is right. It's a constant battle with a multiplicity of rights and wrongs.

First we have to see as a fact that we are influenced. From the start, a child, in the family and at school, is going to be influenced and will not know what is right and what is not right. The responsibility of the parent and the teacher is to relate him with an inner strength which will not be taken over by external influences. Then he will have a voice of his own.

When ethics are fundamental to a culture, the individual

finds his own strength and his own voice. The action begins when one human being sees the need of another and responds to it. This response is something very independent and very free. It comes from the goodness within man. And humanity is abundant with that goodness.

> *QUESTION:* When I look at my own life I see I've got a family and many encumbrances that I've created and carried with me throughout my life. How can I step away from all of this and become more in touch with my center, quiet my life and slow it down? I've got all these responsibilities.

Can we see how detrimental so-called progress is, with less and less possibility for me to find my own "center?" At least I am now beginning to question and that is a good beginning, isn't it? By my very questioning, the dehypnotizing process has begun. But then the next question is invariably, "How?" In this context, the word "how" almost always represents man's helplessness. "How" is always looking for some method or some technique — the means to escape. And then I feel I am not trained enough, I don't know enough and so forth. We may feel inadequate to deal with our external issues, but "how" is not necessary to find my own inner resources. Do you see?

> *QUESTION:* It is not necessary to look externally?

To look externally leads me to dependence. Now, I am not saying that we are not going to be dependent. I am *questioning* anything which leads me to dependence because it does not free me. In creation, there is relationship between you, me, the tree, the air — everything. We are related with one another. In relationship there is sharing. And that is beautiful. However, at the dependence level there is exploitation and taking advantage. Man has to be awakened to some of these basic differences. Then he is not for or against anything. He becomes very objective.

We have become terribly dependent on the externals. And these externals now have control over us. "I have to make a living. I have a family. What to do ?" The individual is feeling more and more helpless, isn't he?

Fine progress this is. It might be progress for the person building skyscrapers. It is not progress for the individual. Having a job has become the single most important factor in today's society. And to take the one step from having a job to having your own work has become nearly impossible. Is this progress? In actuality, we have gone down the ladder.

Again the answer would be for the person to question and ask himself if his job is just routine. Is his heart in it? Is it creative? He must find his own inner calling and his own work. Can we awaken the individual to the realization that he has the energy and potentials within himself to find his own work? Those who have found that energy will not work for another. You and I may cooperate and work on the basis of relationship — because we both like something — but dependence and exploitation are not a part of it.

We must bring this confidence back to man. Externalized society with its potato chips and hamburgers and free sex is not going to do it. The important thing is not progress or external grandeur but the human being — the human being who discovers his own energy. And then that human being is a little harder to influence, isn't he?

QUESTION: Taking that step requires a great deal of courage.

Yes, but when one person has come to it, it is as if light has entered the darkness. There was one Socrates. And he lives forever, doesn't he? Jesus was one person. His words are eternal. They are related with eternal laws. And eternal laws do not change. Can we come to Absolute Knowledge rather than relative? At this plane, Absolute Knowledge might use relative knowledge, but it would not get taken over by it.

QUESTION: Mr. Singh, you are currently working with *A Course In Miracles*. How did you discover it?

I discovered *A Course In Miracles* after spending more than three years in silence. I saw it on someone's desk and read in the Introduction, *Nothing real can be threatened. Nothing unreal exists.* Who has ever heard words like these? Immediately, I felt this was the reason for my being born upon the planet. It was so complete. It's hard to explain, but for me everything else ended.

Whether you read the Gita, the Bible, the Koran, or the Torah — they all tell us about what wonderful things holy beings have done. They talk about Job and Jonah or Krishna. But I want to know about my own bondage, my own frustrations, my own unclarity. These concern me. If Moses parts the sea, God bless him. It is great. But it does not directly affect my life.

A Course In Miracles deals with my own issues. It begins by undoing. We come to wisdom with "Know Thyself." We come to wisdom by unlearning. It begins with us, and it revolutionizes our lives. Every day there is a different lesson — three hundred and sixty-five lessons in all.

They are very simple. You begin to question when it says: *"I am never upset for the reason I think." "I see only the past."* And then you begin to see, *"I am not the victim of the world I see."*

The discovery begins within myself. I see that understanding is incomplete! I can understand and repeat words and yet not know the truth. I was amazed to find *A Course In Miracles* leads to the realization of the truth. It does not teach. It does not preach. It awakens and brings one to that realization.

If one looks at Jesus, one sees a man who was a light unto Himself. His words are eternal. And what He said was very simple — not to judge but to forgive. If I do not judge, then I will not limit myself. And if I can forgive, then I am free from my own memory and the poison I have kept in my mind against another.

So, some of these realizations took place in me. And the Course has helped tremendously.

> QUESTION: It seems that many of us feel depressed by the events around us. One feels powerless and unable to do anything; one becomes paralyzed in the midst of all the negativity that one sees externally.

The few people who would not underestimate themselves can do wonders. This thing that is within man himself is more powerful; it is independent of the externals. Man does not have to give authority to the externals. That does not mean he is going to become critical of them — that would be a reaction. His not giving authority to the externals is the action itself. Then he has a poise and a dignity; whatever he does becomes intrinsic. And whatever he does would take care of his external needs — paying the rent, taking care of the children, and so on.

Man has to make that demand upon himself which brings the action of integrity into his life. It would introduce him to simplicity. And if he is no longer dependent on the pursuit of pleasure, simplicity becomes very natural. Whatever a man does reflects peace when he has discovered that pleasure is in just being.

We are so stimulated. Somehow the individual has to step out of this momentum of tension. It is very important to come to relaxation. Moments of solitude are essential. It is becoming more and more difficult to simply be by yourself or with someone for whom you deeply care. But it is not difficult if we could just step aside.

We need to start with some discrimination. Do you see that everything I am pointing out is something I can do? It is never that I have to go to this shop or to that teacher. It is something I can do. I must have discrimination to see what is and what is not essential in my life. And then I begin to weed out the unessential. I will have more space. And I will give integrity to what I do.

REFERENCES

INTRODUCTION

1. *A Course In Miracles* (ACIM), *Workbook For Students* (II), page 48.
2. Mr. J. Krishnamurti (1895 - 1986), a world renowned teacher and philosopher.
3. John 3:11.
4. John 1:23.
5. Matthew 5:39.
6. As quoted in: *Thus Spake Sri Shankara* (Sri Ramakrishna Math, 16 Ramakrishna Math Road, Madras 600 004, India), page 51.
7. ACIM, *Manual For Teachers* (III), page 2.
8. ACIM, II, page 315.
9. ACIM, II, page 277.
10. Matthew 6:28.
11. ACIM, II, page 376.
12. "In God We Trust" appears to have been inspired by a line from the Star Spangled Banner, "In God is our trust," written by Francis Scott Key in 1814."In God We Trust" first appeared on the coinage of the United States in 1864, during the presidency of Abraham Lincoln. It became the official motto of the United States in 1956. (Editor)
13. ACIM, II, page 132.

CHAPTER ONE: THE LAWS OF PARENTING

1. John 3:5-6.
2. ACIM, III, pages 61-62.
3. ACIM, II, page 277.
4. ACIM, II, page 432.

CHAPTER TWO: THE CHILD TEACHES ONE TO LOVE

1. ACIM, II, page 132.
2. ACIM, II, page 239.
3. ACIM, II, page 79.

CHAPTER THREE: MARRIAGE

1. Corinthians I, 7:3.
2. Corinthians I, 11:3.
3. ACIM, II, page 162.
4. Refers to a prayer in *A Course In Miracles, Text*, page 326. *Forgive us our illusions, Father, and help us to accept our true relationship with You in which there are no illusions and where none can ever enter. Our holiness is Yours. What can there be in us that needs forgiveness when Yours is perfect. The sleep of forgetfulness is only the unwillingness to remember Your forgiveness and Your Love...* " See also CHAPTER 6: DIVINE LEISURE — BIRTH THROUGH PUBERTY, reference no.3. (Editor)
5. The one commandment given by Jesus, ''Love ye one another,'' appears many times in the New Testament. See, for example: John 13:34-35, 15:12, 15:17; Romans 13:8. (Editor)
6. ACIM, II, page 132.
7. ''Twilight'' was originally published as one of the songs in *Excerpts From The Forty Days In The Wilderness* by Tara Singh (Foundation for Life Action, 1981), page 148. It has been reprinted in *The Voice That Precedes Thought* (Foundation for Life Action, 1987), pages 280-281. (Editor)
8. Matthew 6:10.
9. *The I Ching,* The Richard Wilhelm Translation rendered into English by Cary F. Baynes (Princeton University Press, 1950), page 569.

10. ACIM, II, page 464.
11. Ibid.
12. Sri Ramakrishna was a God-lit being who lived in India from 1836 to 1886. He taught that all religions are true, having discovered the truth of each of them himself by practicing them with total devotion. He found that God can be known directly through all forms of spiritual practice. Sri Sarada Devi (1853-1920) was the wife of Ramakrishna. She is often referred to as the Holy Mother. (Editor)
13. ACIM, II, page 464.
14. Ibid.

CHAPTER FOUR: CONCEPTION

1. ACIM, *Text*, (I), page 7.
2. ACIM, I, page 293.
3. ACIM, II, page 396.
4. "Souls who are eternally free and belong to the divine class but come down to earth for the good and guidance of humanity." From *The Apostles Of Ramakrishna*, compiled and edited by Swami Gambhirananda (Advaita Ashram, India, 1982), page 95. (Editor)
5. Guru Nanak (1469-1538 or 1539) was the prophet who founded the Sikh religion. (Editor)
6. "Yuga is a cycle or world period. According to Hindu mythology the duration of the world is divided into four yugas, namely, Satya, Treta, Dwapara, and Kali. In the first, also known as the Golden Age, there is a great preponderance of virtue amongst men but with each succeeding yuga virtue diminishes and vice increases. In the Kaliyuga there is a minimum of virtue and a great excess of vice. The world is said to be now passing through Kaliyuga." From *The Gospel Of Ramakrishna*, translated by Swami Nikhilananda (Ramakrishna-Vivekananda Center, New York, 1977), page 1048. (Editor)
7. *From The City To The Vedic Age Of Shining Beings Extending The Will Of God* by Tara Singh (Foundation for Life Action, 1983), pages 52-53.
8. ACIM, II, page 75.

CHAPTER FIVE: TO BE A MOTHER

1. ACIM, II, page 192.
2. Numbers 6:24-26.
3. *The Gifts Of God* by Helen Schucman (Foundation for Inner Peace, 1982), page 84.

CHAPTER SIX: DIVINE LEISURE — BIRTH THROUGH PUBERTY

1. Mark 9:37.
2. ACIM, III, page 1.
3. ACIM, I, page 326. The prayer which begins with these lines has been referred to as *A Course In Miracles'* version of the Lord's Prayer. *Journey Without Distance: The Story Behind A Course In Miracles* by Robert Skutch (Celestial Arts, 1984), page 68. It is discussed in great detail in *Dialogues On A Course In Miracles* by Tara Singh (Life Action Press, 1987), pages 35-167. (Editor)
4. ACIM, II, page 186.
5. ACIM, II, page 47.
6. ACIM, II, page 63.
7. ACIM, II, page 69.
8. ACIM, II, page 79.
9. ACIM, II, page 239.
10. ACIM, II, page 185.

CHAPTER SEVEN: LOVE, LAW, AND CHILDREN

1. Matthew 16:23.
2. Genesis 1:28.

CHAPTER EIGHT: WORKING WITH A CHILD — CRYSTAL (Part I)

1. Numbers 6:24-26.
2. Refers to Matthew 18:20.
3. Luke 1:38.
4. ACIM, I, page 24.
5. Matthew 24:35.

CHAPTER NINE: THE CHILD AND THE SOURCE OF CREATION — THE NEED FOR REVERENCE

1. ACIM, II, page 271.

2. Matthew 6:10.
3. Matthew 5:40.
4. ACIM, II, page 292.
5. ACIM, II, page 376.
6. ACIM, II, page 58.

CHAPTER TEN: MARY AND HER CHILD JESUS
1. Luke 1:28,31-33.
2. Luke 2:38.
3. Luke 1:13-14.
4. Luke 1:18.
5. Luke 1:19-20.
6. ACIM, I, page 91.
7. Matthew 18:1-6.
8. Refers to Matthew 13:13-23.
9. Matthew 5:3.
10. Matthew 5:8.
11. Matthew 5:44-45.
12. Luke 22:42.
13. ACIM, II, page 459.
14. ACIM, II, page 363.
15. ACIM, II, page 119.

CHAPTER ELEVEN: RELATIONSHIP AND THE DIVINE MOTHER
1. ACIM, I, page 326.
2. ACIM, III, page 25.
3. Edgar Cayce (1877-1945) was a gifted clairvoyant who would enter a self-induced trance state and give readings on a wide variety of subjects. He made a great contribution in the field of health and diet. The Association for Research and Enlightenment, Virginia Beach, VA, maintains a library of his work and makes his readings available to the public. (Editor)
4. ACIM, I, page 7.
5. ACIM, II, page 317.
6. ACIM, I, page 24.
7. See CHAPTER 3: MARRIAGE, reference no. 12.
8. ACIM, I, Introduction.

CHAPTER TWELVE: THE GOD-CHILD AND THE WORLD TODAY

1. *Think On These Things* by J. Krishnamurti (Harper and Row, 1964), pages 11-13.
2. Op cit., pages 9-11.
3. ACIM, I, Introduction.
4. Ibid.
5. ACIM, II, page 317.
6. ACIM, I, page 285.
7. ACIM, II, page 58.

CHAPTER THIRTEEN: THE PATH OF VIRTUE

1. ACIM, II, pages 331-332.

CHAPTER FOURTEEN: TALKS WITH PARENTS (Part I)

1. Refers to Matthew 13:13-23.
2. *Time Magazine* (September 8, 1986), page 22.

CHAPTER FIFTEEN: TALKS WITH PARENTS (Part II)

1. ACIM, II, page 195.
2. See the work of J. Chandra Bose which illustrates something of the same principle in plants. (Editor)
3. ACIM, I, page 49.
4. ACIM, II, page 69.
5. ACIM, I, pages 60-61.

CHAPTER SIXTEEN: WORKING WITH A CHILD — CRYSTAL (Part II)

1. ACIM, I, page 96.
2. Ibid.
3. Ibid.
4. Ibid.
5. ACIM, II, page 101.
6. ACIM, II, page 376.

CHAPTER SEVENTEEN: A CALL TO WISDOM

1. See CHAPTER 4: CONCEPTION, reference no. 6.

2. *Journey Without Distance: The Story Behind A Course In Miracles* by Robert Skutch (Celestial Arts, 1984), page 60.
3. ACIM, III, page 30.
4. ACIM, III, page 3.
5. ACIM, III, page 2.

OTHER MATERIALS BY TARA SINGH

BOOKS

Dialogues On A Course In Miracles
The Voice That Precedes Thought
Commentaries On A Course In Miracles
"Love Holds No Grievances" — The Ending Of Attack
A Course In Miracles — A Gift For All Mankind
The Future Of Mankind — The Branching Of The Road
How To Learn From A Course In Miracles

AUDIO CASSETTE TAPES

Discussions On A Course In Miracles
    (three tape album with the book
    "Love Holds No Grievances" —
    The Ending Of Attack)
"What Is The Christ?" (three tape album with the book
    A Course In Miracles — A Gift For All Mankind)
Bringing A Course In Miracles Into Application
    (three tape album with the pamphlet
    The School At "The Branching Of The Road")
A Course In Miracles Explorations (three cassettes)
"What Is A Course In Miracles?" (two cassettes)
Raising A Child For The New Age (two cassettes)
Freedom From Belief (two cassettes)
Discovering Your Own Holiness (two cassettes)
Finding Peace Within (two cassettes)

Discovering Your Life's Work (two cassettes)
The Heart Of Forgiveness (single tape)
Tara Singh Tapes Of The One Year Non-Commercialized
    Retreat: A Serious Study Of *A Course In Miracles*

VIDEO CASSETTE TAPES

"Nothing Real Can Be Threatened" —
A Workshop On A Course In Miracles
    Part I   — *The Question And The Holy Instant*
    Part II — *The Deception Of Learning*
    Part III — *Transcending The Body Senses*
    Part IV — *Awakening To Self Knowledge*
Finding Your Inner Calling
How To Raise A Child Of God
Exploring A Course in Miracles (series)
    — *What Is A Course In Miracles*
        and *"The Certain Are Perfectly Calm"*
    — *God Does Not Judge* and *Healing Relationships*
    — *Man's Contemporary Issues*
        and *Life Without Consequences*
    — *Principles* and *Gratefulness*
A Call to Wisdom
        and *A Call To Wisdom* — *Exploring*
        A Course In Miracles
Man's Struggle For Freedom From The Past
        and *"Beyond This World There Is A World I Want"*
Life For Life
        and *Moneymaking Is Inconsistent With Life Forces*
The Call To Wisdom: A Discussion On A Course In Miracles
        (Parts I & II)
"Quest Four" with Damien Simpson and Stacie Hunt
"Odyssey" and *"At One With"* with Keith Berwick

Additional copies of *How To Raise A Child Of God* by Tara Singh may be obtained by sending a check, Mastercard or Visa number and expiration date to:

LIFE ACTION PRESS
902 South Burnside Avenue
Los Angeles, CA 90036
213/933-5591
Toll Free 1/800/732-5489
(Calif.)1/800/367-2246

Limited edition, hardbound $22.95
    (plus $3.00 shipping/handling)

Softcover $17.95
    (plus $2.00 shipping/handling)

A Course In Miracles may also be purchased from Life Action Press.

Three Volume, hardbound edition $40.00
    (plus $3.00 shipping/handling)

Combined, softcover edition $25.00
    (plus $2.00 shipping/handling)

California residents please add 6½% sales tax.

Thank you.

Typesetting: Photographics Inc., Los Angeles, California
Printing/binding: McNaughton & Gunn, Inc., Saline, Michigan
Type: Palacio
Paper: 55lb Glatfelter natural (acid free)